MULLET
ON THE BEACH
THE MINORCANS OF FLORIDA
1768 - 1788

A Florida Sand Dollar Book

MULLET
ON THE BEACH
THE MINORCANS OF FLORIDA
1768 - 1788

PATRICIA C. GRIFFIN

The St. Augustine Historical Society

University of North Florida Press/Jacksonville

Griffin, Patricia C.
    Mullet on the beach : the Minorcans of Florida, 1768-1788 /
Patricia C. Griffin.
        p.   cm. — (A Florida sand dollar book)
    Includes bibliographical references and index.
    ISBN 0-8130-1074-8
    1. Minorcans—Florida—Saint Augustine Region—History—18th
century.   2. Saint Augustine Region (Fla.)—History.   3. Florida—
History—English colony. 1763-1784.   4. Florida—History—Spanish
colony, 1784-1821   I. Title.   II. Series.
F319.S2G75   1991
975.9' 18—dc20   90-24798
                                                                      CIP

The University of North Florida Press is a member of the University
Presses of Florida, the scholarly publishing agency of the State Uni-
versity System of Florida. Books are selected for publication by fac-
ulty editorial committees at each of Florida's nine public universities:
Florida A & M University (Tallahassee), Florida Atlantic University
(Boca Raton), Florida International University (Miami), Florida
State University (Tallahassee), University of Central Florida (Or-
lando), University of Florida (Gainesville), University of North
Florida (Jacksonvlle), University of South Florida (Tampa), and University of West Florida (Pensacola).

Orders for books published by all member presses should be addressed
to:
                        University Presses of Florida
                        15 Northwest 15th Street
                        Gainesville, FL 32611

Contents

Tables

Figures

Preface

A few years ago a benighted tourist rushed into the library of the St. Augustine Historical Society wanting to know where he could find the "Minorcan reservation." This amusing misconception has some element of historical truth, for the group described in the following pages was, in the first few years of sojourn in the New World, confined on a Florida indigo plantation under semi-servile conditions.

During the last half of the eighteenth century, when East Florida was a British province, this plantation community, composed of Mediterranean subsistence farmers from Minorca, Italy and Greece, was forged on the frontier seventy miles south of the capital city of St. Augustine. As a group they became known, and are known to this day, as the "Minorcans," after the insular birthplace of the majority. Their geographic, linguistic, cultural and religious isolation in an Anglo-Protestant environment, coupled with intermarriages among the subgroups, built an enduring cohesion which helped them to escape en masse from the adversities of the plantation, and subsequently to reorder their lives again in St. Augustine. When East Florida was retroceded to Spain in 1784, they became the core of the Hispanic population in that city where they have remained ever since as the fabric upon which the community has been built during the years.

The current study of the crucial first twenty years which these emigrants spent in the New World is based on my master's thesis completed at the University of Florida, Gainesville, in the Department of Anthropology (Griffin 1977a). It is revised and expanded to include new data and understandings gained through other research which I have subsequently undertaken in St. Augustine history (Griffin 1983, 1988a, 1988b) and on newly available documentary materials and retranslations.

The community model used is that of Arensberg and Kimball (1972). Community is viewed as a "process involving social structure and cultural behavior" in which settlement pattern, household forms and other features are elements or expressions of the interactional systems, all in turn related to the environment, both physical and human, in which the bounded group finds itself (Arensberg and Kimball 1972:1-3). The Minorcan colonists experienced two quite different environments in their first two decades in the New World—nine years on the indigo plantation and the remaining years in St. Augustine and its environs. In the St. Augustine years, the freedom to heed the cry, "mullet on the beach," was symbolic of the regained right to manage their own lives. Given the disparity of the two environments, it was logical to break the narrative into two parts.

The finished work is in the nature of an ethnohistorical study of the Minorcan community using documents, contemporary accounts, physical remains, and folk memories as "informants." Members of the group in those first years could neither read nor write, with perhaps one or two exceptions, but even those few who were literate left almost no eyewitness reports. The principal documents where the Minorcans speak for themselves are the twenty-one depositions against the plantation proprietor filed with the British authorities in 1777, to seek permission to evacuate the plantation, and even these are filtered through the pen of a translator.

Unfortunately, although we have the Colonial Office records and some private archival materials for the British period in East Florida, intra-province records are scanty indeed. Notorial records have never been found—no land plats for the town, no wills, no Anglican church records.

After the Spanish returned to claim Florida in 1783, records were much more substantial. For present purposes, materials from the second Spanish period furnished the main insights into the Minorcan community at the end of the British domain as well as in the Spanish years. Conversely, a look backward at the community was possible through the many accounts during the United States Territorial period of the "quaint" Old World ways of the Minorcans in the travel stories, letters and newspaper descriptions of that time.

A consistent problem in documenting the story of this group was the many different spellings of the names of people and places. To sort through Minorcan, Spanish, Greek, Italian, and English spellings, not to mention the imprint of Irish priests on the parish records in Spanish St. Augustine, has taken an inordinate amount of time. For example, Minorcan Josep became Spanish José which in turn was Anglicized to Joseph. In general, the line taken has been to use the most common spelling in the New World, particularly when that spelling survives in the St. Augustine of today. The exceptions are those cases where the individual died in the early days or instances in which a certain spelling has a distinguishing meaning in the person's life or in one particular document. For towns and geographical locations in Minorca, the arbitrary decision was made to use the names on the map of Minorca in figure 1.1. Even though they are not faithful to the Minorcan dialect of Catalan they are the spellings generally employed in Spanish St. Augustine.

Lastly, Minorcan is the spelling adhered to in this work because the bulk of the documents use this spelling. The proper dialect spelling is *els menorquins*, and in very recent times some New World descendants have adopted the spelling "Menorcan," which is an intermediate rendering.

In carrying out this project many people have given me assistance. Especially I acknowledge my original academic committee: Brian M. du Toit, chairman, Solon T. Kimball (now deceased), and Michael V. Gannon.

Although some of my research was conducted at the P.K. Yonge Library of Florida History, the library of the J. Hillis Miller Health Center, and the library of the Historic St. Augustine Preservation Board, my primary debt of gratitude is to the board and staff of the St. Augustine Historical Society for the use of their research library and other facilities. I especially thank Jacqueline Fretwell for her help and encouragement through the years that this work was in process, and Page Edwards for his support in publication plans.

I am also in debt to the following individuals, among others, for help on various aspects of the manuscript: Eugenia Arana, Luis Arana, Father Robert Baker, Deborah Rekart Buckingham, Bruce Chappell, Charles S. Coomes, Stephen L. Cumbaa, Kathleen A. Deagan, James D. Dilbeck, Overton G. Ganong, Eugene Lyon, Albert Manucy, William R. Maples, Susan Parker, Daniel R. Schafer, Robert H. Steinbach, Charles A. Tingley, Jean Trapido-Rosenthal, Jean Parker Waterbury, and the late J. Leitch Wright.

Those scholars who have written on the Minorcans need acknowledgement for their labor and varying insights which add to our growing knowledge of this significant but little known New World colony. They are Carita Doggett Corse (1919), Kenneth H. Beeson (1960), E. P. Panagopoulos (1966), Jane Quinn (1975), Philip D. Rasico (1987a), and Naaman Woodland, Jr. (1989).

Of the descendants of the Minorcan colony who have given assistance and support, I am proud to consider many as my friends.

I owe a special debt to my husband, John W. Griffin, who has worked and written extensively on the archaeology and history of Florida. His library of Florida materials was an invaluable resource, and he furnished much practical help including the drafting of maps and charts. His insistence on scholarly standards was ever-present.

Lastly, I owe a heavy debt of gratitude to Herbert E. Bolton who first kindled in me as a lowly undergraduate fifty years ago a spark of interest in the Spanish borderlands which has continued to grow through the years, and it is to his memory that this volume is dedicated.

I

The New Smyrna Years

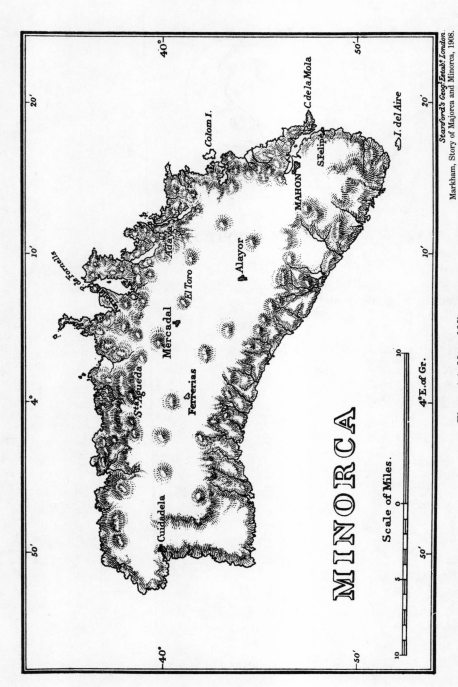

Stanford's Geog.l Estab.t London.
Markham, Story of Majorca and Minorca, 1908.

Figure 1.1. Map of Minorca.

1. A Scotsman's Dream

When the tree is fallen, everyone takes its wood
Old Minorcan saying

By the end of March, 1768, more than 1,400 people were waiting to sail to the New World from the port of Mahón, Minorca. The colonial venture of which they were a part was perhaps, on later analysis, foolhardy, but at the outset its backers saw it as promising, even visionary. The plan was to bring heat-inured Mediterraneans, thought to be already well versed in agriculture in the warm climate of their homelands, to carve out a plantation in the wilderness of East Florida. The proprietor and his associates would profit, the colony of East Florida recently come under English domination would gain responsible and productive citizens, and the settlers themselves would in a few years benefit by making a fresh start in virgin territory where they would eventually acquire some of the lands they tilled—or so it was thought.

In those last days before sailing, a number of this polyglot crowd of potential settlers, composed of Minorcans, Italians, Greeks, and other nationals, were already on shipboard while others stayed in the port town with friends or relatives. Most, however, probably lived in hastily constructed quarters where some had waited almost a year for the expedition to begin. Twice more in the next two decades, before their fortunes were at last secure in East Florida, they were doomed to live in shantytowns—those would be after they first found themselves in the wilderness at New Smyrna, the plantation area, where inadequate preparations had been made for their arrival, and again in the north section of the city of St. Augustine where the English governor gave them refuge after they fled from the rigors of the plantation.

But in that early spring of 1768 when the cold north winds, which sweep over the rocky island of Minorca with more force than in the

other islands in the Balearic archipelago, had finally abated, optimism, which mirrored the brilliant return of the sun after the
winter rainy season, prevailed. In fact, so bad were times on the
island and so enticing were the prospects outlined by Dr. Andrew
Turnbull, the proprietor of the venture, that two hundred potential
stowaways were found when the doctor took a last minute recount
after hearing that one hundred people had deserted. Thereupon, with
an optimism equal to that of his recruits, Turnbull allowed them to
sign on when more reflection might have reminded him that preparations had been made for no more than five hundred on the other side
of the Atlantic. This confident outlook particularized a naivety on
both sides. The emigrants knew little of their destination, and while
Turnbull may have known his medical profession he had never before
planned or managed an agricultural enterprise.

To set this strange encampment on a remote island in the middle
of the Mediterranean into its eighteenth-century context we must
examine the international situation of the times. England had just
gained both Minorca and the Floridas from Spain, part of the terms
of the Treaty of Paris of 1763 under which a much-prized Havana
was restored to Spanish hegemony. While Minorca had experienced
British domination for a period earlier in the eighteenth century, the
Floridas had known no other rule than that of Spain for the preceding
two hundred years.

Unlike the Spanish dominion during which Florida was mainly a
military outpost, England intended to emphasize agriculture and settlement in the newly acquired territory. To carry out this policy,
inducements were given to small grantees, and West Florida largely
followed this settlement pattern. East Florida, on the other hand,
diverged considerably from this ideal. Highly placed individuals,
close to the Crown, were encouraged in securing large holdings for
the development of a plantation economy. It was hoped that Protestant families from depressed European areas could be induced to
emigrate as settlers to work the land. To many planters in the southern colonies this was an impractical idea, for they believed that only
Negro slave labor could do this work. There was considerable agreement, however, that the tropical crops which could be raised, and
for which England was paying dearly in the world market, commonly
required large acreages in order to show a profit.

In accordance with an intent to secure large landholdings, a group of select individuals in London formed the East Florida Society which began to hold monthly meetings in 1766 to explore the process by which this could best be accomplished (Rogers 1976:480). Scotsmen, including Dr. Andrew Turnbull, formed a substantial part of the group, and in fact Rogers (1976:479) regards the Florida venture as "a part of the larger story of Scotland." Scotland was undergoing a renaissance in the last half of the eighteenth century, not the least part of which was an attempt by many Scots to secure sizeable land-holdings in the colonies. Moreover, Scottish governors were appointed in all four of the new colonies acquired by Britain in 1763— Quebec and the ceded islands of the West Indies, as well as the two Florida provinces. These appointments and the heavy Scots membership of the East Florida Society can largely be laid to the influence of the Earl of Bute, a Scotsman who was George III's tutor and cherished advisor and who enjoyed the position of prime minister for a short time.

As it turned out, Turnbull was one of the few entrepreneurs to establish a proprietary project of any consequence in East Florida. Yet, in many ways his enterprise was an anachronism. To secure farm labor he returned to the proprietor-indenture system so successful in earlier British colonial enterprises in North America, a system increasingly out of favor in the very places where it once flourished. With an opening frontier and in a time of rapidly expanding industrialism in the western world, white indentured servants did not remain on the land as peasants on shares as it was hoped but instead emerged into the yeoman class as they took up lands of their own or developed mercantile interests, or, even before their indentured time was served, vanished westward into the obscurity of the forests. Furthermore, those in power in England were discouraging the recruitment of farm labor from the British Isles. The Earl of Hillsborough, who had become president of the Board of Trade in 1763, himself having a large estate in Ireland, was worried about the possible reductions in the labor force which might occur, especially noting that Spain had depopulated her peninsula by extensive immigration to the New World (Bailyn 1986b:29-30). A major segment of the indentured emigrants in the American colonies to the north by that time were craftsmen and skilled laborers seeking expanded opportunities, and their indentures were for no more than three or four years. The "typical pattern was that of artisans and laborers from

European villages, towns and cities settling on the land in America rather than that of peasants thrust into strange . . . worlds" (Bailyn 1986b:26). Undependable for other reasons were the convicts who were being sent in substantial numbers to the colonies as indentured servants in the eighteenth century.

The only successful plantations of that era were those in the southern colonies manned by black slaves—a new kind of feudalism based on a caste system in which those subjugated were easily recognized by their skin color. Plainly put, a plantation in the southern colonies worked by a dependable labor force of black slaves showed a much higher profit than was possible under any other system.

However, by the end of the eighteenth century the cost of American-born slaves was becoming prohibitive, and raw recruits from Africa posed special problems, especially for large scale operations. Turnbull thought that he had hit upon a viable alternative to slave labor and one which would satisfy the grant requirements as well. He had traveled much in the Mediterranean and had married Maria Gracia Dura Bin, the daughter of a wealthy Greek merchant in Smyrna. Why not colonize this new English possession, he reasoned, with those hardy Greeks who, like the African slaves, were already habituated to farming in warm latitudes? It is likely that Turnbull was influenced by a pamphlet written by another Scotsman, Archibald Menzies, entitled *Proposal for Peopling his Majesty's Southern Colonies on the Continent of America.* This early promoter made the following proposal:

> The people I mean, are the Greeks of Levant, accustomed to the hot climate and bred to the culture of the vine, olive, cotton, tobacco, madder, etc. etc. as also to the raising of silk; and who could supply our markets with all the commodities which at present we have from Turky [sic], and other parts. These people are, in general, sober and industrious; and being reduced, by their severe masters, to the greatest misery, would be easily persuaded to fly from slavery, to the protection of a free government. (Menzies 1763:2).

Menzies had special plans for the women whom he described as "remarkably handsome." "This circumstance," he concluded, "would naturally prompt inter-marriages between our people and them, and soon put an end to all distinctions."

Turnbull found among his friends in London a willing partner for his project—Sir William Duncan, a baronet and a fellow member of the East Florida Society. Both were well known to the highly-placed and influential Earl of Shelburne, so their requests for 20,000 acres each were expedited. They were later joined in their venture by Sir Richard Temple, acting for George Grenville, prime minister of England. Including subsequent grants to the principals and to the Turnbull children, the total land area in East Florida eventually reached 101,400 acres, some of which was at a distance from the area where the main plantation was located. All three of the partners were to provide capital and other resources, but Turnbull alone was to act as the colonizer and manager of the plantation.

Reports on prospects in Florida were conflicting. Some publications on Britain's American colonies reinforced the prevailing stereotype of Florida as a sandy desert with its "pestiferous sea coasts" and aptly named "dismals," i.e. swamps (cited by Mowat 1943:51). A note of caution also came from Henry Laurens, a successful South Carolina businessman and planter, and agent for some of the would-be proprietors including Andrew Turnbull. He warned that location of uniformly good land in large tracts in Florida was almost impossible (Rogers 1976:485). However, members of the East Florida Society of London preferred to believe the enthusiastic report in the pamphlet written by Dr. William Stork who visited Florida in 1765 on behalf of some of his clients, most of whom were members of the East Florida Society. So popular was this work that a second edition of his work appeared immediately upon the heels of the first, this time supplemented by a series of observations by the naturalist John Bartram (Stork 1766).

To fulfill some of the conditions of the grant, and in order to begin plans for the colony, Turnbull sailed for Florida in the fall of 1766 taking his wife and children with him. The immediate friendship formed between Governor James Grant and Turnbull flowered as much from expediency as from their being fellow Scotsmen. Each saw how the other could be useful.

The choice of James Grant as the first governor of the newly acquired province of East Florida had been a wise one. He had already distinguished himself in a diverse career in the Carolinas, Canada, Havana, and in the Indian Wars. This background coupled with an adroitness in handing difficult and ambiguous situations made him valuable for the transition period when he would deal with the Indians, the remnants of the Spanish occupation, and the settlement of the new colony.

In the first several years, Grant's attempts to populate the colony had been unsuccessful. The only previous settlement of potential consequence was that of Rollestown, near the present location of Palatka on the St. Johns River. From the first, Denys Rolle's venture had suffered from the quality of its settlers—vagrants, beggars, prostitutes, and debtors from the London streets and prisons, plus a collection of footloose frontiersmen from the southern woods—and from the absenteeism of its proprietor. Just prior to Turnbull's arrival, Denys Rolle had published a petition charging Governor Grant with obstruction (Rolle 1765). Consequently, encouragement and support of Turnbull's project became especially vital after this setback as Grant was under a mandate from the Colonial Office to settle the new lands with all possible speed.

Turnbull, for his part, could ask for no more important ally than the governor of the colony in which he planned his settlement. Until his return to England in 1774, Grant remained Turnbull's chief friend and intercessor with the English authorities, a strong bulwark for the new plantation venture.

The first grants to Duncan and Turnbull were on the east central coast of Florida in the area graphically described as "The Mosquitos," near present Ponce de Leon Inlet, and partly encompassed in the modern city of New Smyrna Beach, about seventy-five miles south of St. Augustine. These lands were surveyed in 1765 and again in 1767, by William Gerard De Brahm, the surveyor-general of the province (De Vorsey 1971), the latter survey specifically to fix the boundaries of the Turnbull colony lands.

Both of the original 20,000 acre grants were long, relatively narrow pieces of land stretching back diagonally for miles from the Hillsborough River (figure 1.2). The naturalist, William Bartram, who accompanied De Brahm on the 1767 survey, noted that there were no cleared fields or human habitations, but Indian mounds, one of them quite large, and numerous orange trees attested to prior inhabitants (Bartram 1958:91-92).

The land on the large tracts was far from uniform. Along the river side of the property ran a relatively high ridge, underlaid by a vein of coquina rock and overlaid at least in part by the shell kitchen-middens of earlier aboriginal occupants. It was the ridge which sup-

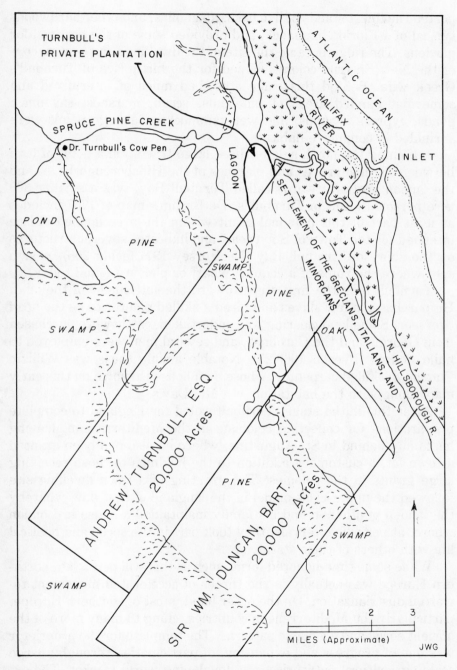

Figure 1.2. Land Grants of the New Smyrna Colony. Adapted from De Brahm (1769), with additions.

ported the finest stands of live oaks, magnolias, and other hardwoods typical of a Florida hammock, and provided some of the best soil for gardens. The ridge became the site of the dwellings and central core of the New Smyrna colony, named for the birthplace of Turnbull's Greek wife. Behind this ridge stretched miles of intermixed and somewhat banded areas of pinelands, scrub, marshes, savannas, ponds, cypress swamps, and wet hammocks. Cabbage palms were sprinkled in conducive habitats.

Adjoining the north side of these large tracts, on a point of land between the mangroves and marshes of the Hillsborough River and the lagoon arm afterwards called Turnbull Bay, was a smaller 300 acre personal grant of Turnbull's. De Brahm's map of 1767 includes at least part of this personal grant within the area labeled "Place intended for the Town of Smyrnea," and indicates several structures on the shore of Turnbull Bay (De Vorsey 1971:facing 206), near a spot where the ruins of a coquina wharf or pier are found today.

Turnbull took the first steps toward the settlement of the land. He purchased a few slaves and hired a skilled planter to be the head overseer. Some land clearing was undertaken, cattle were purchased from Georgia and the Carolinas, and several men were employed to build houses (Beeson 1960:27). Notable among these was William Watson, a skilled carpenter, whose own house is shown on this early map, along with the habitation of a Mr. Davis.

After this initial stage, Turnbull sailed for England to complete preparations for collecting colonists in the Mediterranean, leaving his family behind in St. Augustine, where he also had been granted a town lot, a customary addition to the holdings of those receiving large grants in the colonies. The granting of a town dwelling site followed the upper-class model in the England of that day, whereby the landed gentlemen and his family maintained a house in London where, at periodic intervals, they took part in the social and political life with others of their status.

While some time-honored forms such as this still persisted, northern Europe was actually in the throes of accelerated movement toward industrialization. On the other hand, most of southern Europe, particularly the Mediterranean countries, clung to many more of the ancient social and economic patterns. The template for the proprietor was one of progress and expansion, of participation through a large scale agricultural enterprise in a developing world market. The expectations of the recruited settlers contrasted sharply. Their aim, exclusive of the inevitable few who quest adventure for its own sake, was to re-establish their traditional way of life in a better environment—to escape disease, famine, and ancient wrongs. This was not a marriage made to last.

2. Children of Tyranny, Plague and Famine

A year of fig blossoms is a year of tears.
Old Minorcan saying

The port of Mahón, where Turnbull arrived in June, 1767 ready to begin his venture, was a logical place for the expedition's Mediterranean headquarters. Its strategic placement, its ownership by the British, and its unparalleled deep and sheltered harbor—still one of the best in the world—made it a natural choice. Ships could provision and set out in good weather, and on return, recruits could be quartered and fed while others were being sought. Moreover, the British governor, James Johnston, was very willing to house and provision the emigrants since he had previously been removed from office for mistreatment of the Minorcan populace and had only recently been reinstated, with orders to make amends. Undoubtedly, then, the port of Mahón was an excellent staging area, but ultimately this choice was the contingency which controlled the composition of the settler group.

The collection of colonists took almost a year. The story of Turnbull's adventures and mishaps as he gathered people for the venture has been described by several historians, that of Panagopoulos (1966) being especially well documented. As it turned out, considering the difficulties encountered in recruiting Greeks for the colony and the ease with which the Minorcans and Italians signed on, time and money might have been saved if the entire recruitment effort had been confined to the western Mediterranean.

An exact breakdown of the national origin of Turnbull's colonial group was never recorded, making it necessary to depend on the conflicting numbers included in the reports of Turnbull, his compatriots in London, Governor Johnston of Minorca, Governor Grant, and his successor Governor Patrick Tonyn in British East Florida. Each had special reasons for inflating the total number or for altering the size of national origin groups at the expense of others. Historians have muddled matters even further in arriving at various totals for the ethnic subgroups, or are advisedly vague. No one studying this group can go with any certainty beyond the two simple statements—that 1,403 people set sail for the New World, and that the majority of these were Minorcan islanders.

The only new light on this puzzle shed by the present study is in a look at the survivors. No even partially accurate count of the places of origin is possible until the still-living original colonists show up as named individuals in the censuses and other documents some sixteen years later in Spanish St. Augustine. By then, of course, many had fallen away from disease, accidents, or old age and the resultant count pictures imperfectly the original composition of the colony.

Nevertheless, a look at table 2.1 which indicates the place of origin of colonial survivors tells us, among other things, that eighty percent were Minorcan islanders, a somewhat larger proportion than previously speculated. The probable low mean age of the immigrat-

Table 2.1

Place of National Origin of Survivors of Colony (Circa 1786)

	Number	Percent
Minorcans—town not known	50	
Minorcans—town known	177	
Alayor 44		
Mahón 39		
San Felipe 38		
Cuidadela 40		
Mercadal 15		
Ferrerías 1		
Total—all Minorcans	227	80%
Italians 22		
Greeks (Corsican) 11		
Greeks (other areas) 12		
French 6		
Mallorcans 5		
Spanish 2		
Total—all other nationals	58	20%
Grand Total	285	100%

Source: Figures compiled from St. Augutine census reccords of 1784, 1786, and 1787 and from the Parish Records.

ing Minorcan group, which included children coming with their parents, and the higher death rate among the mainland Greeks, dealt with in a subsequent chapter, are variables which affected this result.

Setting aside this table for the moment, a glimpse at the eighteenth-century Mediterranean world is in order. In the last half of that century, the tremors of the industrialization beginning in northern Europe were having some effect further south, particularly on the trade networks of the Mediterranean. Nevertheless, the common people's traditional way of life changed little, subject as always to famine, pestilence, wars and political oppression; exacerbated, or at least influenced, by the changing economic fortunes of southern Europe.

However, because of these changes in the world situation as well as other factors, eighteenth-century Europe was marked by a long, slow increase in population. For example, Italy, the native land of some of Turnbull's colonists, showed a population increase from eleven million in 1700 to over eighteen million in 1770 (Anderson 1961:48). Dwindling of the great plagues and improved nutrition played a part in this change. In addition, a dramatic shift in climate occurred in the middle of the century. A warming trend with milder winters and cooler, rainier summers extended the growing season, increasing crop yields (Brooks 1970:376).

However, short term fluctuations could cause temporary, although often severe, imbalances. Anderson (1961:49) concluded that "it is clear that throughout this period both birth and death-rates for every part of Europe for which reasonably reliable figures are available tended to fluctuate, in the short term, in sympathy with the state of the harvests and the ease or otherwise of obtaining food." Equally important, and the result of a few years of lush harvests in any area, were the rises in population beyond the carrying capacity. Such temporary imbalances provided ready recruits for a New World venture.

With the Greek mainland many miles away, Turnbull easily postponed going directly there when he heard of a group of Italians ready and willing to leave the seacoast town of Leghorn, Italy. In the good summer weather, when the Mediterranean is often calm and unruffled, the coast of Italy was only a few days away. There he recruited 110 Italians (Lansdowne MSS 88:135). Some were new residents of

Leghorn, having come from inland areas to seek their fortunes in a city decimated by one of the last great epidemics of the plague. Strangers in a hostile city, mostly unemployed, they were regarded by the civil authorities with mixed feelings and were subject to deportation without notice.

Based on later statistics as well as Andrew Turnbull's statements, these Italians were all young single men. Of the twenty-two Italians in later St. Augustine counts, no last names were duplicates, although some of the original immigrants were probably related. According to the proprietor (Turnbull 1788) these men were all, with the exception of one, in dire circumstances. They were escaping the fate of their families who Lopreato (1967:15), in describing Italians of the eighteenth century, refers to as "peasants languishing in hunger, disease and exhaustion." From these exigencies came the beginning nucleus of the New Smyrna colony.

At last on July 11 Turnbull departed for the Levant to fulfill his intention of recruiting Greek families. While this search proved more difficult than anticipated, his agents meantime found to their surprise a contingent of Greeks closer by on the island of Corsica who were ready and willing to leave that island.

The undetermined number of Greeks, probably about fifty individuals, who came from Corsica, were mostly members of one kinship group. The Stephanopoli family had immigrated to Corsica en masse in 1676; altogether 730 men, women and children had fled the Greek mainland after the ascendence of the Ottoman Empire. In the ensuing one hundred years they had become a sturdy sector of the island population, even blending in by forsaking the Greek Orthodox religion to embrace Roman Catholicism. Contributions of these Greeks to Corsica were many, including the introduction of new agricultural methods and trade development (Panagopoulos 1956:109). However, in 1767, facing the unpleasant change from Genoese to French control of their adopted homeland, some chose to sail in Turnbull's ships.

Meanwhile, Turnbull contended with unforeseen problems in recruiting the anticipated Greeks from the western Mediterranean. His mission was suspect there, and several times he had to wait for letters from London to smooth the way for him. Other times he encountered conflicting elements in the local communities. This was natural since he aimed his efforts at places where the brewing discontent made his offer tempting. It was a slow process, and he ranged

around the Aegean Sea for so long that he was overtaken by the
winter storm season. In the days of sail it was the rare seaman who
cared to ply the Mediterranean between late November and April,
but the ships carrying the eastern Greeks negotiated the passage
without disaster, arriving in Mahón in February at the height of the
rainy season.

About two hundred Greeks had been recruited from among the
peoples of Mani in the Peloponnesos—the entire membership of a
group which had been resisting Turkish oppression, an oppression
endemic in those times in that part of the world. Harassment had
forced them higher into the mountains where they barely subsisted,
working rocky patches of land and engaging in some pastoral activities. These transhumant pastoralists were a warlike group, both
men and women bearing arms in raiding parties to the plains. Their
priest-leader had recently been murdered and many of their number
killed in ambush, so that Turnbull's offer of opportunity in the New
World was timely (Panagopoulos 1966:30-32).

Campbell (1964:57) describes a Greek mountain community which
he studied recently as patrilineal and virilocal, meaning that descent
is reckoned through the male line and newly married couples live in
the locale of the husband's family. The traditional way of life of that
group has probably changed little in the last two hundred years, and
we can assume that social organization today differs little from that
of the highland Greeks in the Turnbull colony.

In addition to the above Greeks, Turnbull picked up several
people in the Aegean islands, some on the coast at Coron, and an
adventurous seventeen-year old, Gaspar Papi, from Smyrna in Asia
Minor. According to Panagopoulos (1966:45) several members of a
Greek colony in Mahón, Minorca, chose to sail with the Turnbull
colony, although John Grammatos is the only such documented individual.

The largest number of settlers were Minorcans, certainly of such
numbers, probably no less than 1,000, that the entire colony was
eventually named for them. The social organization and life patterns
developed by the colonial group were built on the dominant cultural
themes of these Minorcan natives; hardly surprising since they probably constituted at least two-thirds of the colony.

Cleghorn describes Minorca in the eighteenth century:

The Surface of the Island is rough and unequal; and in many Places divided by long narrow Vales of Considerable Depth, which are called *Barrancos* by the Natives. . . . Near the Towns and Villages the Fields are well cultivated, and enclosed by Stone Walls; But the rest, for the most part is rocky or covered with woods and Thickets. . . . The Soil is light, thin and very stony, with a good deal of Sea Salt, and some calcareous Nitre intermixed. . . . if the Peasants may be credited, it would always yield a Quantity of Corn [i.e. grain crops], and Wine sufficient for the Natives; did not the Violence of the Winds, and the excessive Drought of the Weather, in different Seasons frequently injure the Crops (Cleghorn 1779:11-12).

Minorca raised mainly winter crops, notably wheat and barley (Cleghorn 1779:13; Armstrong 1756:125). The barley was cut by the twentieth of May and the wheat in June, "so that the whole Harvest is commonly got in by Midsummer Day [June 24]" (Cleghorn 1779:13). Then in late summer grapes were harvested and made into wine. In between, the natives grew diversified gardens, hunted, fished and engaged in some gathering activities. The last became crucial in time of food scarcity. Cleghorn (1779:24-25,39) furnishes us with a long list of foods gathered by Minorcan islanders at the time. In lean years, Indian figs used as fences for the gardens provided sustenance for whole families in September. Fortunately, these trees fruited abundantly in poor grain years, the early and profuse flowering of which was viewed as a sure sign of trouble ahead (Cleghorn 1779:53).

We are indebted to Cleghorn, a medical doctor like Andrew Turnbull, for a physical description of Minorcans of that day:

The Natives of this Island, are commonly thin, lean, and well built, strong and active, of a middle Stature, and an Olive Complexion. Their Hair for the most part, is black and curled; in many Chestnut coloured, in some red. In a Word, the young People are either of a sanguine or cholerick Constitution; while those of more advanced Years, become dry, meagre, and, what the Ancients called atrabilious (Cleghorn 1779:59).

A decade before the Minorcan group sailed to Turnbull's New World colony, Armstrong (1756:213) reckoned the population of

Minorca at 27,000. Of these, 12,000 were female and 3,000 were of the proper age for fighting men. Considering the scarcity of good soil on the island and its small size—35 miles long and 10 miles at the widest—it must have been suffering from overpopulation.

Historians (Corse 1919; Panagopoulos 1966; Beeson 1960; Quinn 1975) all agree that Turnbull found so many ready recruits in Minorca because of the severe famine existing at the time. Quinn (1975:42) attributes the beginning of the famine to the mid-March freeze of 1766, leading to starvation conditions among most of the population by 1767-68.

In an apologia written after the breakup of the colony Turnbull himself (1788:684) described the plight of the Minorcans:

> In regard to the families he carried from the island of Minorca, they were also very poor and in miserable circumstances, two or three families excepted, for provisions were so scarce that year in Minorca, that many families were almost starved; some of the men that the doctor [meaning himself] engaged often declared that if he had not relieved them, they must have perished for want of food; it was only the indigent that he wished to engage, and to take such as could not have any reason to look back, nor regret leaving their own country. . . These people were all engaged as farmers before they left Europe.

The island of Minorca (figure 1.1) was divided into five geographical areas called *términos*, each with a major village or town, namely, Cuidadela, Ferrerías, Mercadal, Alayor, and Mahón. Clearly, from the list of survivors in table 2.1, colonists came from all of these subdivisions. The largest number, if we can regard survivors as an accurate index, came from the *término* of Mahón, with an almost equal number hailing from that port city and from nearby San Felipe whose ancient fort guarded the entrance to the harbor. Alayor, an inland farming area, accounted for the next greatest number of survivors with Cuidadela close behind.

The folk tradition that many people in the original colony were from Mercadal is either erroneous, using the survival figures as an indicator, or, if correct, perhaps Mercadal natives were felled by malaria and other diseases in the New World. Armstrong (1756:51) did not find those from that inland town to be robust for he tells us that, "there is something squalid and haggard in the countenances of these people, beyond what we observe in the rest of the natives of Minorca, especially in the women."

The Minorcan group were patrilineal, with some mixed matrilineal influences—a confused picture characteristic of the Mediterranean (Casselberry and Valavanes 1976:215-226). This was a likely consequence of the variation of early tribal and Greek/Roman assimilation, influenced locally by specific environmental zones.

No accurate information is available on eighteenth-century Minorcan residence patterns. However, the mapping of the group after they reached St. Augustine in the present study establishes the Minorcan group who came with Turnbull's colony as primarily uxorilocal. Adam's (1947:678) definition of the term uxorilocal, as opposed to virilocal, refers to residence of a married couple in the locale, sometimes the actual domicile, of the wife's family.

Among those enumerated as "Minorcans" in later census counts in St. Augustine there were a few people listed of other than Minorcan, Greek, and Italian origin. Six French nationals who evidently signed up to join the colony at Leghorn were in the group. We also know, for example, that Pedro Osias was from Provence. As a speaker of *provençal*, a French dialect which is close to *menorquin*, the dialect of Catalan spoken in Minorca, he could easily communicate with María Ortagus, the Minorcan girl whom he married. Likewise, Juan Columinas and Francisco Marin came from Catalonia, the closest area of Spain to the Balearic Islands. Whether they embarked directly from there or by way of Minorca, which seems more likely, the documents do not tell us. No mention was found in the accounts sent to the Colonial Office of recruits from Mallorca, the largest island of the Balearics, but five such men were in the surviving group, four of whom had taken Minorcan wives. We can only conclude that news of the promising expedition reached many corners of the Mediterranean during that crucial year.

While many aspects of this venture were unique, there were similarities to other ventures of that time. Emigration from Europe to the New World followed customary migratory flow patterns which were the westward extensions of often-used migratory pathways. Many times, and we have just such a case with the Italians recruited for this venture, there were two or three stage migrants, who, when they first left their original homes, had no intention of making the trans-Atlantic passage (Bailyn 1986b:186).

Even before they sailed, these separate peoples, gradually collected together in Mahón, commenced the process of becoming a
distinct community. How did this happen? Pre-existing similarity of
culture certainly played a part; the fact that "the Mediterranean
Basin represents a cultural unity" (Gilmore 1987:3) furnished a starting point. The amount of cultural contact through the centuries
among various areas of the Mediterranean, through the development
of trade and migration routes, the constant shifts in personal and
political allegiances, made contact much easier in an era when the
best and most reliable roads were those made of water. The settlers
from coastal areas or even from inland areas in insular locales probably knew the trade language of the Mediterranean, the kind of pid-
gin scramble which grows up naturally in areas of constant inter-
change and which is codified by usage. Easing communication even
further in the present instance was the fact that the languages of the
Italians, Spanish, French, and Minorcans were mutually intelligible
at least to a degree, remembering, too, that the Corsican Greeks
undoubtedly had facility in the Italian language.

This mutual culture was, and of course still is, grounded in an
environmental similarity. The Mediterranean climate is such that it
offers the outsider a false welcome masking its harsh realities, while
Mediterraneans themselves have long adjusted themselves to the
scourges of drought, heat, and the fierce winter storms with their
high winds sweeping the watery expanses which border their homelands. They had made do for centuries in that climate and with the
poor rocky soil, where with their skillful adaptations they had found
means to sustain themselves.

The colonists were of this old Mediterranean stock, mostly small
agriculturalists who combined farming with other subsistence activities such as fishing, hunting, and gathering wild edibles. Except
for the highland-dwelling Peloponnesian Greeks, they were tied
loosely to a town economy for economic, political and trade purposes
in the characteristic Mediterranean pattern. Even though these were
folk peoples used to a limited life, this country-city relationship
bridged them across to the larger Mediterranean world. This duality
is treated as a general Mediterranean feature by Caro Baroja (1963).

Of major importance for this microcosm community was the
strong binding force of the Roman Catholic religion, with its integral
world view and value system, a religion which was Mediterranean

born. The Corsican Greeks had within the previous century taken on Roman Catholicism, and even the Greeks from the eastern Mediterranean practiced a form of Christianity which was a branch of the original spread of the Christian religion.

Notwithstanding the commonalities in the various heritages, the numbers and domination of Minorcan islanders set the cultural tone. The designation of the whole group after they reached the New World and even until this day as the "Minorcans" tells the story. It was their variant of the Mediterranean life-style and their social system and cultural themata into which the others blended and adapted their ways. At times in the English documents they are referred to as "Mahónese", which, aside from the eighteenth-century habit of referring to the nearest city of residence instead of to national origin, might also demonstrate more prominence in numbers as well as status. We see by table 2.1 that those hailing from Mahón along with those from nearby San Felipe together numbered 77 out of the 177 Minorcan islanders for whom town of origin is known. Also, of course, Mahón was the embarkation spot. Other documents from the early days of the colony in Florida referred to the whole group as "the Greeks," "the Greek colony," or the "Doctor's Greeks," most likely because the original intent was to people the plantation with Greeks. Within the first few decades, however, these other terms largely faded from use, leaving Minorcan as the common name for the group.

In spite of the ultimate Minorcan cast to the little community, the original core group of recruits was the more than one hundred Italian men who were first brought to the embarkation site. However, through a natural process, these being young unmarried men, they soon recruited Minorcan girls to the enterprise as brides. Through these marriages and in other ways they began to adopt the lifeways of their new milieu. Having shifted their living locales several times in their homelands, it was easy for them to accommodate to new places and new people. Later living patterns in the New World as well as godparent exchanges, lead to the conclusion that of all the nationals, these Italians blended into the dominant Minorcan island group with the greatest ease.

As to those of Greek descent, the Corsican Greeks were already accustomed to carving a niche for themselves in an alien culture. The eastern Mediterranean Greeks, on the other hand, were a different

matter. Not only were they used to the practice of the Greek Orthodox religion, but they varied somewhat in marriage and residence
patterns and in other cultural practices from the rest of the settler
group. Moreover, they spoke a different language. Those from the
highland areas particularly had kept themselves isolated to guard
against being overwhelmed by invaders. Things became even more
problematic on the other side of the Atlantic when their lack of natural disease immunity, because of that very isolation, began to take
a toll. It is no surprise then to find the Greeks several decades later
in St. Augustine somewhat different from the rest of the group in
marriage, household and residence patterns, definitely on the
periphery of what came to be known as Minorcan.

Two Catholic clergymen, both Minorcan islanders, both from
humble families, embarked with the group, providing the kind of
leadership needed in facing the rigors of life on the Florida frontier.
As apostolic missionaries they were granted temporary faculties for
their work in the New World by the vicar-general of Minorca. Since
the seat of the bishopric was in Mallorca, which was under Spanish
domination, communication was disrupted and full credentials could
not be secured before sailing. Perhaps if they had waited for permission from the bishop in Mallorca or from the higher church authorities
in Rome, given the slowness with which the ecclesiastical and political wheels moved, they might have lost their chance for the ocean
passage. Several years after arriving in Florida and after lengthy
exchanges through ecclesiastical and civil channels, extended faculties for administering the New World parish were finally granted.

Father Pedro Bartolomé Camps was at that time thirty-eight
years old and had for twelve years held the position of pastor and
vicar of the San Martín parish in his native Mercadal (Quinn 1975:45).
Father Camps always signed documents with the designation "Reverend Doctor Camps" leading later scholars to assume that he had
earned a doctorate in theology. His actual education is unclear, but
perhaps he began his religious dedication at the Augustinian Monastery on the nearby mountain, *El Toro*. After that it is assumed that
he completed his doctorate at the University of Blessed Ramon Lull
in Palma, Mallorca. If so, it is possible, given the time element involved, that he was taught by Father Junipero Serra, who was teach-
ing religious philosophy at that University until 1749 when he embarked on a missionary career eventually resulting in the founding

Figure 2.1. The Virgin of El Toro.

of the California mission chain. Even if their periods at the University did not overlap, Father Camps must have rubbed elbows with other students there who later undertook a call to missionary fields. It would have been easy for Father Camps to catch the missionary fever prevalent at the time, and to carry it into his life's work in a foreign land. In all of his work he was never spoken of as other than an exemplary pastor.

With Father Bartolomé Casanovas who became Father Camps assistant, it was another story. Father Casanovas was an Augustinian monk, probably also educated at the monastery at *El Toro*, who had been given license to preach and hear confessions, and who had been for some time serving the parish at Alayor. Somewhat younger, he did not have the even, saintly temperament of Father Camps. In contrast with the glowing report on Father Camps' work in Minorca, Father Casanovas rated the lukewarm statement from his superiors that there was "nothing wrong in his conduct." His volatile disposition led him into activities in Florida causing Andrew Turnbull to deport him for insurrection six years after the colony began.

As in any venture of this magnitude, the last days before sailing must have been hectic. The Minorcan islanders were saying good-bye to relatives and friends with the certainty that they would never see them again. The lives of those going would be totally severed from those of their compatriots and since they were not able to read or write, it would be a rare instance when either would hear of the subsequent fortunes of the other. It was as clean a break as death.

All were busy sorting out their own belongings, and in accordance with Turnbull's request, wrapping and storing in barrels the seeds and cuttings of plants for future use in starting crops as well as kitchen gardens in a land whose soil and climate they did not yet know (Beeson 1960:44). In addition they were disposing of property and taking care of other legal matters. Most important of all these business affairs was the matter of indenture contracts with the proprietor.

The whole matter of the contracts between the colonists and Turnbull is very cloudy indeed. Unresolved are such questions as whether all of the settlers signed a written contract and how many years were contracted for. Contracts were evidently for variable periods, anywhere from three to ten years, the length being a function of the plight of the recruit or group of recruits or the skills which the householder would bring to the plantation.

The only actual surviving contract available for study is the one
for the Minorcans published later by Ruidavets y Tudury (1887:1381-
1383). This document carries Turnbull's signature only, the supposition being that the Minorcan signee list was lost. The terms are
similar to Turnbull's own later description of the contracts:

> ... the agreement or farming lease (signed by him and them in
> Europe) being that the whole of the expense after their landing
> in East Florida, should be paid out of the first produce; that
> they were to cultivate the same lands for ten years more on
> shares with the proprietor; that is, they were to share the neat
> [sic] produce equally, the proprietor's share being to reimburse
> the expenses of bringing them to America; the whole, however,
> of the expense of maintaining the farmer and his family was
> first to be taken from the gross produce, before the division
> mentioned was made, so that the farmer's share, for the most
> part, could not be less than two-thirds, even from good crops,
> but in a bad season, these expenses would take the whole, which
> actually happened to the lazy and indolent; by this agreement
> the farmer was always certain of a living, for even in a total
> failure of a crop, the proprietor could not suffer the farmer to
> starve; ... The doctor offered them leases for ninety-nine years
> wishing to fix them and their children (Turnbull 1788:684-688).

More favorable contracts were made with the specialized
craftsmen who were part of the colony, but we do not know how
many of these craftsmen there were in the original group. In addition, certain individuals were later selected from among the colonial
group for their special skills and still others were enlisted from the
American colonies. As well as land and the promises of good rations,
some, such as Juan Portella, the shoemaker, were to receive cash.
Portella contracted to work for five years at five pounds sterling a
year. Likewise, Turnbull had contracted to pay 300 and 260 pesos a
year respectively to Fathers Camps and Casanovas according to a
letter written by Father Camps to the Bishop of Cuba in 1772 (Connor Collection, Doc. 82, 1772).

It is certainly possible, given no positive evidence to the contrary
and considering the fact that all but a few were illiterate, that in
most cases the contracts were read to them, and they were not entirely aware of what they were signing with an X, or that in some
instances, particularly the stowaways, that they gave verbal agreement only. Such casualness about the formal agreement is not sur-

prising considering the trust inherent in the patron-client relationship in the eighteenth-century Mediterranean world. "The rich man employs, assists and protects the poor man," as Pitt-Rivers (1961:140) describes it, "and in return the latter works for him, gives him esteem and prestige, and also protects his interest by seeing that he is not robbed, by warning him of the machinations of others and by taking his part in disputes." The patronage system, still extant in the lands of the Mediterranean basin, and of great importance today in the social structure and economy of Central and South American countries, carries with it rights and privileges, and consequent cultural sanctions should the delicate balance in the system not be maintained. Many of the agreements in this system are verbal and implicit. Each man's word is a matter of honor.

In contrast, Andrew Turnbull came from another culture with a different social and economic structure, so that his understanding of the agreements carried no such baggage as the proper Mediterranean patron would be expected to acknowledge. Moreover, in a rapidly industrializing nation such as England, labor had assumed the nature of a commodity, a "thing" to be employed for profit. Individuals with rights and privileges and human feelings of their own were often forgotten. For instance, Turnbull's statement that those who were "lazy and indolent" would be unable to get any share of the proceeds provided a loophole for him. In turn this loophole could furnish a means for blaming the victims in the years, particularly in the lean years, that followed in the New World, an excuse for not honoring the terms of the contracts as the settlers had been led to expect. Even more telling is the statement made by Turnbull in a letter to Governor Grant on April 29, 1768, in which he advised the governor that "the families are engaged to stay on our grounds ten years after they have paid the expense of settling in the province, so that it carries them for thirteen or fourteen years at least" (Bailyn 1986b:457) From statements made later in St. Augustine, we are made clearly aware that this long indenture period was not the colonists' understanding.

As a postscript to a description of recruits for the colony another matter must be disposed of. An early German traveler (Schoepf 1911:234) who visited St. Augustine in 1783-84 told of another group of recruits destined for the colony. "To be sure, for making the work easier the company had provided for negroes who were to be hired out among the Greeks; but unluckily the first ship, bringing 500 negroes from Africa, was wrecked on the coast of Florida and the whole number was lost."

This intelligence, found only in this source, and sanctified by repetition in subsequent accounts, is questionable. Turnbull did use slaves and other blacks on the plantation, particularly on his own acreage, but nowhere does he indicate other than his avowed intent to use Mediterranean peoples as primary labor on the plantation. Nor at a time when he had already oversubscribed his labor force, and was short on resources, was he likely to engage in such a venture. Certainly a loss of this magnitude would have been reported in the official documents of the province. We can also expect that, if true, Turnbull would have used the occurrence as evidence of good intent when later defending himself against detractors accusing him of inflicting harsh conditions on his colonists.

It is probable that this shipload of Africans, if indeed it existed at all, was intended for one of the other more conventional plantations in the general Mosquitos area, perhaps Mount Oswald plantation. The owner of that plantation, Richard Oswald, had extensive holdings in the British colonies and imported slaves on his own ships from his staging area in Africa (Taylor 1984).

3. A Colony Begins

A year of thunder is a year of death.
Old Minorcan proverb

T he journey to the New World was a nightmare. On April 17, 1768, eight ships, with such colorful names as *Charming Betsy, New Fortune, Hope,* and *Friendship,* put out from Gibraltar loaded with 1,403 colonists. The ships varied considerably in size and rig—brigantines, brigs and a snow are mentioned—and carried from 120 to 232 passengers each. An average load would not tell us much, although a cursory examination of shipping for that era does suggest overcrowding, an overcrowding nearly comparable to that of ships carrying slaves.

Four of the ships dropped anchor in St. Augustine on June 26, 1768, a trip of two and a half months. They were the lucky ones. The other four ships were blown off course, and the last one did not straggle into St. Augustine until early August. Documents of the day, nevertheless, tell of a stormy passage for all, even those who arrived at their destination the earliest, and this at a time of year when a trans-Atlantic passage is ordinarily the easiest.

The hardships aboard ship are manifest in the number of reported deaths. The figure of one hundred and forty-eight deaths reported by Turnbull is questionable. The actual mortality was probably slightly higher because the replacement by births is not figured in. The official figure is the difference between the 1,403 people leaving Mahón and the 1,255 who arrived in Florida. Turnbull himself reported five births between Mahón and Gibraltar (Lansdowne MSS Vol. 88:145), but no births for the much longer passage period are reported. Yet the parish records show three babies born at sea and baptized later in New Smyrna, presumably because neither of the priests were aboard the ships on which they were born. We can assume that others were baptized on shipboard and therefore do not enter into any official count. Even ten births would have replaced ten people who died, thereby pushing the death toll to one hundred fifty-eight. Regardless, using the lowest death toll still yields a 10.5% mortality figure; equal to that of slave ships of the time, where an average mortality of ten to fourteen percent could be expected.

But statistics do not tell of the agony of individual suffering. Unfortunately, we do not have any eyewitness accounts of that suffering except in the reports to the authorities by Turnbull. His terse report noted that scurvy and infections caused most of the deaths during the crossing, with the highest toll among the young and old. Even those who survived must have suffered from the debilitating effects of a long sea voyage belying the confidence earlier expressed by Turnbull.

Before leaving the Old World, Turnbull with rosy optimism had reported that his colonists were "healthy and Fit" (Lansdowne MSS Vol. 88:145). However, in preindustrial times, those voyaging in the spring when most long ocean voyages were undertaken, suffered from an extension of the seasonal deprivation of fresh food (Tannahill 1973:271). Add to this the inferior nutritional status of Turnbull's colonists which had led many to sign on in the first place, and the high death rate is partly explained. For example, scurvy requires about six months to develop to the acute stage, so that deprivation of fresh food on the high seas merely contributed to already incipient problems. Therefore, when they landed in the New World the settlers were not in top physical condition, nor mental condition for that matter since mental depression is a symptom of scurvy.

Nevertheless, when the first four ships carrying 700 passengers dropped anchor at St. Augustine on June 26, 1768 spirits rose. June, of all months in Florida, is most like the warm, dry climate of the Mediterranean. Perhaps the sight of houses packed close together on the narrow streets and the old Spanish fort which guarded the port of St. Augustine as the Castle of San Felipe guarded the port of Mahón, was reassuring. The land was low and monotonous, however, unlike the rocky cliffs of their homelands. In a like manner, the vegetation, dense and tropical in appearance, was an untidy snarl compared to the hardy, sparse scrub of the Mediterranean.

Part of the group, whether by choice or assignment is not known, went overland by path to New Smyrna. The shipping space vacated was doubtless filled with provisions for the plantation. The colonists, heartily sick of being on shipboard, may have considered the seventy-five mile walk to the plantation a lesser hardship. Known grandly as the "King's Road," the path, which wound through the palmetto scrub skirting marshes and with here and there a stream to be forded, partly followed an old Indian trail. Governor Grant had recently commissioned a group of Indians to widen it, and had plans for building bridges to make the southern plantations more accessible to St. Augustine. Just before the group of settlers made their weary way to their new homes an Indian named Grey Eyes had driven a herd of cattle, purchased in Georgia and the Carolinas by Turnbull, down that same path, perhaps widening it further as they went and doubtless causing a certain amount of mess.

At last, at the beginning of August the sea-scattered settler group was once again reunited. It had been six months since they had all been together. People had died and sickened, been born and some maybe married in the interim. Now they faced together the task of taming the wilderness in a little known part of the world. What manner of place was this where they expected to spend the rest of their lives?

In 1768 when the Minorcan colonists first landed in Florida it was a lush, subtropical area teeming with animal life but almost devoid of human beings. The province showed little impact from the two hundred years of Spanish occupation. The Franciscan missions had tumbled into ruins and the converted Indians had been exterminated in Spanish days by European diseases and English raids from the north. The new groups of Creek Indians (later called Seminole) migrating from the north, were still in the process of settling in.

The town of St. Augustine, the capital of the province, had gained the reputation in the centuries of Spanish rule of being an isolated station. Under the British it changed little, especially at first. In spite of big plans for its development, it was still an outpost, dependent on the mother country and the northern colonies for food and necessities. Settlers were badly needed.

The few plantations in operation by 1768 were along the St. Marys River, or were, including Rollestown, scattered in a gentle curve down the fertile banks of the St. Johns River to about the latitude of the Mosquitos. As many as ten plantation tracts had been granted by this time in the Mosquitos. Most, such as Mount Oswald, had absentee owners. Others, the Bissett plantation for example, comprising 5,000 acres and lying south of the Turnbull plantation, had resident owners and were smaller scale operations. In the immediate New Smyrna area all of the agricultural enterprises were manned by black slaves.

The impact of this sizable group of Minorcans forever changed the landscape and altered the course of events in British East Florida. Using available figures, and with particular reference to Mowat (1943:64) who reconciled various figures to guess at a population of 3,000 in Florida in 1771, it seems likely that the population in 1768 (i.e. three years before) was around 2,000±. Of these, probably 1,000 were Indian, 900 black and 300 white. The impact of over 1,200 Minorcans all arriving at once had a unsettling effect on the other segments of the population. Their "foreignness" made them additionally suspect.

The neighboring Indians were the first to react to so large an invasion of Mediterraneans. Knowing the profound hatred of most of the Indians for the Spaniards, Governor Grant was concerned when the Minorcans first came to East Florida. His fears were justified, for within one month of the arrival of the first part of the settler group in New Smyrna, a group of Creeks, faces painted black, signaling potential hostilities, visited St. Augustine demanding to know on what footing the settlers had been brought into the province. The Indians had observed the complexions and the language of the colonists to be very like that of the Spanish.

Governor Grant, who had considerable skill in dealing with Indians, explained that the Minorcans were not "white people," that is, Englishmen, but that nevertheless they were loyal British subjects and had once, like the Indians, been oppressed by the Spaniards on the little island from whence they came. They were now in the New World to help their brothers, the English, to cultivate the new lands, lands which were like their warm homelands (C.O. 5/549:284). The Indians believed Grant, took off their warpaint and, for the moment at least, left the Minorcans in peace.

The confrontation with the Indians over the settlers, although it was only temporarily halted, was of less moment initially than the revolt which occurred among the settlers themselves in the early days on the plantation. In retelling this occurrence one writer

(Luther 1987:8) concluded that "in some beginnings the end is foretold." Certainly an extensive description of this open rebellion is worth detailing not simply because of its dramatic quality, but for what it tells of life on the plantation as well as the beginnings of community among the Minorcans, of a sense of peoplehood.

To set the scene, the outbreak happened on August 19, 1768, about two months after the first half of the settlers had arrived in New Smyrna, but only a few days, or if we can credit Turnbull (1788:687) only forty-eight hours, after the last colonists finally reached the plantation. August, every year, then as now, is insufferably hot and humid, the cloying, velvet air punctuated by insects. A bad storm easily turns into a hurricane, and the resulting low barometer causes tempers to flare. Added to the shipboard scurvy were the summer dysenteries and the new threat of malaria brought on by the vector-carriers for which "Los Mosquitos" had been so aptly named by the Spaniards many years before. The settlers had undertaken the onerous work of clearing the wilderness and building shelters to supplement the few structures built before their arrival. All of this strenuous work was done under the direction of black drivers imported from the Carolinas and Georgia, aided by a few colonists, mostly Italians, promoted as task foremen. Moreover, the hard work was fueled by improper food and questionable water. We can picture the settlers, bone weary, many half sick or even dying, taking communal food, then dragging to their crude, damp, insect-infested homes only to be kept awake at night by insects and by babies made fretful by scurvy. The latest arrivals, viewing the circumstances to which they had come, could see little hope in their futures. It is was not a scene of promise.

None of this was apparent to Governor Grant. He gave a glowing report of the new colony in the first part of a letter to officials in England on August 29, 1768 (C.O. 5/549). Considering the large number of people in the colony and the tremendous task of building shelter, clearing land and planting fall crops, things were going well, he thought. The people were described as pleased with their prospects and obedient to their overseers.

The second part of this letter, added before it was dispatched, tells a different story. Turnbull, it seemed, was so proud of his plantation that he invited some planter friends down from the Carolinas to admire his settlement. They were most complimentary about the progress that had been made declaring that "the same number of Negroes could not have done more, and that it must turn out to be the best settlement upon the continent of America, if they went on as they had begun."

On the surface all was calm on August 19, 1768, the morning after the visiting planters left with Turnbull to view another plantation in the area. But like a time bomb the community erupted into violence, a culmination of the festering anger of the Italians and Greeks over their hopeless plight:

> . . . Carlo Forni, one of the overseers [Turnbull early appointed several of the Italians as sub-overseers, sometimes called drivers or corporals] at 11 o'clock in the forenoon declared himself Captain General and commander-in-chief of the Greeks and Italians, seized a vessel which had been sent with provisions, made himself master of the storehouses and firearms, confined and wounded the doctor's principal manager [Mr. Cutter, head overseer], declared his intention of proceeding to Havana, and gave orders to put any of his people to death who should attempt to make their escape and desert the service. Rum was given in plenty, which is a prevailing argument in those woods, and the rioters who did not consist of above twenty, soon increased to two or three hundred. The confusion was great, the store houses were plundered, casks of rum, wine, oyl [sic] which could not be put on board the vessel were staved and all of the rioters loaded themselves with the poor doctor's slops, which he had provided for their use. They even plundered the Mahonese [Minorcan islanders] who did not join them (C.O. 5/549:282-283).

The overseer, Cutter, whose first name is unknown, eventually died of his wounds. Another casualty was Dr. William Stork, the pamphleteer, part of the distinguished coterie visiting the plantation, who had chosen to stay behind when the others left and was strolling about the settlement when the revolt began. What happened next is not clear. Bernard Romans, who was not an eyewitness, insisted that Stork died of fright, while Andrew Turnbull said that the distinguished gentleman tried valiantly to defend himself with his umbrella, but was felled by a fatal stab to the groin. In a third account at variance with the other two, it was reported by Spencer Man, a St. Augustine storekeeper, that Stork "was ill of a fever there [New Smyrna] & hearing there was a Mutiny amongst some of Dr.

Turnbull's Settlers, went into convulsions, in which he continued two days & then expired" (Rogers, et al. 1978:74).

This affair followed a common Mediterranean pattern. "In the lands of the Mediterranean, it was common for the 'plebs' to indulge in periodic agitations of a revolutionary character against the established social order, especially during periods of famine. The furious mobs would rally to the call of some man unknown until that day, a leader born to tragic destiny" (Caro Baroja 1963:35).

Carlo Forni, appointed as a driver, or leader of a work gang, probably all fellow nationals, was just such a temporary leader. All reports, even by Turnbull's detractors, paint Carlo Forni as a despicable character, one who had already been in trouble because of the rape of one of the women on the plantation. However, he must have had some incipient leadership skill to be elevated in the first place and the thread of order in the melee and the systematic departure plans speak of organizational ability. As examples he saw to it that a cow was killed for meat on the voyage, other foodstuffs loaded on board and firearms distributed. About three hundred people boarded the ship in preparation for sailing.

Two Italians who were loyal to Turnbull managed to get word to him. He was alarmed and made for the settlement with all possible haste after dispatching a message to Governor Grant in St. Augustine. Grant immediately sent men overland and others aboard the *East Florida* by sea. On the morning of the August 22 the government ship sighted the rebel vessel, still within the harbor, waiting for the tide. In the subsequent confrontation a round of shot was fired. One historian, Panagopoulos (1966:60-61) says that it was fired by the *East Florida* crew. Another historian (Beeson 1965:53) reports that the mutineers fired first. All agree that most of the rebels disembarked and were taken into custody, except for thirty-five who put off in a small boat down the coast and were captured a few weeks later in the Florida Keys.

All but five of the insurgents were eventually released. These five were taken to St. Augustine, tried and found guilty. Three were condemned to death: Carlo Forni for piracy; an Italian, Guiseppi Massiadoli, for cutting off two fingers and one ear of Mr. Cutter; and a Corsican Greek, Elia Medici, for killing a cow. The other two were convicted of felonies, for stealing a boat and breaking into Dr. Turnbull's warehouse. An eyewitness account of the hanging is given by Bernard Romans:

Governor Grant pardoned two, and a third [Elia Medici] was obliged to be executioner of the other two. On this occasion I saw one of the most moving scenes I ever experienced; long and obstinate was the struggle of this man's mind, who repeatedly called out, that he chose to die rather than be the executioner of his friends in distress . . . till at length the entreaties of the victims themselves, put an end to the conflict in his breast, by encouraging him to the act. Now we beheld a man thus compelled to mount the ladder, take leave of his friends in the most moving manner, kissing them the moment before he committed them to an ignominious death (1775:272).

The execution of these two men was intended to be a lesson to the remaining colonists. The riot made the authorities nervous about the future of the colony, and other plantation owners in the vicinity demanded protection. The governor requested 100 soldiers to maintain order at New Smyrna, and he reactivated plans to build a fort, plans earlier formulated when it was thought that a large group of Bermudians would settle in the Mosquitos area. Although the fort was never built, an officer and initially twenty-two men were assigned to the plantation.

What of the colonists themselves? The governor's actions had sent a clear message to them. The insurgents and their followers had been treated like runaway slaves, and the tone was thereby set for the future servitude of the settler group on the plantation.

In addition, it is significant that the Italians and Greeks banded together in the endeavor while the Minorcan islanders, and presumably the Italian men who had married into that group, while probably in sympathy with the rebellion, chose to wait it out. However, the course of events may have been set in motion by the simple fact that the young single men, principally the Italians and some of the Greeks, lived together in dormitories giving them more opportunity to plan such an undertaking. Also, the Italians and the Corsican Greeks spoke the same language and given this fact and the married status of the eastern Mediterranean Greeks plus the reported early mortality from malaria among the Greeks from Mani, it is likely that the Italian speakers among the settlers formed the nucleus of overt discontent.

In one sense this cleavage in the settler group is what one might expect in a colony, or any other human group, in the process of amalgamating into a community. A frequent stage of such a process is the development of a two-part system. It happened in Jamestown, it happened at Plymouth. Is it any wonder that it happened in New Smyrna? If no splitting-off occurs, each part lives in tandem with the other in a state of dynamic equilibrium. This cleavage of the colonists closed in as time and intermarriage intervened and as the Italian language was subsumed by the Hispanic tongue, but it was still somewhat evident when the group reordered itself in St. Augustine less than a decade later.

The hardships on the plantation which led to the rebellion were only beginning. The first year in New Smyrna followed the scenario usual for New World colonies—starvation, inadequate housing and clothing, failed crops, disease and misery. Governor Grant, to soften some of the alarming figures sent to the home office, insisted that the settlers were undergoing "seasoning." This was the word most commonly used to describe the process by which slaves became accustomed to a new environment and working conditions, and during which time one expected the less hardy to succumb.

By the end of 1768 a total of 450 people had died, a rate of 320.74 per thousand (table 3.1), a population crash (see graphic representation in figure 3.1) equaling that of a natural disaster such as a flood or an earthquake. Of these, 300 were adults and 150 were children. It is assumed that the 450 figure includes the deaths during the ocean crossing, but whether it includes deaths for the first few months of 1768 spent in the Mediterranean before embarkation is unclear.

Depopulation resulted from the falling birth rate as well as from the rising death rate. The birth rate dropped to a low of 5.12 per thousand in 1769, well below the level of 32.5 per thousand considered by Wrigley (1969) as average for preindustrial European populations. This low rate is especially significant considering the number of couples of child-bearing age in the population.

A note of caution is in order. The death and birth rates in table 3.1 are crude, coming as they do from totally different sources. The deaths for the period were reported all at one time in Governor Patrick Tonyn's official report to the colonial office (C.O. 5/558) after the colony was dispersed.

No official birth records were ever sent to England, so for these figures, baptismal records must be relied upon. Baptismal records do not customarily include as live births those babies who die in early

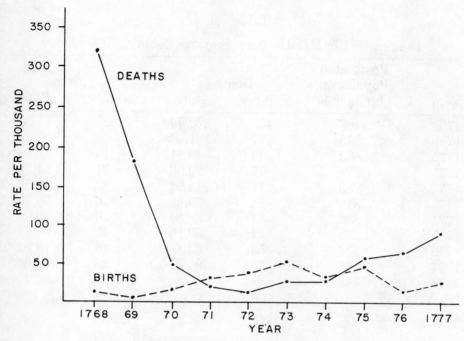

Figure 3.1. Birth and Death Rates, New Smyrna, 1768-1777.

infancy before the sacrament can take place. However, unlike the
lump figures for deaths, parish records of those baptized do name
actual individuals, so that although error may be in either direction
in the case of deaths, error in the baptism figures would be in the
direction of under-representation of births. Aside from the possibility
of mistakes in the statistics as here presented, the seriousness and
magnitude of the population crash of 1768-1769 is well documented
in narrative form in the Colonial Office records.

Later census figures from the period after the move to St. Augustine also reconcile well with the postulated population figures derived
for January first of each of the New Smyrna years. The early crisis
years weeded out the vulnerable in the group, and the total population leveled out to perhaps about eight hundred individuals.

Immediately apparent from table 3.1 and figure 3.1 are the three
periods of life on the plantation. The period from 1768 to 1770 was
the starving time, the first disastrous years of anguish, hardship,
and death. During the middle years, from 1771 to 1774, things partially righted themselves and the settlers, as well as the proprietor,

Table 3.1

Death and Birth Rates New Smyrna Colony, 1768-1778

Year	Postulated Population (January 1)	Deaths		Births	
		Number	Rate	Number	Rate
1768	1403	459	320.74	22	15.68
1769	975	177	181.53	5	5.12
1770	803	40	49.81	15	18.68
1771	778	16	20.56	27	34.70
1772	789	11	13.94	32	40.56
1773	810	24	29.62	46	56.79
1774	832	24	28.84	30	36.06
1775	838	51	60.86	43	51.31
1776	830	53	63.85	15	18.07
1777	792	72	90.91	23	29.04
1778	743				
No Year		34*			
Totals		1052		258	

*34 Greeks stated to have died, but years not indicated.
Sources: Death statistics derived from reports of the Governor to the Board of Trade, London, (C.O. various). Birth statistics based on baptisms recorded in San Pedro Parish records (Camps 1768-1784), It is believed that these baptisms are roughly equivalent to births since nearly all of the families were Roman Catholic.

looked forward to even better times. Then for a number of reasons—drought and soil depletion, greed of the proprietors, war and the alteration of political fortunes—matters deteriorated from 1775 to 1777, leading ultimately to the collapse of the plantation enterprise.

As we turn now to look at the calamitous first years, it must be borne in mind that there was in the middle of the New Smyrna years a period of promise, even though brief. It is easy to concentrate on the negative aspects of the nine years on the plantation since so much of what floats up through the documentary material is focused on these aspects while ignoring the partial and fragmentary information on the adjustments made in the middle years. However, while keeping a necessary balance in mind, the fact that those positive years were gained at a great cost to the colonists in terms of starvation, disease, and deaths cannot be ignored.

For any population under stress, a number of specific interacting causal factors for a high death rate can usually be established. Poor diet or outright starvation, polluted water, disease, exposure, accidents (even murders), filthy conditions all take their toll.

The majority of the colonists, especially those from Minorca, were accustomed to a clean environment. Every work consulted about the island of Minorca and its people mentioned the cleanliness of the people. One writer (Calvert 1910:97) called it the "Holland of the Mediterranean," adding that "cleanliness, well being, industry and good conduct are characteristic of the inhabitants." In the eighteenth century, Armstrong (1756:209) noted that "The very poorest of these people eat good brown Bread, made of Wheat, which is their principal Nourishment; and lie in tolerable Beds, the Sheets of which they frequently shift; so that we are not shocked here with the squalid Poverty and Wretchedness, which display themselves in the Houses of the Poor in other countries. . . . They take pride in keeping their House and Utinsels clean."

In New Smyrna even people from a clean tradition had the odds against them. Most of the families were forced to reside in temporary palmetto huts (casas de guano), and with few clothes and one blanket apiece, the white-washed walls and swept stone floors and other amenities of their homelands were only a memory. Insect bites could easily become the infected pustules called "Florida sores."

Food was an equally serious problem. The food rationed by Turnbull to the settlers was meager at best and by some accounts was taken communally. Romans (1775:269) says that each person was granted a quart of maize per day, presumably in the form of hominy grits, and two ounces of pork per week. He added that "they were forced to join all together in one mess, and at the beat of a vile drum, to come to a common copper, from whence their hominy was ladled out to them." He believed that, "this might have sufficed with the help of fish which abounds in the lagoon, but they were denied the liberty of fishing."

Turnbull later insisted that he had allowed the colonists to fish saying, "they became so dextrous and successful that many families had for the most part great quantities of dried fish in their houses; fish being so plenty in the river . . . that one man could generally catch as much in one hour, as would serve his family for twenty-four, almost all having small canoes for that purpose" (Turnbull 1788:685-686).

The colonists told another story in their depositions against Turnbull. Rafael Ximénez along with George Calamaras and Michael García were responsible for cutting fodder for the horses each morning. Ximénez reported that the three men were "very weak with hunger and bad usage, and were not able to fetch much grass, for which Turnbull whipt them severely with the Horse Whip every morning and if they happened to fetch some Oysters or fish, they were taken away so that this Deponent and many others were obliged to kill snakes and any other vermin, or otherwise starve" (C.O. 5/557).

A note of caution is in order here. These polarized accounts were written at the time of the plantation's end. The depositions were taken from a selected group of the colonists to justify abandoning the plantation while Turnbull's account refutes the stories told by the settlers as well as some of Turnbull's detractors. The truth probably lies somewhere in between. Fishing was possibly out of the question at first when the land was being cleared and shelters erected and doubtless later at peak cropping times of the year. But documents mentioning the Minorcan's small boats as well as the extensive knowledge of local fishing which they possessed by the time that they reached St. Augustine speaks to the other side of the question.

Cleghorn, describing the Minorcan diet usual in the homeland at that time says:

> . . . scarce a Fifth of their Whole Food is furnished from the animal kingdom; and of this, Fish makes by much the most considerable Portion. Bread of the finest Wheat Flour, well fermented, and well baked is more than half the Diet of People of all Ranks. Rice, Pulse, Cuscassowe, Vermicelli, Herbs and Roots from the Fields and Gardens, Summer Fruits, pickled Olives and Pods of the *Guinea* Pepper, make up almost the other Half. A Slice of Bread soaked in boiled Water with a little Oil and Salt, is the common breakfast of the Peasants, well known by the name of *Oleagua*. Their ordinary meals are very frugal, and consist of little Variety; but on Festivals and other solemn Occasions, their Entertainments are to the last Degree profuse and extravagant (Cleghorn 1779:61-62).

Three factors leading to protein starvation in the diet in the early New Smyrna years are evident. The amount of animal protein was a much lower proportion of the total diet than that to which they were accustomed. Also, pork, with which the settlers were provided, is a lower quality protein (lacking in some essential amino acids) than fish. Thirdly, extra food, especially protein, at ceremonial and holiday times no longer offered a safety margin. The conclusion of protein starvation is reinforced by documentary reference to "dropsies," probably renal failure, brought on by a combination of low and poor quality protein intake, bacterial toxins and general stress.

Lack of meat and fish was only part of the problem. Corn alone as a major grain in the diet falls far short of wheat as a carbohydrate. Furthermore, a quart (four cups) a day is not a very large portion if it constitutes almost the total diet. Added to these diet shortfalls was a lack of fresh food to overcome the ravages of scurvy and other vitamin deficiencies.

The health and vitality of the colonial group was further compromised by the water available for drinking. No archaeology of consequence has been done at New Smyrna, but it can be assumed from Deagan's (1974) excavations in St. Augustine that shallow-water wells were the rule in East Florida. Rain-water cisterns and deep-water wells were the customary sources of water in the Mediterranean, posing different pollution problems from shallow wells. The Minorcan islanders usual cistern purifying methods (Armstrong 1756:47) of throwing in several live eels or green tops of myrtle, would have been insufficient for cleaning up the shallow-water wells in New Smyrna polluted by animal and human wastes. Such wastes were probably used to fertilize the kitchen gardens. Armstrong (1756:178) describes such use for animal waste in Minorca and implies also the use of human refuse. To compound the pollution problem, the colonists had no immunity to the new strains of water-borne bacteria which they found in the New World. We can therefore surmise a certain amount of misery, if not actual deaths, from the Florida equivalent of "Montezuma's revenge."

In addition to outright starvation, people continued to die of scurvy residuals such as gangrene of the mouth, and when winter set in pleurisy and fevers took their toll. Malaria probably accounted for more deaths than any other disease although it is difficult to assess the incidence of the malarial pathogen, and deaths resulting

from it. Many of the vague references to "fevers" in the documents
may well refer to malaria. More specifically, the fact, but not the
extent, of the high mortality from malaria among the Greeks is stated
in the Colonial Office reports. One of the Governor's reports on
deaths in the colony refers separately to the deaths of thirty-four
adult Greeks but does not state the causes (C.O. 5/558:107).

Most severely hit were the Greeks from Mani, the mainland
Greeks. Of the twenty-three surviving Greeks counted in the censuses in St. Augustine two decades later, only two came from Mani.
Coming from an isolated mountainous area, these Greeks did not
carry the gene for Thalassemia major (Cooley's anemia). This condition when expressed in its full-blown form, a result of inheritance
from both sides of the family, is lethal at an early age. In spite of
this fact, there is a high gene frequency in many parts of the Mediterranean, especially in the lowland areas. It is believed by
epidemiologists that Thalassemia minor, a lesser expression of this
inherited defect in which the gene is inherited from only one parent,
is a protection against malaria. In this regard it is much like sickle
cell anemia which in its mild form, inheritance from one parent only,
protects peoples on the African continent from the same disease
(Harrison et al. 1964:243-248; Hulse 1971:317-321).

Guessing from our crude survival rates, those who did not contract malaria, or had a mild case, came from lowland, mosquito-in-
fested areas in the Mediterranean. The incidence of the Thallassemia
gene on Corsica is high. If, as we guess, approximately 50 Corsican
Greeks sailed with Turnbull, the survival of eleven of these eighteen
years later is a good showing; equally as good as the one in five
survival rate among the Minorcan islanders.

Cleghorn includes an entire chapter entitled "Of Tertian Fevers"
in his book on Minorca, noting with surprise (1779:134) the capri-
ciousness with which the disease attacked some areas of the island,
and some families. It is possible, aside from their generally poor
physical health, that deaths from malaria explain the low proportion
of survivors from inland Mercadal. Finally, leaning on recent evidence, the fact that "Cooley fever," another designation for this
Mediterranean anemia and the name by which colonial descendents
knew it, still occurred at an above chance level in the descendant
population at least until the middle of the twentieth century, argues
for its survival significance (Griffin 1976).

Photo courtesy of LUTHERS, New Smyrna Beach.
Figure 3.2. Ruins of the Stone Wharf.

On a social level the deaths of so many Greeks increased the dominance in numbers and influence of the Minorcan island majority. Keeping the Greeks alive and well was proving as difficult as recruiting them in the first place. Nevertheless, none of these pioneers, no matter their place of origin, was immune to all the new strains of disease on the western side of the Atlantic. Life was precarious, and someone reasonably well one day could be receiving the last sacraments from the Catholic fathers the next day.

*   *   *

The plantation was laid out without any reference to spatial organization common to Mediterranean agriculturalists. Turnbull settled the two hundred families along eight miles of ridge fronting the tidal lagoon, each on a plot of land 210 feet along the water's edge and extending inward many acres in depth. The kitchen gardens were to be near the houses and the communal land behind was to be worked on shares with Turnbull until such time as the indenture was over and the land theirs.

There was no town as such, although near the center of the north-south spread of habitations there was a clustering of some structures close to the substantial stone wharf which served as a link to the outer world (figure 3.2). Here were the warehouses and three long-houses, or barracks, for the fifty or more single men. There were work sheds for the craftsmen such as carpenters and masons, and a blacksmith is specifically noted in the documents. Quarters for the small garrison, usually no more than eight men, and a double-stockaded powder magazine were added after the early insurrection.

A church, San Pedro, and a residence for the priests were built by the parishioners early in the colony's existence. They were described as comfortable and decent by a visiting Cuban fisherman in 1769 (Santo Domingo 1777). He also reported that the church, the priest's house, and Turnbull's residence were built of bricks (ladrillos). While some bricks were imported from Charleston, for example 2,000 in November of 1768 (Rogers et al. 1978:155), the amounts were sufficient only for small projects, not for major buildings. It is, therefore, far more likely that the three buildings mentioned were constructed of the available local coquina stone.

The exact location of the religious complex, including the cemetery, has long been uncertain, but given its significance to the Mediterranean colony, it was probably near the other structures just mentioned as representing the core of the community. A recent report has suggested that the long-enigmatic coquina foundation ruins in the New Smyrna Beach waterfront park (figure 3.3), variously referred to as "the old fort" or "Turnbull's mansion," are most likely those of the Church of San Pedro (Griffin and Steinbach 1990). This location is just north of the north canal bounding the central secular area.

Turnbull's residence was located about four miles north of the main wharf area, on the 300 acre personal grant which adjoined the larger grants of the partners (figure 1.2). While somewhat apart from the plantation proper, it was accessible from the sea and from the King's Road leading to St. Augustine (Coomes 1975:40). It was on this area that Turnbull had concentrated much of his initial construction efforts in preparation for the arrival of the colony. William Watson, the experienced carpenter who had been employed to supervise the construction of structures, built Turnbull's own house there, and listed a cost of £270. This may have been the figure for only the carpentry work on the masonry house.

The eventual number of structures, their placement and the building materials used at New Smyrna are all somewhat open to

Photo by Griffin.

Figure 3.3. Disputed Ruins.

question. While a number of small frame houses had been constructed in advance of the arrival of the colonists, they were certainly insufficient for the numbers of people that Turnbull actually brought with him. Palm huts were hastily erected to take care of the overflow. Some later writers have pictured the colonists as living in their crude huts for the entire nine-year period. But there are indications from tools and materials known to have been shipped in that some more substantial homes were built for or by the settlers. Also, William Watson said he built 145 houses at £35 each by 1777 (T 77/7), and these were presumably of frame construction. In 1785 an anonymous visitor to the site of New Smyrna supported the prevalence of frame construction, saying, "I had the curiosity when there, to count all the houses both in Town & Country, & to the best of My recollection there were some few more than 100 framed buildings left standing or unburnt" (T 77/7).

Tabby floors and coquina rock chimneys, common in nearby St. Augustine, were probably introduced to the plantation also. However, the ruined remnants noted by nineteenth-century travelers to

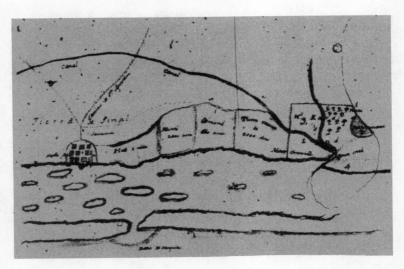

Figure 3.4. Map of New Smyrna Area in 1803.

the New Smyrna area, and presumed to date from the original plantation, could also have come from abandoned plantations slightly later than the Turnbull colony.

The only plat of the settlement which has been found (figure 3.4) is both later, 1803, and drawn for another purpose, a land dispute not concerning the Turnbull colony. As such, it cannot be considered a completely accurate source. It indicates a cluster of occupation labeled "Smyrna," enclosed in a semi-circular area bounded apparently by the two major canals. The road from St. Augustine also terminates here. This has, by some, been interpreted as showing a series of city blocks and a central plaza. It would seem much safer to regard it as purely schematic, although the central area is definitely indicated.

Lacking a satisfactory contemporary plan of the plantation, a conjectural plan, projected onto De Brahm's map of 1769 as a base, is presented as figure 3.5. Given the limitations of the available documentary evidence and the lack of substantial archaeological evidence it must remain just that, conjectural. It does, however, show the important facts of the settlement pattern; the lineal residential zone, with its small nucleus near the wharf, the proprietor's estate to the north, and the plantation fields with their indigo vats and sheds and the cattle pens to the west.

In general, the schema presented in figure 3.5 has many of the

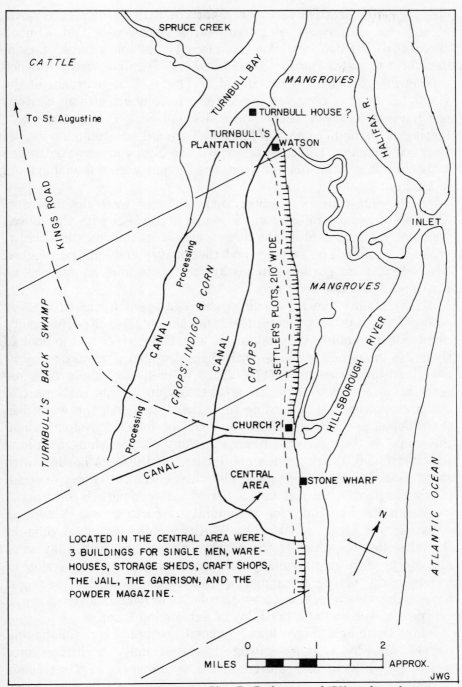

SPRUCE CREEK

CATTLE

TURNBULL BAY

MANGROVES

HALIFAX R.

To St. Augustine

TURNBULL HOUSE ?

TURNBULL'S
PLANTATION

WATSON

KINGS ROAD

INLET

Processing

CANAL

CROPS; INDIGO & CORN

CANAL

CROPS

SETTLER'S PLOTS, 210' WIDE

MANGROVES

Processing

TURNBULL'S BACK SWAMP

HILLSBOROUGH RIVER

CHURCH ?

CANAL

CENTRAL
AREA

STONE WHARF

N

ATLANTIC OCEAN

LOCATED IN THE CENTRAL AREA WERE:
3 BUILDINGS FOR SINGLE MEN, WARE-
HOUSES, STORAGE SHEDS, CRAFT SHOPS,
THE JAIL, THE GARRISON, AND THE
POWDER MAGAZINE.

0   1   2

MILES   APPROX.

JWG

Figure 3.5. Conjectural Plantation Plan; De Brahm map of 1769 used as a base.

elements of a Scottish settlement pattern with its dispersed farm-
steads and crossroads congregate area (Arensberg and Kimball
1965:74-96). Its design is also reminiscent of a "line village," dependent on the waterway for communication. Turnbull wrote to Lord
Shelburne, president of the Board of Trade, "The nearness of the
Hutts to one another gives the whole a Resemblance to an Eastern
or Chinese plantation" (Lansdowne MSS vol. 88:155), such statement
hinting at Turnbull's image of himself. Turnbull's contemporary critic
Bernard Romans (1775:268) described the New Smyrna venture as
a "bashawship" transplanted from the Levant with a feudal system
of land management.

Eighteenth-century Mediterranean villages were far different.
They were usually roughly in the shape of a wheel with the church
frequently at the center, the houses close together on the narrow,
crooked streets. The farmers and their wives and children walked
out to tend their garden patches by day, sometimes as much as an
hour-and-a-half trip each way.

Their Mediterranean evenings the men spent in the taverns or
coffee houses, usually among the same assemblage of people every
night. Or in summer they might sit with their wives at the door of
their dwellings and socialize with their neighbors or passers by as
described in Armstrong (1756:210). Women had their own assemblages related to domestic affairs. As late as the early part of
the present century, according to Calvert (1910:98), the women in
the villages and towns of Minorca could be found "gossiping along
the walls" as they gave their houses a daily whitewashing with lime
water. Holiday times were amplifications of these gatherings with
some special fetes of their own. The village was the center of social
life for the people, not just a place to rest between periods of work.

Turnbull's rationale for community structure was based on
economic, not social, considerations. Although he may have thought
the huts close together, to the people who lived in them, they were
far apart, with an unfriendly, unprotected aspect. The string of
houses made evening groupings difficult if not impossible. One might
have to travel several miles to see a relative or friend, not a congenial
prospect at the end of a hard day of exhausting labor.

Only the single men's houses, mostly occupied by Italians and
Greeks, afforded easy assemblage in the evenings, a circumstance
which, as we have seen, nurtured the development of a rebellious
nucleus.

4. The Plantation

Time to go back to Minorca.
Expression used by St. Augustine
Minorcans when times are bad.

A plantation is a tight, self-contained world in much the same way that a university is or a factory town can be. The geographical bounds are set, relationships with the wider world are set, tasks are set and even the social relationships of the labor force tend to become set as time goes on. The cash crop(s) plus the labor and technology to produce those commodities are the controlling factors. Gray (1941:444 ff.) in his classic definition described a plantation as "a capitalistic type of agricultural organization in which a considerable number of unfree laborers were employed under unified direction and control in the production of a staple crop." He spoke of four special characteristics: (1) the sharp separation of worker and employer classes, (2) the aim of continuous commercial agriculture, (3) monocrop specialization, and (4) the capitalistic nature of the enterprise, with the planter as businessman, not farmer.

In the eighteenth and nineteenth centuries, management, whether good or bad, had to depend ultimately on the muscular energy of the plantation work force. Large plantations as microworlds were characterized at that time, therefore, by a similarity one to the other wherever they were and no matter under what regime they were established. Notwithstanding these commonalities, the character of the labor force could ultimately be the deciding factor in the success of an enterprise.

In the present instance, we have already seen how the settlement pattern caused customary Mediterranean life patterns to be fractured. However, nowhere were the differing elements of British and

Mediterranean world view and culture more evident than in the work situation. Cleghorn described the work/leisure situation in Minorca at that time:

A Fourth of their Time is made up of Holidays, on which, tho' Work is prohibited, Sports and Pastimes are allowed. A considerable Part of those Days is spent in the Churches or in Processions: At Night the more Sedate divert themselves in their Houses with Musick and Cards; whilst the young Men serenade their Mistresses, in the Streets, with the jarring Musick of their Guittars, and extemporary Love Songs of their own composing. . . . In the Interval between the Harvest and the Vintage, there are a Number of publick Diversions in different Places of the Island (Cleghorn 1779:64).

The Scotsman Armstrong took a much less positive view of this pattern:

The multitude of feasts that are maintained by the people in a voluptuous indolence, set a dangerous example to the inhabitants of any country. The great number of holy days which they are obliged to observe indispose them to labour; and the diversions which are so laudable at those festivals, though it is sinful to exercise an honest calling for the support of a poor family, make the returns to business irksome and the workmen careless and lazy; on the other hand the trade and manufactures of a Protestant country are carried on with briskness and alacrity. The people have but few holy days and are not very strict in the observation of them (Armstrong 1756:248).

There can be no doubt that Turnbull's attitude toward his work force, judging by the way in which he ran the plantation, accorded with the latter viewpoint. The colony became an agricultural factory.

During the first disastrous year, as a result of a request by Governor Grant, Parliament awarded a £2,000 relief grant to the New Smyrna colony. This grant stipulated that the plantation concentrate on growing crops such as silk, olives, raisins, wine and honey which had heretofore drained British gold into foreign countries. The colonists had early unpacked the seeds and cuttings brought from Minorca. There were starts for grapes, olives, figs and mulberries; seeds of many kinds, and also silkworm eggs. The oil was carefully

drained from the barrels and saved for later use, the plants wiped
dry of the oil and then rubbed with ashes until the ashes came off
dry; the empty wooden barrels then being sawed in half and used for
buckets or pails. The silkworm eggs were given special attention
with repeated blottings with ashes and absorbent paper (Beeson
1966:58-59).

Although these imports were planted and nurtured with some
care, and later "the vines and mulberry trees . . . thrived astound-
ingly" (Schoepf 1911:235), Turnbull's hurry to turn a quick profit
prevented their ever being successful cash crops. Schoepf, who visited Florida in 1783-1784 says:

It was not found practicable at once to engage largely in vine
and silk culture, which were the main objects of the plan, such
enterprises requiring a good many years before any profit is to
be expected from them. Attention must first be given to the
necessary support of these people and to the interests of the
undertakers. Maize and indigo were thus the first products had
in view, the land once being cleared (Schoepf 1911:234).

The main cash crop on the plantation became and remained indigo
(*Indigofera tinctoria*). It is not now easy to understand the importance at that time of the brilliant blue dye derived from indigo. With
its color depth and slight reddish glow it was considered the "king
of dyestuffs." A tropical crop, it brought a high price in the countries
of Europe, and continued to do so until aniline dyes were developed
in the mid-nineteenth century (Schery 1972:256). As a special induce-
ment to growers in the British colonies, Parliament in 1748 placed a
bounty of sixpence per pound on American colonial indigo, which,
however, was reduced to fourpence in 1771.

Because of the expensive and extensive equipment and the complicated processing required for its production, indigo was profitable
only on large plantations (Wolf 1959:179), such as the one at New
Smyrna. It is a perennial, yielding three to five cuttings a year between March and November. For processing, three vats were required, usually made of hardwood timber (figure 4.1). In the first,
or steeping vat, the weed was thrown in the water, pressed down
with pieces of wood and allowed to ferment. When it bubbled and
assumed a purplish hue—anywhere from eight to twenty-four hours
depending on the temperature of the air—the plug was pulled and

Figure 4.1. Indigo Works.

the liquid drawn off into the second vat. In the second vat the liquid was beaten continuously, the beating usually done by men drawing bottomless buckets up and down in the thickening purple-blue mass in a churning motion. After some solid parts had begun to coalesce, the churning was terminated and the sediment was allowed to settle. At a certain stage the solution was let into the final vat for further evaporation. Diderot's pictorial encyclopedia, originally published in 1750, refers to this last tank as the "devil's tank" (Gillispie 1954:Plate 36) because it was said that long exposure to the vapors was usually fatal to the workers.

When the semisolid mass reached the right consistency it was put in bags the shape of a Hippocrates sleeve (a conical cloth used for straining) and left to drain in the shade. After a few days the mudlike remainder was put into shallow boxes and left to dry further. To make certain that these blocks dried thoroughly, it was necessary that they be turned three or four times a day and the flies fanned away so that the bricks were not contaminated. Finally the dyestuff was ready for shipment.

Romans outlined other unpleasant aspects of indigo cropping:

An indigo work should always be remote from the dwelling house on account of the disagreeable *effluvia* of the rotten weed and the quantity of flies it draws; by which means it is also scarce possible to keep an animal on an indigo plantation in any tolerable case, the fly being so troublesome, so even poultry thrive but little where indigo is made; nor is there scarce a possibility to live in a house nearer than a quarter of a mile to the vats; the stench at the work is likewise horrid (Romans 1775:139).

Indigo production in colonial South Carolina, upon which Turnbull probably modeled his operation, has been characterized as "rather smelly," in part because human urine was used as a catalyst, having been collected in tubs in the slave quarters. The unpleasant odors necessitated the placement of the operation "well away from the residential areas of the plantation and where prevailing winds would carry the odors away from the living quarters" (Leland 1976?:11).

While it is questionable whether human urine was used in East Florida, since potash replaced it as the preferred catalyst in the late eighteenth century, there can be little doubt but that indigo was a

demanding and difficult crop. While not so strenuous for the labor
force as was rice growing, it was more arduous than cotton culture
(Wallace 1961:190).

Corn was the secondary crop grown on the plantation in New
Smyrna, and was actually a poor second to indigo. It was used locally
and exported to Charleston but not to England. Also exported were
dried legumes, probably beans and peas. A little cotton was grown,
and rice and sugar were probably planted experimentally.

In the early days of the colony a small amount of barilla, an
impure soda (sodium carbonate) produced by the ashes of various
plants of saline regions, was exported to the London market. Naval
stores—tar, pitch, and turpentine—were also produced on a limited
scale from the surrounding pine forests. Considering the demand for
these products by the British Navy and Merchant Marine, it is surprising that more of the colonists' time was not allotted to their
production. The overwhelming success of indigo must remain as the
explanation for the little effort spent on other crops.

Settlers accustomed to growing diversified crops on their small
landholdings in the Mediterranean chafed under the tyranny of a one
crop system, a demanding crop to deal with, and an inedible one at
that. They were required to work long hours, often at night, and in
the rain, for according to Romans (1775:135) indigo is best harvested
in rainy weather. Also, care had to be exercised in harvesting to
keep the "blush" on the leaves, the presence of which assured a
quality product.

During the intensive harvest periods the colonists probably had
to neglect their own gardens and to eschew what little fishing, hunting, and gathering for which they could ordinarily spare some time.
Furthermore, the indigo was harvested in the summer, the time
which had always been devoted to ritual, relaxation and joyful diver-
sion in the Old World. The profound effect that raising and processing the indigo crop had on their lives is dramatically illustrated by
the monthly birth statistics.

The 258 births on the plantation (as represented by baptisms but
using the dates of births) show a seasonal pattern, with births clustering in the months of September through January, with the peak
of the curve in December (figure 4.2). This clustering was more sharply marked in the middle years of the colony when indigo crops were
optimal. The conception time of the largest number of babies was

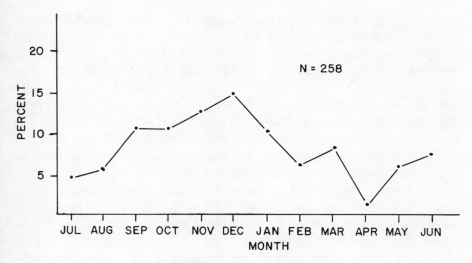

Figure 4.2. Births by Month, 1768-1777.

therefore September through April, nearly coinciding with the period when the indigo required no cultivation or harvesting. In all of the nine years of the colony only four babies were born in April having thus been conceived in July at the peak of the indigo season, and two of these were born in 1768 before cash cropping had begun.

The work force was managed by the overseer system common to the slave plantations of the American colonies. Of the seven "overseers" mentioned in the documents, only Cutter and Watson, the carpenter, actually fit the category of "overseer." Cutter is referred to as "plantation manager," and also was appointed as a justice by Governor Grant. The others were "drivers," the day-to-day foremen of the work crews, whom the settlers addressed as "corporal." Several, Nichola Moveritte and Simon for example, were blacks trained for their positions in the other southern colonies. Others, such as Luis Soche and the ill-fated Carlo Forni, were from among the Italian group of the colonists.

The drivers known from the documents probably did not constitute the whole group. Possibly there were as many as ten or twelve. Estimating the work force at 450 in the years of highest indigo yield—figuring 200 married men, 150 women, 50 single men and 50 children and adolescents at that time—then each of ten drivers would have had an average of 45 or so workers under his control.

From casual reference in the sources, we can conclude that women toiled in the fields, even when pregnant. In his deposition against Turnbull, Giosefa Lurance described the way in which his sister-in-law, Paola Lurance, "being in the field at work" was propositioned by the driver, Simon, and upon her refusal was beaten by him. He continued to beat her in spite of her entreaties and three days later she was delivered of a dead child (C.O. 5/557:445-447). However, craftsmen's wives ordinarily did not labor in the fields, if we note the outrage this occasioned in Louis Margan, the blacksmith. When, upon completion of his contract, he asked for his discharge, he was beaten and thrown in jail and his wife was required to work in the fields and leave her nursing infant behind at the house, the mother being allowed to come only twice daily to give the infant the breast (C.O. 5/557:441-442).

The horrible story told in the deposition of Michael Alamón suggests age-grading of the boys in work groups. Guillermo Vens, age ten, was beaten and driven to work by Lewis Pouchintena, a driver whose origin is unknown. When he reached the fields, the boy said that he was too sick to work. Pouchintena ordered the other boys to stone him, Alamón being one of those boys. This they did, and Guillermo died there in the field (C.O. 5/557:554).

There is no record of the age at which girls were required to begin regular plantation work. Possibly they stayed home to take care of small children and tend the kitchen gardens.

Working children were no novelty in the Mediterranean, but the jobs given them in their homelands were easier and had their playful elements. "As the corn ripens," according to Armstrong (1756:177), "a number of boys and girls station themselves at the edge of the fields and on the tops of the fence walls to frighten away the small birds with their shouts and cries. . . . They also use for the same purpose a split reed which makes a horrid rattling as they shake it with their hands."

Six craftsmen on the plantation at New Smyrna have been definitely identified: Louis Margan, blacksmith; Juan Portella, shoemaker; Christopher Flemming, carpenter; Lorenzo Bertani, clerk; Luis Capelli, cartwright, and Babpina Patchedebourga (Peso de Burgo), who seems to have held a quartermaster type position. This is possibly a selected sample of the craft or skilled labor group, emerging in the documents as they do because of their disgruntlement over Turnbull's treatment of them. They complained of broken contracts, poor food, no wages, physical abuse, and Capelli and Margan were affronted by being forced to work in the fields. They also chafed when they had to take orders from one of the drivers or overseers. Luis Capelli, we find, was working in a shop putting the spokes in wheels when Mr. Watson complained that the spokes the cartwright was working on were bent. Capelli, perhaps out of spite, cut them shorter and when they warped in the sun and were too short he was beaten for his pains (C.O. 5/557:459).

While some Minorcans were used as servants at the main house, a personalized circle or house cadre with special privileges, frequently the pattern on plantations in the other southern colonies, never evolved. Several cases will illustrate. Francisco Seguí, for example, was Turnbull's cook. He would have needed no special training because the art of cooking was part of the male as well as female repertoire in the Minorcan tradition. We know of Seguí's job because a visitor to the plantation gave Seguí a dollar, whereupon Turnbull took the money away from him in anger.

Another small piece of evidence tells us that house servants, unlike their counterparts on colonial American plantations, were detailed to the fields when needed. One day Mateo Triay, who is identified as one of Turnbull's house servants, being temporarily pressed into service in the fields, probably at the peak of the indigo season, was accidently killed by an axe aimed by the driver, Moveritte, at another Minorcan workman (C.O. 5/557:477).

The three distinct groups on a typical southern colonial plantation were field workers, craftsmen, and house servants, and in the ordinary course of events the lines between these categories were rigid. The evidence in the present case, on the contrary, points to the lines being blurred among these categories on this East Florida plantation.

Those of the regular laboring settlers who cleared the land used the slash and burn technique. De Brahm described the way in which this was accomplished on other southern plantations at the time:

The planters set out their weak hands (Women and Boys) to cut down the bushes and Shrubs with Hoes and Hatchets, before the tasks are laid out and marked, and after this, the Trees are all cut down; this is *daywork*; but the lopping and burning is

nightwork vide, at Sun-set all Slaves leave the fields and retire
to their cottages to rest an hour; then all hands are turned to
lopping and firing, which they continue until 9 o'clock. The fires
are made but small, and in many Places, in order not to burn
the Soil, yet to destroy all the Branches, Shrubs and Bushes,
whereby they scatter the Salt in the Ashes all over the Ground;
the bodies of the Trees remain on the Land (De Vorsey 1966:92).

We can be reasonably certain that logs were left in the fields in
New Smyrna, since several complaints tell of men being chained to
logs in the fields for punishment.

In contrast, although it is true that the fields of Minorca were not
totally cleared of stones until the eighteenth century, agricultural
work there was relatively easy. "The tillage is neither a laborious,
nor an expensive Work," Cleghorn (1779:13) tells us of that time,
"for a Plough so light as to be transported from Place to Place, on
the Ploughman's Shoulder, and to be drawn by a Heifer, or an Ass
sometimes assisted by a Hog, is sufficient for opening so thin a soil."

Plows do not appear on any of the shipping lists of the New
Smyrna colony and were most likely made in a traditional style and
fitted with plowshares forged on the plantation. Hoes were imported
in large numbers—grubbing hoes, felling hoes, Philadelphia hoes and
the husky Crawley's broad hoes. Along with the hoes there were
other hand implements such as indigo sickles and axes. The main
source of energy was obviously human muscle, supplemented by a
few draught animals as time went on.

The long-handled implements favored by the English forced an
adjustment of muscle use and work rhythms by the colonists. Foster
(1951:320-321) describes the Iberian preference for short-handled in-
struments (see figure 12.5), even to the women's preference for short
brooms.

In whatever spare time they had, the householders planted
kitchen gardens in the fertile land by their houses. Indian corn, peas,
beans, potatoes, peppers, onions and greens were all eventually
grown for household consumption. Cucumbers and melons were also
raised as confirmed by an incident told by Pompey Possi in his deposition against Turnbull:

. . . that sometime after Nichola Moveritte having taken the
Cucumbers and Melons belonging to this Deponent . . . that the

said Nichola Moveritte, a Blacksmith and a Negro [and also a Driver according to other documents) came to the Field where the Deponent was working and he was stript and tied up and whipt by the Negro, by the direction of Mr. Andrew Turnbull, for which piece of service the said Negro received a Bottle of Rum (C.O. 5/557:437-438).

Watermelon was much valued, for in addition to being enjoyed for its taste, in Minorca it was given to "children at fevers" (Armstrong 1756:180).

A long catalogue of vegetables and fruits grown at that time in Minorca is furnished by both Cleghorn (1779) and Armstrong (1756). Probably in their New World gardens the variety was more restricted, especially in the New Smyrna years when the time spent on cultivation was limited.

The datil pepper (believed to be *Capsicum sinense*), a strain of hot pepper seemingly unique to the St. Augustine area and strongly linked to the Minorcan group, must have traveled to North America with the immigrants. Peppers were a vital ingredient in the *sopas* or vegetable stews which were the mainstays of the Old World Minorcan diet; composed of vegetables, bread, oil and accented with spices, garlic and peppers. Today, many Minorcan recipes for chicken pilau, gopher stew, and homemade sausage call for these peppers, and a condiment commonly made by pickling in vinegar affords a pungent seasoning as well.

The colonists had to manage without olive oil, so prominent a part of Mediterranean cookery. Although olive trees flourished and accounted for the name of Mount Olive given to a portion of the former New Smyrna settlement by 1804, their yield, as in other Florida plantings, was probably insignificant. Even in Minorca the oil had been imported, for as Postlethwayt (1757:274) noted, "they have abundance of olive-trees, yet they make no oil of the fruit, and are utterly ignorant of the right method of pickling it." A book written in the mid-nineteenth century (Johnson 1851:328) but based on earlier reminiscences mentioned that the New Smyrna colonists "murmered for their olive oil, raisins, chestnuts and light table wine. For fat in the diet they had to rely on animal fat, either domestic or wild." Sesame seeds may have been grown for their oil as Schoepf (1911:243) observed the "culture of sesamun oriental" in Florida in 1783 and notes that it makes an oil which does not grow rancid.

In the productive middle years of the colony the settlers realized a small amount of income selling excess produce to the residents of St. Augustine. Turnbull (1788:685) mentioned great numbers of poultry sold in the St. Augustine market. "A Captain Brown once purchased above twelve hundred poultry at one time," he reported, "and above eight hundred in another trip with his schooner, for which he gave tobacco, sugar, and . . . little articles of luxury."

A few other domestic animals were kept by the colonists; pigs and cows were mentioned and beehives were kept for honey. However, the ubiquitous goat of the Mediterranean did not thrive in the Florida climate, nor did sheep do well.

Homegrown produce was not enough, so to survive the settlers engaged in a multitude of hunting, fishing and gathering activities. Some wild plants and animals were familiar from their homelands, others were variants or close to the homeland species, and, in a third category, were edible plants and animals with which they were totally unfamiliar. All other things being equal, the environment would have been exploited in descending frequency in each of the three categories. However, all things were not equal. Turnbull and his subordinates appear to have outlawed some activities, such as deer hunting, and, especially when the cash crops required attention, discouraged others, including fishing. The fatigue of the settlers at peak cropping times and the general weakness consequent on the near starvation in the early years restricted many of the gathering activities to a close-to-home radius. The strength and expertise of the young children and nursing mothers, neither being in the regular plantation crews, may have limited the kind of gathering activities.

During famine times in Minorca the islanders, according to Cleghorn (1779:39), "have been obliged to have Recourse to Acorns, wild Dates, the Berries of the Myrtles, the Bramble, the Arbutus, and the like." He further mentions (Cleghorn 1779:24-25) the eating of wild foods such as dandelions which "in Times of Scarcity they have served as common Food." Plenty of wild rabbits were available, "as also Hedge-hogs and Land Turtles which are sometimes eaten by the poor" (Cleghorn 1779:54). A picture emerges of a people with a repertoire of contingency foods to fall back on in time of need, with the expectation of periodic necessity to reactivate this subsistence knowledge.

Probably various roots and berries were gathered in New

Smyrna, and most certainly the easily recognized dandelion. Varieties of dandelions and acorns found in their new location were not as bitter as the ones they had known. As recently as the depression of the 1930s there are reports of Minorcan families near St. Augustine weathering hard times by eating acorn broth (Manucy 1975). Even palmetto berries could have been used, as probably were palm hearts, or "swamp cabbage," as they are called.

The New Smyrna area was well populated with deer, which must have multiplied after land clearing, thriving as they do in "edge areas" of plant succession (Harlow and Jones 1965:153). However, Dr. Turnbull in good English fashion kept a hunter, an African named London, to supply his table and may have considered deer hunting by his workers as poaching. The prohibition against hunting did not deter resourceful members of the group from taking deer when they could.

The settlers fished at every available opportunity, finding fish much more abundant in the tidal lagoons at New Smyrna than they had been in the Mediterranean Sea. They also collected or caught small reptiles and mammals including snakes, lizards, possum, squirrel, and rabbit. Before they had chickens they discovered that sea-turtle eggs, collected from the beach during the July laying season, were a good substitute for chicken eggs, and even into the twentieth century their descendents favored those eggs for the rich texture they imparted to cakes.

Of birds, many, such as ducks and quail, resembled their Mediterranean counterparts. As hungry as the people were during the starving times, birds eaten were not always the tastiest. If we can give credence to his deposition, Juan Portella and his wife were reduced to eating a turkey buzzard killed by one of the drivers and traded to them for two weeks ration of pork (C.O. 5/557). Like many hungry Floridians of a later day, the settlers found the wood stork to be tolerable fare, calling it "gannet" according to the naturalist John James Audubon (Proby 1974:156). This new meaning for gannet was later picked up by Webster's Dictionary, the only lexical contribution of any consequence made to American English by the Minorcan colonists. Much tastier, the marsh hens, abundant along the shore, were called even into the nineteenth century "everybody's chickens."

The gopher, a common land tortoise in East Florida, often made the difference between starvation and survival. An average gopher

Photo by Griffin.

Figure 4.3. Gopher Tortoise.

(*Gopherus polyphemus*) weighs six pounds, of which roughly seventy percent is edible meat, including selected portions of the viscera (Stephen L. Cumbaa, personal communication). The gopher has not been assayed for food value, but is probably close to sea turtle which has a high protein value of 19.8 grams per 100 grams, and 89 calories per gram of edible meat. The gopher is easy to catch with bare hands. With a taste somewhere between pork and chicken, it became and remained for two centuries, until it was declared a threatened species, a preferred food for the Minorcan group, It was usually served in a peppery hot "gopher stew" at gatherings and ceremonial occasions, with old timers still declaring today that it is tastiest if it contains the claws. The gopher population unfortunately depletes easily because of the size of the individual territory, the sixty-year average life span, and the slow reproductive rate of the species. They are also garden marauders, so the settlers may have found it necessary to erect low log fences or barriers to discourage their depredations.

Oysters, growing right off shore in the estuaries, were easily obtained by an individual working alone. In contrast, diving for oysters off the rocky coast of the Mediterranean was a hazardous procedure, requiring two or more men working together from a boat (Armstrong 1756:20-21). Although not high in calories, oysters were a rich protein addition to the diet, as were other shellfish, particularly clams. In his thorough description of the lush fauna of the Mosquitoes area in 1765, surveyor William Gerard De Brahm noted the "fine oysters, turtles, & fish, as trouts, mullets, sheep heads, drums, bass & porgies" (De Vorsey 1966:38).

A fish familiar to these Mediterraneans, and found in their new home waters in vast numbers, was the mullet (*Mugil cephalus*). Its abundance, schooling behavior, and the ease with which quantities could be netted, made it a central and important resource. The waters near New Smyrna teemed with mullet; within a mile of that place Gregg (1902:45) "met a school which extended from shore to shore . . . Some eight or ten boats of fishermen were in the school, and had loaded their boats to the gunnels by using their cast nets." Mullet have been known to jump into boats in their paths, particularly at night. It is small wonder that the Minorcans became fishermen, and that to this day the cry of "Mullet on the beach!" speaks to the importance of this subsistence source. It was probably mullet to which Turnbull referred when he said that "many families had for the most part great quantities of dried fish in their houses" (Turnbull 1788:386). To this day, smoked mullet remains a prized delicacy in St. Augustine.

The colony was situated, we see, in a natural environment rich in resources and truck garden potential, but cash cropping for the proprietor seems to have prevented a well-rounded resource utilization by the colonial group. On the whole, the balance between cash cropping and subsistence activity remained an uneasy one for the nine-year duration of the plantation operation.

Problems in the economic life of the plantation were many—structural as well as ideological—nor were such problems unique to the New Smyrna enterprise. Thompson (1959:31-34) outlines the rocky process by which the family forms and lifeways of a new plantation work force were attenuated and adapted to the economic life of an American plantation. In order to break down the cultural baggage of his workers and to fit them into his economic mold, the estate

manager fell into a certain ruthlessness, often quite different from
the ways in which he related to the other parts of his life. Thus, while
taming the wilderness on a new plantation, the proprietor had the
equally onerous job of taming his work force.

First of all, the way in which the work groups were structured
caused problems. For efficient production, the labor gangs were
formed on the model of American plantations where the usual work
force was of African origin. In this model trusted slaves were often
used as drivers. Turnbull's use of this system seems to have caused
much resentment among the colonists, especially since the imported
black drivers were accustomed to rule by force. As mentioned earlier, when the large number of colonists necessitated the naming of
drivers from the settler group, those named were Italians and
Greeks. It would appear that any potential leaders among the Minorcan islanders were, for unknown reasons, slighted.

The way of managing work outlined above varied greatly from
the cultural patterns of the Mediterranean labor force. The diffuse
leadership pattern of the kinship-affinal-neighbor work group, a consensus model congenial to these indigenous Mediterranean peoples,
found its only expression in New Smyrna in informal work groups
structured by the colonists themselves in the leisure time they had
away from their daily work for the planter. One wonders what might
have happened had natural leaders been identified by Turnbull and
his overseers and put in charge of groups composed of those who
would ordinarily work together; if respect had been substituted for
force, if natural, not artificial, patterns had been followed.

Secondly, the colonists' relationships with the proprietor were
never viable. Turnbull evidently had no idea of the importance of the
mutual relationship expected by his workers, of the usual quasi-kin
bonding between a patron and his clients. This, of course was not a
unique failing. "Patronage is good when the patron is good," says
Pitt-Rivers (1961:204) of that relationship gone wrong, "but like the
friendship on which it is based it has two faces. It can either confirm
the superiority of the señorito or it can be exploited by the rich man
in order to obtain a nefarious advantage over the poor people."

Turnbull never recognized the friendship relationship as any part
of his planning. When Giosefa Marcatto was "put in Confinement in
the Stocks" and given nothing but hominy and water, Turnbull "stir-
red the Hominy about, to see if there was any meat or fish in it, and
allowed no person to speak to him" (C.O. 5/557:435). In another inci-

dent Pompey Possi complained "that the said Dr. Turnbull beat him on horseback, and afterwards dismounted and beat him again, and struck him on his private parts, which obliged him to lay in a Palmetto house in the field all night, not being able to go home" (C.O. 5/557:435-436).

The lack of an effective manager to take over when Turnbull was absent presented another difficulty. Neither of his own sons was old enough for this job so his nephew, also named Andrew Turnbull, barely in his twenties, and as far as is known with no plantation experience, was usually left in charge. One imagines that young Andrew Turnbull relied heavily on the overseers and drivers.

The third stumbling block in the successful working of the plantation has already been alluded to, that is, the difference in world view between the Scottish planter and his workers. Turnbull assumed that he could easily turn subsistence farmers into plantation labor, not anticipating that his disruption of the ritual, seasonal work/leisure patterns of his workers might have profound consequences for the success of the plantation. He was dealing with a group for whom work as an end in itself had no meaning, for whom being a "good worker" and "good person" did not necessarily equate. A man's skill in some area might be admired, it is true, but discharge of kin and community obligations and fulfillment of religious requirements were at the core of a person's value among his Mediterranean fellows. Hard labor had its place but not center stage.

Greeks, Italians, and Minorcans alike complained later of the continuous toil expected and the work required on sacred days. Pedro Cocifaci, one of the Greeks, testified that "he hath served Dr. Turnbull Sundays, Holidays and all times whatsoever but that he hath always been badly used by the said Dr. Turnbull" (C.O. 5/557:437-440), and Giosefa Marcatto described "working days & nights, not even Sunday excepted without any rest" (C.O. 5/557:435-436). Probably the afternoon siesta, so dear to the hearts of those of southern European extraction, was banned on the plantation. If so, this was contrary to the advice later given newcomers: "Experience has taught the natives to sleep in the middle of the day. Emigrants should at least be equally cautious" (Williams 1837:304). In any case the long accustomed web of activity and rest, part and parcel of the complex cultural core of these Mediterraneans, was seriously out of balance.

Lastly, the variety of languages, symbolic of the differing cultural models on the plantation, posed a problem in the work sphere. There was Catalan, Spanish, Greek, Italian and a sprinkling of French among the settlers. The significant language in terms of power and authority on the plantation was English, while the black slaves spoke English shaded by their African dialects. Notwithstanding Governor Grant's belief that the foreignness of their languages would help to keep the colony in line, the actual day-to-day operation of the plantation was doubtless rendered difficult, especially at first, by the multitude of tongues. Difficulty of communication was a possible contributory factor in the drivers' adoption of excessive physical control methods.

However, English was not entirely unknown to those of the Minorcan islanders who had been exposed to British garrisons on the coast of their island, or to others from coastal areas in the Mediterranean. Luis Bertani, an Italian who became Turnbull's clerk was most certainly fully literate in English. Also, Juan Portella must have had enough English at his command to make him the logical choice for petitioning the proprietor on behalf of the settlers. Portella said that, "in the name of the people," he went to Turnbull sometime in 1770 to complain of the ill treatment of the plantation workers by the drivers (C.O. 5/557:449). Turnbull's answer, according to Portella, was to confine him in irons in the guardhouse where he received twelve lashes. He had his own personal grievances as well since he had been originally hired as a shoemaker, but was required to work in the fields instead. His wife, he reported, had the temerity to roast an ear of corn where she was working in the field, and was beaten for this "affront."

The question remains, why, in view of all the slippage described, plus the climatic factors and soil depletion that eventually interfered with production, did the plantation become, at least for a time, a successful one. Unilateral answers such as the high price of indigo and its subsidy by the British government, the temporarily optimum soil and climatic conditions, or the effective toil of the workers as they looked forward to land ownership, do not answer this fully, if indeed it can be answered at all. The case of Luis Soche may help to solve this puzzle.

We know that Luis Soche was from Italy, that he was thirty years old at the colony's beginning, and that he was illiterate, since he signed his deposition against Turnbull with an "X." He was married three times. Two children were born in New Smyrna of his first marriage to Catalina Pons, but their failure to appear in any of the St. Augustine records may indicate their deaths prior to 1777. Catalina also died, and Soche married Juana Llopis in 1776. Two years later in St. Augustine, again widowed, he married Antonia Tremol, twenty years his junior, the widow of a Minorcan man murdered by a driver. Soche's second and third marriages were without issue.

On the plantation, Turnbull, or maybe the head overseer, selected Soche to be one of the drivers. We can only speculate on the reason. He was of a prime age for the job, perhaps he was physically strong or distinguished himself as a hard worker, or even that he might have been bilingual in spite of his inability to write.

More surprising than being chosen for a foreman's job was his retention of it, given his humane treatment of his fellow colonists. As Juan Portella later told it, when he (Portella) fell out of favor with Turnbull, he was sent from his shoemaker's bench into the field to work under Soche's direction. One morning, Portella claimed that he heard Turnbull tell Soche "to beat the People very hard, not to mind killing a Man for that was nothing, the said Luis answered, if you want to kill a Man you may do it yourself, for I will not. Dr. Turnbull then said if you don't I will break you and put another in your place" (C.O. 5/577:449-450).

Luis Soche was the last of the seventeen complainants to execute a deposition against Turnbull:

Lewis Sauche being duly sworn saith that he agreed to serve Dr. Turnbull six years in the Province aforesaid. That about six weeks before this Dept's [deponent's] time was out, he applied to the said Dr. Turnbull for his discharge to be given him when his time was out, upon which Dr. Turnbull put this Dept. in gaol, with irons to his leg and nailed them to the wall and remained in that manner for about an hour, when Dr. Turnbull came to the gaol and told him if he did not go to work he would tie him up and flog him. That this Dept. was afraid of being flogged (as well he knew in what unchristianlike manner the people were used and expected to be used in the same manner) went to his work. That then the said Dr. Turnbull shewed [sic] this Dept. a false Contract to which this Dept's name was subscribed and said to him he was for ten years and that he had

two witnesses Pietro Merlin and Gaspar Trotti upon which this
Dept. went to call the witnesses and Dr. Turnbull desired him
to go to his work and let it alone. That Dr. Turnbull always
desired him to beat the People very much and make them work
hard else he would flog him and make him work in the field.
This Dept. told him that he would rather work in the field than
to use the People cruelly, and this Dept. was always badly used
upon that Account. This Dept. further saith that the aforesd.
Pietro Merlin and Gaspar Trotti told him that they forged the
said ten years Contract on Dr. Turnbulls order, otherwise they
would have been flogged. And this Dept. further saith that all
the People upon the Plantation were always badly used.

his
Lewis X Sauche
mark
(C.O. 5/557:479-480)

Later in St. Augustine, Soche's career was not a distinguished
one. He was listed as a ropemaker/fisherman in the 1784 census and
as a mariner in the 1786 and 1787 censuses, employed on a "small
boat." However, by the latter date he must have been tired of the
seafaring life as he stated that he "has no land but desires to farm."

On the Rocque map of 1788 his residence was close to the center
of the Minorcan quarter in a dwelling described as a "timber-frame
and shingle house, in bad condition, palm thatch roof, owned by Luis
Soche; lot owned by the Crown."

He owned neither livestock nor slaves and his name and mark
was twenty-fourth of twenty-nine on the Greek-Italian memorial of
1784 swearing loyalty to the Spanish Crown. Since these names appear to be roughly in rank order, this fixes him close to the lower
part of the range in status. He was, however, godfather to five children, attesting to continuing good relations with his fellow colonists.

Returning to Soche's role on the plantation, Turnbull must have
retained him as a driver because of Soche's ability to extract work
from his crews. If so, Turnbull's good judgement in this instance may
represent more basic managerial capability on his part than the thin,
perhaps distorted, documentation has so far indicated.

5. Social Life

Rue in a garden will keep off evil spirits.
Old Minorcan saying

The holy oils stored aboard ship by Father Camps upon leaving Minorca were almost gone before 1769 ended. The sacraments administered to the dying, more than six hundred dead in the first two years, an average of nearly one a day, had almost exhausted the supply. Luckily, two Cuban fishermen put into Mosquito Inlet in October, 1769, for on their departure they carried away with them a note from Father Camps to Bishop Echevarría of Cuba. Communications being what they were at the time, the bishop had never heard of Father Camps, and since a Catholic parish in British East Florida seemed highly unlikely this cautious prelate undertook to make inquiries of church authorities in Mallorca and Spain and finally the Vatican. This took time, and by October, 1771, Father Camps was desperate. The temporary faculties under which the fathers administered to the people had expired, and they were still without holy oils. He wrote two more letters. At last on December 3, 1771, again via Cuban fishermen, the two priests received notification that their faculties, greatly expanded this time, were extended for twenty years. They could minister every necessary sacrament except confirmation. Holy oils and other ecclesiastical supplies were also included in the packet.

The Roman Catholic church, so vital a part of the past lives of a majority of the colonists, was the only formal Mediterranean institution transplanted to the New World with them. Catholicism was the faith of the Minorcans, Italians, French, Mallorcans, Spanish, and Corsican Greeks. In the absence of their own Greek Orthodox clergy, many of the other Greeks became Roman Catholic. Perhaps they followed the example of Turnbull's Greek wife who regularly attended mass at the Church of San Pedro. More likely, though, the presence of an unbaptized baby in the family pushed them toward the Roman church. Indeed, godparent exchanges do point to increasing incorporation of Greeks into the parish church. Later in St. Augustine when asked to declare their religion only one Greek, Demetrios Fundulakis, listed himself as Greek Orthodox. Next to the family, and an integral part of it, the church was the strongest cohesive force for the total community. A Minorcan descendant (Wickman 1974:9) describes "the strength of the Catholic faith which sustained all the members of the colony throughout their years of hardships and united them into one group."

In New Smyrna the church was not merely the most important institution in Minorcan social life, it was the only one. Its sacraments moved each person through life, from birth to death, its processions celebrated a favorite saint or acted as intercession for good crops, and its liturgical year was the foundation of the great ceremonials and festivals of the people. The connections made through the sacrament of marriage and the godparent ties, hardly to be taken lightly when one had scarcely enough resources for oneself, were the cords that tied them to each other.

After arrival in New Smyrna the Catholic fathers lost no time in regularizing their work and ministering to the families. The parish formed for the community they named San Pedro, probably because the arrival in Florida was close to that saint's day.

If the documents are cloudy on the location of the Church of San Pedro, they are much clearer on its interior decoration and its activities. As described by Father Camps in a letter to the bishop in 1772, the main altar of the church was adorned with a crucifix and statues of San Pedro and San Antonio de Padua, both favorite saints of the island of Minorca. The bishop was requested to send a wooden cross, whether to grace the outside of the church or to use in processions, is not known. Dr. Joseph Johnson, a later apologist for a fellow doctor, says that Turnbull "even employed a carver to supply their wants for saints and other images" (Johnson 1851:328).

An Anglican congregation of some sort also existed at New Smyrna during the plantation years. The fact that the ministry of Reverend John Forbes to the Protestants in the Mosquitos area predates the arrival of the colony (C.O. 5/550:8), is strong evidence that such a ministry was not set up specifically for members of the Turnbull colony. In fact, Forbes, in order to get married, left for Boston in the autumn of 1768, soon after the colonists arrived, and did not return for some time. Subsequently, the pulpit was filled by a succession of ministers, several in residence, but after 1775 sent on a periodic basis from St. Augustine. There is a question as to whether a church was ever built although De Brahm (De Vorsey 1966:206) hints at such a structure in his description of the colony. More convincing is the approval in 1772 of the proposed expenditure of £700 for "a church at Hillsborough" (C.O. 5/545:116,151).

The only logical conclusion is that the Protestant congregation must have been composed of the personnel of the other plantations in the area, swollen by Turnbull's black and white recruits from the other colonies, and perhaps a few stray Protestants from among the settler group. One shred of evidence suggests peaceful coexistence between the Protestant church and the Church of San Pedro. In a letter dated February 14, 1784, Reverend James Seymour, who served the Protestant congregation in New Smyrna from time to time in the late 1770s, described Father Camps as "a very discreet and prudent man . . . much respected for his good conduct in Florida" (Pennington 1927:199).

We are much clearer on the parishioners of San Pedro. Writing at the beginning of 1772, Father Camps informed Bishop Echevarría that "the families that make up my parish number one hundred and seventy-five, comprised of five hundred communicants, sixty of the age of confession, and forty innocents who have not yet attained the age of seven years." He alerted his superior to the fact that "not all are Minorcans, but almost all; we have some Italians, Leghorn; of Corsicans, there are fifty, and in all these cases they have Minorcan wives and families" (Quinn 1975:56-57).

Besides the two clerics, the parish household of San Pedro included Lorenzo Capo, the sacristan, who was twenty-two years of age at the colony's start. He had been a parishioner in Father Camps' parish in Mercadal, maybe especially recruited to serve the parish in the New World. Although he contracted two marriages to Minorcan girls later in St. Augustine, he was a bachelor in New Smyrna. In St. Augustine he continued to serve as sacristan.

Among his other duties the sacristan oversaw the burial of the many who died, although how the bodies were disposed of in New

Smyrna remains a mystery. Customs varied in the Mediterranean and differing reports on burials in Minorca have been set down by eighteenth-century writers. Armstrong (1756:68) claims that bodies were put in the vault in the churches of Minorca, covered with lime and later disposed of in mass burials; while Cleghorn (1779:70) mentions that although bodies were not put in coffins, they were carried in open litters to the grave. All that can be said with certainty for New World practice is that cemetery burial was the standard form after the Minorcans reached St. Augustine.

While there was only one birth to every three deaths in the New Smyrna years, the joyous occasion of baptism relieved the somberness of life. On August 25, 1768, just six days after the rebellion, the first four babies were baptized in the new parish. Two had been born at sea and were already four months old. The very first entry is for Florida-born María Famanias, a two-day-old infant at the time of baptism. María, though, was not the first baby born in New Smyrna. This distinction goes to María Alguina (now spelled Usina), born August 1, 1768, but not baptized until August 26th. Thus began the "Golden Book of the Minorcans" as it is called (Camps 1768-1784).

In this parish register certain names occur over and over. Of the 123 boys baptized at New Smyrna, Juan was either the first or second name of 48 (31%). Next in popularity were Antonio with 23 (19%) and Pedro with 21 (17%). Predictably, María and its derivatives was included in the names of 69 (51%) of the 135 girls baptized in New Smyrna. Next in popularity, Juana, was included in 18 (13.3%) of the female names and Antonia and Agueda each were part of the names of 15 (11%) of the girls.

The names most commonly used equate with favored saints of the Minorcan group, noting that Juana and Antonia are feminine counterparts of the male names, Juan and Antonio. The Holy Mother's name, María, is common in all Catholic groups, and in the Iberian tradition a girl bearing this name was thought to have special grace (Pitt-Rivers 1961:190). The name of Pedro (Peter), the patron saint of fishermen, is frequent throughout the Mediterranean, and naturally of significance to the settlers through the naming of their church.

Agueda as a frequent name for girls baptized at New Smyrna deserves a special explanation. Agueda (Agatha) is the patron saint of the women of Minorca. On top of *Monte Agueda*, northwest of Mercadal (figure 1.1), stands a chapel to this saint much visited by women suffering from complaints of the breast. Armstrong (1756:56-57) vividly describes the altar "hung with votive figures of the seat of the distemper, and there are some hundreds of the representations of little breasts in wood, wax, and silver, which have been placed there, in gratitude to the saint." According to contemporary accounts (see particularly Brydone 1773:128-129), Agueda was greatly reverenced throughout the Mediterranean in the eighteenth century.

As for other joyous occasions and holidays, the strait-jacket of the indigo season put a damper on the annual celebrations based on the liturgical year. The most significant time of the year in Christian Mediterranean countries was the Easter season with its pre-Lenten carnival and other festivities and the special events of Eastertide itself. While the serious parts of the Easter celebration were not eliminated—the Catholic fathers would have seen to that—the wild ribaldry of the carnival, described in detail by later observers in St. Augustine, with its elaborate parades, masquerading and feasting, must have been in a minor key in the plantation years.

Probably the Fromajardis (properly *formatjades* in the Minorcan dialect of Catalan) on the Saturday night before Easter was largely eclipsed also. Bryant (1850:114-120) and later Dewhurst (1886:164-168) gave full descriptions of the Fromajardis Serenade as it later appeared in St. Augustine, and more recently Catalan scholar Philip Rasico (1987a:291-305) has studied the practice and furnished a new rendering of the words. According to the many accounts of this custom, on the night before Easter Sunday the young Minorcan men went about in groups serenading the households of the town. They sang the Fromajardis Song; a song to the Virgin assuring her of her Son's resurrection. At the end of the song a request was made for a token gift of food. The traditional cheese pastries, fromajardis, composed of cheese wrapped in a "womb" of pastry, or other cakes or eggs, were then handed out through the shutters and dropped into a bag carried by one of the serenaders. At a generous household a bit of wine might be added also. The ending of the song varies according to whether the treats were forthcoming. Either *"Es homo de compliment"* or *"No es homo de compliment"* was sung, the loud emphasis on the *No* announcing to the neighborhood the stinginess of any family unwilling to take part. The serenading ended abruptly at midnight as Easter day began. It is not likely that guitars were available in New Smyrna, given the limited space aboard ship on the

journey over, but even if serenading was a *cappella*, family larders
did not permit of much open-handedness. Those who tried to keep
up the tradition could often expect a resounding *"No!"*

The second most important holiday, especially for those from the
Balearics, was St. John's Eve (Midsummer's Eve), June 23. A continuance of the ancient summer solstice celebration, this ceremony
in the Mediterranean, and indeed throughout Europe, was a mixture
of Christian and pre-Christian elements. In addition to being the day
of longest daylight, in Minorca it marked the end of the grain harvest, and initiated the summer festive season which ended at wine
making time in early fall.

Cleghorn (1779:65) mentions the importance of St. Johns Eve
celebration in eighteenth-century Minorca. Chamberlain (1927:138)
in a much later description of the holiday in Minorca called the Fiesta
of San Juan the "most prominent show of the year." "It has always
been," he adds, "a great celebration of the stallions of the island.
They are bedecked with flowers and be-ribboned in the most bewil-
dering color schemes and ridden by youths as gaily caparisoned in
procession after procession."

Although no longer at harvest's completion, the celebration of St.
John's Eve persisted for many years among the Minorcans who came
to Florida with the Turnbull colony. John Bemrose, writing of his
tour of duty in St. Augustine in the 1830s, outlines its form at that
time:

> St. John's Eve is the great drama of this light hearted people
> [Minorcans]. It is then the custom to promenade the city in
> masquerade, by day. The ladies represent the ancient chivalry,
> mounted upon handsomely caparisoned steeds, whilst the gent-
> lemen wear the costumes of the ancient dames.
>
> There are generally two or three altars throughout the city.
> These are large wooden frames, forming a recess, beautifully
> and tastefully decorated with flowers and draperies. In the
> center of the recess is placed a representation of Our Savior, in
> silver. This is lit by a hundred tapers. The beauty of the "Toute
> ensemble" is more than fancy can paint.
>
> The rule is to present the gentlemen who view the altars
> with a bunch of flowers, taken from the decorated pile. This he
> gracefully received from the hand of the lady proprietress (Bem-
> rose 1966:10-11).

Coming as it did in the heart of the indigo season, and commonly stretching over two or three days, or longer, this summer carnival was doubtless regarded as an unnecessary interruption of work on the plantation. Rafael Hernández may have been describing a confrontation over this holiday in his deposition (C.O. 5/577:453). "About six years since [around 1771]," he reported, "there was a Holiday amongst the People when this Dep. was Ordered to Work by the said [overseer or driver] Brace, but refused to do so upon which the said Brace beat this Dep. several times that day, and allowed him no Victuals that day and likewise told him if he did not go to work he would shoot him."

On the plantation it was much easier to follow certain more strictly ecclesiastical customs, the Palm Sunday mass and procession for example. To secure the necessary palm leaves it was only necessary to step out of the door. It was a simple, sober occasion. Bryant (1850:104) who observed the Easter customs among the colonial descendents in St. Augustine told of how the leaves of the palmetto, blessed by the priest, were distributed first to the men in the congregation in order of age, from oldest to youngest, and then to the women in like manner.

The proprietor evidently did not discourage the rogation processions since they are mentioned in one of the letters sent by Father Camps to the Cuban Bishop. On the day of Ascension each year a mass was said in the church and as the last verse of the litany of the saints was chanted the procession of the priests and people proceeded to the fields to ask for God's blessing on the crops, ensuring a bountiful harvest. The traditional purple for the occasion was no problem, as hues of indigo resemble this color. Turnbull may have smiled on this particular ceremony thinking it might encourage the laborers to put more effort into the plantation work. It was also a celebration easily understood by him since it was close to "the common riding," or walking of the bounds, known from his youth in Scotland and founded on the ancient Christian, and before that pagan form, which insured spiritual benevolence on the processes of the natural world (Neville 1979:102-103).

If proprietor and settlers found some connection in this ceremonial form, in the matter of Christmas celebrations they were far apart. To those of British extraction the Christmas festivities composed the main ceremonial cycle of the year, a time of no work and much frolic. The custom of giving the "hands" three days off at Christmas was a well established one on plantations in the southern colonies. While the Minorcans no doubt appreciated any time off from work which they might be given, they probably would willingly have exchanged the time for more significant festival days of their own cultures. In most of the Christian Mediterranean countries at that time the day of Christ's birth was treated as little different from any other saint's day, and it was not until the end of the eighteenth century, decades after the New Smyrna colony left the Mediterranean, that even manger scenes began to appear in the houses of the rich at Christmas time.

In addition to the church-centered events, social life and customs brought from the Old World continued in some cast on the plantation. While wine was scarce, we still can imagine the men gathered together in the evenings for talk and camaraderie, with the young boys hanging around the edges of these groups fascinated by tales of the Old World and absorbing easily in this way an understanding of a man's role in the world. The men could also in their own cooperative undertakings such as hunting and fishing settle into in the groupings natural to them—a network of brothers and cousins and brothers-in-law. Similarly the women, used to the daily gossip sessions in the lanes of the Old World towns and villages, must have found time to carry on the common life of the sisterhood. There were babies to birth, marriages to approve or disapprove, honors to be paid to those who had died, and celebrations to plan.

Although the documentation is slim on such things in the New Smyrna years, there were no doubt angers and jealousies among the people, feuds even. The proprietor insisted later that "he was often obliged to interfere in order to keep peace particularly between man and wife, for the women at times provoked their husbands to treat them harshly" (Turnbull 1788:685).

Intermediate between the forms of the established church and the day-to-day associational networks was the gray area of folk beliefs—values, concepts and practices existing in tandem with approved religious doctrine. Such beliefs and their solidification into practice are a part of the culture of all traditional groups, and, in fact, are not totally absent in more sophisticated societies, or for that matter in any communal life even today. At times the Catholic church worked actively to purge these allied customs from formal worship.

As an illustration, the St. Johns Eve celebration was one of the eight celebrations targeted by the church for elimination in the New World, where it was the intention that Catholicism be imported in its pure form, with all festivals based on pagan ceremonies eliminated. However, the two Minorcan priests, themselves men of the people, would likely not have been aware of this. It would be nearly a century later in St. Augustine that Bishop Augustin Verot discouraged the people's celebration of St. John's Eve.

Roughly, folk religion, such as the customs attached to the festival of St. John, can be divided into those practised by men, those by women and those where joint participation is the rule. In long ceremonial cycles, male and female elements are interwoven. The Fromajardis serenade, for example, is a Easter custom associated with men.

In contrast with many other Hispanic colonial ventures in the New World where women's folk religion was not imported because the early colonizers and missionaries were men, women were a significant part of the Minorcan group. The typical bower altars erected at carnival times were among their imports. Less obvious were their venerations of female saints such as Santa Agueda and Santa Elena. In the latter instance a nine-day series of devotions, a novena, was said in the saint's honor, a solemn practice which preceded the Posey Dances which were a significant feature of the pre-Lenten carnival celebration. Santa Elena, or St. Helen, the mother of Constantine and the discoverer of the true cross, was enjoying a great deal of favor in southern Europe in the late eighteenth century, almost amounting to a cult. Among the Minorcan women she was accorded special honor on each of nine successive evenings in the home of a woman of status in the community, the ceremony taking place around a bed made into a bower embellished with flowers and crosses. We hear of this custom not from the many men who later described the Posey Dances in St. Augustine, but from a female eyewitness, a descendent of Francisco Phelipe Fatio, a Swiss gentleman and a Catholic, who came to Florida in the British period and whose descendents are still in Florida today (Taylor 1916). An event such as this could have remained well submerged, and probably much simplified in the New Smyrna years, only to emerge in fuller practice in post-plantation days.

Several surviving words, in use until recent times, are clues to other extra-ecclesiastical beliefs. *Brusha*, from the Catalan word *bruixa* meaning witch, is one of the words which has survived more than two hundred years of impact from English and other languages. It was included in three out of the four word lists consulted. It is glossed as "witch" in one list, as "a person with a heavy head of hair" in another list, and as "a wild head of hair, uncombed" in yet a third. The word *mamalutta* glossed as a "secretive conversation between two people" also hints at the mysterious.

Turning now to look at the connections formed on the plantation outside of the settler group itself, more of a puzzle is confronted. As already discussed, the relationship between the proprietor and the settlers, off on a good footing when the little fleet left the Mediterranean, does not appear to have been very cordial once on the plantation. It further deteriorated as time went on. Again, it must be borne in mind that the depositions, the main source of data about life on the plantation, were written to justify leaving New Smyrna, just as Turnbull's later defense of himself was from the opposite position.

However, the placement of Turnbull's house, offset from the center of plantation life speaks to an image of himself as the lord of the manor. He and his wife were, of course, of gentle birth and their St. Augustine social life and their contacts in London, Charleston, and the Mediterranean set them into an elite class. The couple were cherished members of the aristocratic set in St. Augustine where Dr. Turnbull was a member of the provincial council whose membership was composed entirely of gentlemen. "St. Augustine became, under the direction of an affable gourmet and 'bon vivant,' the bachelor governor James Grant, the unlikely seat of a glittering social life" (Schafer 1983:101-102).

Notwithstanding the disparate places of birth of Andrew Turnbull and Maria Gracia Dura Bin, portraits of them (figures 5.1 and 5.2) show a remarkable similarity. There is in each an upright hauteur, a generous but determined set of the mouth, the same born-to-be-in-charge look, and moreover, the aspect of plump affluence afforded only to the gentry in those spare times. However, whereas the elaborate headdress of the "fair Greek," as she was called by her contemporaries, gives the overall impression of a ship under full sail, the berobed doctor's straight-on look while his left hand rests on a human skull on a table beside him, gives the appearance of assured management of lesser humans. It is difficult to look at that skull and not think of the legions of dead settlers buried in New Smyrna.

Courtesy of John D. Corse.

Figure 5.1. Dr. Andrew Turnbull.

There can be no doubt that Turnbull had a definite and grandiose goal, but in trying to attain that goal he was defeated by his own inflexibility. He was fit to initiate an enterprise but was little equipped to carry it out. "His relationships, outside his family and a very restricted circle of acquaintances, were completely devoid of emotionalism," Panagopoulos (1966:171) concluded. His mode of operation was that of an empire builder; his laboring force was the tool to acheive that end. The distance that Turnbull put between himself and the group of people he brought to the New World, was not just the physical separation he maintained on the plantation but a social

Figure 5.2. Maria Gracia Dura Bin Turnbull.

separation as well. However, this was not Turnbull's perception of the state of affairs as he later claimed that his "care of all at Smyrnia was more that of a Father of a Family, than a hard Master" (Turnbull 1777).

Nevertheless, a recent analyst, Bernard Bailyn sets the Turnbull enterprise in a more general context. In fact, he uses the New Smyrna case as a prime illustration of the characteristic "mingling of primitivism and civilization" which occurred on the American frontier, whereby men of gentle birth deteriorated into despots in the fluid situation at the settlement fringe (Bailyn 1986a:130-131). However, the respect accorded to the Turnbulls during the last years of their lives, which were spent in Charleston, presents an ameliorating image of this eighteenth-century couple.

As to the colonists' relationships with the blacks on the plantation, little is known. Of the blacks imported by Turnbull to initiate and carry out the plantation work, those who were drivers were no doubt chosen for their tough-mindedness. Whether they brought their families with them and where they were quartered is unknown, but they probably lived close to the central work area. Only a few of these blacks, usually the ones accused of cruelty, do we find mentioned by name, although there may have been as many as five or six employed as drivers, plus at least several dozen common laborers, some working on Turnbull's private plantation.

The unfortunate confusion among the designations of driver, overseer and corporal prevents a clear picture of the hierarchy on the plantation. In contrast with New World plantations, the position of overseer or manager of an agricultural enterprise in southern Europe in the eighteenth century was never important. There was the *Señor* or Lord of the manor, and directly below him were the leaders of the work gangs, men of the people, never very powerful, who maintained their positions through the respect of their comrades. The English system as it was practiced in the Americas was totally foreign to the labor force in New Smyrna. Those of the Italians chosen as foremen appear to have operated under the mind-set of the Mediterranean system, and therefore were aligned with their fellow colonists by the time of the disintegration of the plantation. Their participation in the Minorcan community overrode their role in the plantation structure.

It is difficult to know who was the head overseer or overseers. Cutter was evidently the principal overseer of agricultural work at the beginning. After he died from the maiming he experienced in the rebellion, no head manager is mentioned in the documents. Of William Watson we have more knowledge. Even before the settlers

came he was overseeing the building work of the plantation; sub-
sequently he appears in documents about New Smyrna and is later
prominent in British St. Augustine where he lived next door to
Father Camps. Neighborly relations must have been good for when
Watson left with the British he left his property in charge of Father
Camps to sell.

Others among the Minorcans, though, found Watson to be a hard
taskmaster in the plantation days. In his deposition Rafael Hernández told of being sent "nine years since" (in 1768) ten miles out of
town to a pine barren to saw timber. While there he received word
that his wife was dying so he returned to the plantation. Watson sent
a note to the overseer, Cutter, saying that Hernández had run away.
Cutter put him in irons, gave him 150 lashes and sent him back
without seeing his wife. He was then assigned to teach a black slave
how to saw. When not much production was evident, and in explanation Hernández said that the black had never sawn before, John
Brace, called "one of Turnbull's overseers" (probably a driver), beat
him and issued him no food that day. Watson on his return had him
tied up and beaten further. We have in this little scene the interaction of a Minorcan, probably a typical colonist, with two overseers,
a driver, and a black slave showing the breakdown of relationships
outside of the Minorcan community itself.

It is now obvious that while community cohesion of the various
settler sub-groups increased and community life contined to grow in
strength and depth, relationships with other elements on the plantation suffered a growing distance. Tradition met with modernity, and
the end was at hand.

6. The End of the Colony

When you are the mortar take the blows;
When you are the pestle do the striking.
                                    Old Minorcan proverb

O ne day in July, 1776, the people of New Smyrna were terrified when Indians invaded the settlement and broke into some of the houses. There were only twenty-two of them, but the resulting commotion made it seem like many more as they pilfered a random assortment of things. They were especially attracted by the women's clothes. The bits of data we have suggest that Turnbull's request for yard goods for the "Distressed settlement" made in September, 1770, (C.O. 5/551: 156) had, given the sluggish way in which such orders were filled, arrived sometime in 1772 or after. We can, therefore, picture the Indian braves prancing about garbed in dresses of "best blue plains," "checkt linins," of "stript cottons," hollering and chanting and making a general hullabaloo.

Except for the nearby marshes, the alarmed settlers had no place to hide. A dash to the wharfside area, for those close enough, could afford some protection since the small garrison was stationed there. However, the clothes must have put the Indians in a good mood. Calming down a little, they stole some of the precious corn supply and raided the settlers hives for honey, but otherwise left the frightened populace unharmed.

While nearby Indians had kept the colony under surveillance off and on for five years and had carried on some minor harassment, this raid was the first one of any consequence since a terrible time in 1771. Then, Cowkeeper, a chief of the Oconee, a group of pastoral nomads living on the Alachua prairie, had come to the settlement under the pretext of having heard of a number of the Yamasee tribe in the vicinity.

These Yamasee, not part of the Creek nation, had been allies of the Spaniards and mortal enemies of the Oconee. By 1771 the Yamasee no longer existed as a tribe, having been dispersed and scattered by the British in the early 1700s in the Carolinas and later by the Spanish in the Floridas (Swanton 1946:208-211). Cowkeeper, it seemed, or so he wanted the English to believe, did not consider his traditional adversaries so completely vanquished.

The Indians were apparently less interested in the Yamasee than they were in checking on these foreigners in the Mosquitos who spoke a Spanish tongue. Accordingly, Cowkeeper with two allied chiefs, Long Warrior and another whose name is lost to history, marched overland from the interior with a force of seventy-two warriors. At the north edge of the settlement they encountered a Minorcan boat crew. After beating up these boatmen for good measure, they camped at the edge of Turnbull's cowpen on Spruce Creek.

Turnbull, who was in St. Augustine, upon receiving word that a large body of Indians was near the plantation, hurried home and approached the Indian encampment. After ceremonious greetings were completed and Cowkeeper had told him of the reason for the visit, Turnbull assured him that there were no Yamasee or Spaniards nearby. Cowkeeper and twenty of his men were royally entertained at the Turnbull mansion, and after the food and drink had put them into a better humor, the Indians were persuaded, for the moment at least, that the Minorcan settlers were not Spaniards although they spoke a similar language.

It was suggested to the Indian chief that he should call on Lt. Governor Moultrie, Governor Grant then being absent from the province. Cowkeeper agreed and as an article of faith sent Long Warrior back to the interior with half the force. As an assurance to himself and with Turnbull's permission he proceeded with his own contingent to comb the area south of New Smyrna to assure himself that no Yamasee were lurking there. After a cursory look around, he came back to the plantation where he and his men were again wined and dined. This time, full of drink, some of the warriors went wild and stole some of the Minorcans' provisions, and, before they were stopped by Cowkeeper, were about to kill a calf belonging to a Minorcan family. Cowkeeper, described by Turnbull as "a Sober manly

Indian" and "very watchful over the others for fear they should do something wrong" had the unruly men flogged for their transgressions (Panagopoulos 1966:97). Turnbull, to show good faith, contributed another calf from his plantation. When the Indians reached St. Augustine, Moultrie complimented Cowkeeper on controlling his men and extracted a promise from him not to make similar visits to the plantation in the future.

The Indian visit had made the Minorcans uneasy, afraid for their lives. Of Turnbull's and Moultrie's negotiations they knew little, but they had seen the Indians with warpaint on their faces running wildly about the settlement.

Turnbull, also uneasy, requested additional troops for the settlement. Moultrie at first replied curtly to Turnbull that the Indians appeared to be loyal British subjects, not likely to engage in any acts of hostility. However, later, upon advice of council and as a consequence of the alarm of the other planters near New Smyrna, Moultrie requested Maj. Alexander McKensie, commander of the detachment of the 31st regiment in St. Augustine, to send reinforcements to New Smyrna. McKensie refused and there ensued a series of requests, refusals and petitions to the authorities in England, all resulting in a stalemate, the final result being no additional assignment of troops to New Smyrna. Nor was a requested fort ever built; a reactivation of one originally planned when it was thought in the prior decade that a group of Bermudians would be settling a colony in the Mosquitos.

After that time, nonetheless, the Indians kept a close watch on the settlement. "The Indians, too," Curley (1940:35) tells us, "kept a steady guard on the boats about the New Smyrna Inlet, threatening to kill any Spaniard unlucky enough to fall into their hands." The Indians were well aware of the Cuban fishing boats putting into the estuary from time to time. The Minorcans for their part became accustomed to the few Indian scouts lurking about and kept a careful eye out when they went fishing.

Now, however, five years later, in the summer of 1776 some Indians were again back inside the actual settlement itself causing a disturbance. The settlers this time, in Turnbull's absence, took matters into their own hands and complained to Governor Patrick Tonyn, who had replaced James Grant in 1774. Tonyn's response was to threaten death to any Indians caught in such crimes again, a warning

that did not deter a large group of Indians from camping on the edge
of the plantation near Turnbull's cowpen most of the following fall.

This parasitical encampment at the settlement's border makes a
statement to us. The Oconee were economically dependent on their
cattle herds and their small corn fields, and the severe drought years
from 1773 to 1775 had dried up the pastures and fields in the interior
of the state. As in any time of hardship, an alternative solution was
to raid a neighboring people. Even in a dry year, cattle close to the
seacoast could use marsh grass for forage, a situation which enticed
the Indians coastward to supplement their hunting and fishing activities with stolen cattle and purloined supplies.

The arrival of the Indians was just one more calamity to add to
the other woes on the plantation. Was it simply by accident that the
Indians were there in the new "starving time" just as they had been
during the first disastrous years of the plantation? For, once again,
the bell of San Pedro rang out all too often to announce the death of
one of the parishioners. Like the Indians, the people on the plantation were also trying to recover from the drought years, as they once
again watched the young and old and ill felled by malnutrition or
outright starvation and disease.

The old adage about the end recapitulating the beginning applies
here, for, as noted earlier, the nine years on the New Smyrna plantation exhibit a cycle; a swing from bad years to good years and back
to bad years again. The bad years at the beginning—the time of
rebellion, of Indian raids, of population collapse—were still times of
trying to make a go of things. Gradually production outran consumption and optimism crept in. The Minorcans were learning something
about wresting a living in the New World and eventually they could
look forward to owning the plots of land they worked. The settlement
began to look less and less like a death camp.

Regardless of the hardships of those early years the 11,558
pounds of indigo exported from the plantation in 1771 set the tone
for better times. Similarly, by then the settler's gardens were offering up enough produce to feed the populace and to prevent nutritional
deficiencies, especially scurvy, and the initial dieoff in the new disease environment had ceased taking as large a toll. Babies were
being born who had more chance of living to adulthood.

The demographic situation for the three middle years, 1771, 1772,
and 1773, reflects the steady state that developed within the colony.

Referring again to the crude statistics of deaths and births in table 3.1 and figure 3.1, an optimum state was achieved around the beginning of 1773. The death rate fell to a low of 13.94 per thousand in 1772, the lowest for the entire time of the plantation years. The following year, with the characteristic year lag usual in preindustrial population statistics, the birth rate (using baptism figures) climbed to a high of 56.79 per thousand.

Another index of prosperity was the indigo exports for this three year period. Table 6.1 lists indigo exports for the New Smyrna plantation and also lists the total exports for the province for years when these were documented. The bumper crop of indigo exported from the Turnbull plantation in 1771 was 41 percent of all East Florida indigo exports for that year. The years 1772 and 1773, before the drought began in the fall, were also good harvest years.

Table 6.1

Indigo Exports (in pounds)

Year	New Smyrna	Total East Florida
1770		6,189
1771	11,558	28,143
1772	9,065	
1773	10,262	
1774	1,633	22,119
1775	1,948	
1776	6,390	58,295
1777	2,397	
1778		29,260

Note: New Smyrna figures from Panagopulos (1966:76); East Florida from Mowat (1943:77-78). During these same years the exports from Charleston averaged about 500,000 pounds annually (Mowat 1943:78).

The kitchen gardens do not admit of quantification, but the vital statistics and reports to England argue for their bounty. In October, 1770, Governor Grant's official report (C.O. 5/551) said, "Tho the season has been remarkably unfavorable, our planters have contrived for the first time to raise provisions for themselves." The "Life-Produce" referred to in Grant's report was augmented by hunting

and gathering, for by that time the people of the colony had developed the requisite knowlege and skills to exploit the environment
effectively when they were allowed time away from their plantation
chores.

Statements in the 1777 depositions against Turnbull reveal the
first and last years of the colony as times of trouble. In the middle
years the farm workers had made a tentative peace with plantation
work requirements. Most of the contracts with Turnbull would soon
be completed and hardships were temporary, to be suffered until
they became landholders themselves.

The Church of San Pedro was well established by this time, and
the Indians at bay. With relief funds granted to him, Turnbull had
even purchased some things to makes his worker's lives more bear-
able. He ordered, in addition to the yard goods for women's clothes,
heavy material for the men's work pants and "600 Neger blankets"
to replace the by-that-time threadbare ones brought by the colonists
from their homelands (C.O. 5/551:156).

To judge from a list made by William Watson, carpenter, which
appears to be a cumulative statement, 145 houses were constructed
on the plantation sometime during the nine year period (Treasury
77/7):

List of work done on Smyrnea settlement during 1777
Carpenter Work on the Smyrnea Settlement

Mr. Turnbulls Dwelling House	270.	0	0
Two large Stores for Provisions	500.	0	0
One Smaller d°	100.	0	0
A Wind Mill	300.	0	0
A Horse d°	30.	0	0
One Indigo House	100.	0	0
145 Other Houses at £35 Each	5075.	0	0
4 Bridges all of Cedar at £30 Each	120.	0	0
22 Double Setts of Indigo Vatts at £50 Each . . .	1100.	0	0

The Whole of the Above Work
were all Compleat in 77 & as
near the Prime Cost as I can
Recolect

Willm Watson

What was it that upset the working adjustment attained with such effort in the colony? The answer lies partly in the fact that the equilibrium was always a precarious one, easily eroded by outside and inside forces. The steady state had not achieved the level that accommodates to minor fluctuations in crop yields, political fortunes, and the harassment of outside groups.

Environmental conditions played as much of a role in tipping the delicate balance as any other set of factors. The several drought years unfortunately coincided with the depletion of the soil. For five years the colonists had tolerated the unaccustomed humidity, counting on the accompanying rains to keep their crops watered. The droughts of 1773 and 1775, the most severe, did serious damage to cash and subsistence farming in all of East Florida. These three years were times of generally freak weather. The drought was preceded on February 22-23, 1773, with "white rain," as those in the province who had never seen snow called it. It was "the greatest [snowfall] ever known" at that time; stretching from the Carolinas, through Georgia, and deep into Florida (Ludlum 1984:23).

According to the *Yearbook of Agriculture* (U.S.D.A. 1941:818) "droughts [in Florida] usually occur in the spring and autumn at about the time of the annual minimum of rainfall." These two times are crucial for the growing of crops in a sub-tropical climate; in spring water is needed for germination and in the fall it is needed to keep the crops from burning up in the hot Florida sun.

Just as the drought years were beginning, the soil began to leach out. John Bartram (1942:54) recorded in his 1765-1766 diary the effect on indigo. "I observed ye adjacent higher ground which was nothing but sand . . . there was indigo planted, but it was thin and poor, but produced much seed. . . . when ye ground is more mellow & ye roots rotten [right after the slash and burn process] it may do better but I believe it soon wears out."

Specifically descriptive of indigo crop failure in New Smyrna itself, Francis Fatio reported in 1785, "In 1771 some of the inhabitants tried the planting of indigo. The quality was good (or nearly so) as that of Guatemala; but the light soil did not yield the same quantity as in the neighboring provinces. Moreover, the soil was exhausted in three or four years."

If left to their own resources, traditional agriculturalists such as the settler group, entirely familiar with the problems of poor soil, might have managed the land quite differently. Diversified cropping and land fallowing would have been followed. In eighteenth-century Minorca, so Cleghorn (1779:13) tells us, "the fields commonly lie fallow for two years and are sown the third." Certainly the farming skill of the Minorcans is attested to by their later success in growing crops near St. Augustine.

Turnbull obviously did not lean on the ancient wisdom of his farm workers. He blamed the crop failures and the dramatic drop in New Smyrna indigo exports in 1774 and 1775 (table 6.1) entirely on the drought. Always one to do things on a grand scale, he had the Minorcan workmen greatly expand the elaborate canal system to incorporate irrigation in addition to the original drainage functions. It was, he said, modeled after similar ones he had seen in Egypt, but the exact methods he employed remain to be worked out. Oral tradition in New Smyrna has it that the men did the hard digging work while the women and boys carried the loosened dirt up in baskets to dump. The main canals were cut into the underlying coquina rock in places and the sides were sometimes faced with quarried coquina. All of this extra labor required of the colonists was far from welcome, coming as it did on top of trying to save the indigo crop and carrying water to irrigate their own parched gardens.

The canals, although so well constructed that remnants of them can still be seen in New Smyrna, did not solve the problem entirely. The yield in 1776, a wet year, of 6,390 pounds of indigo was a temporary recovery but still not up to the production level of the early years of the decade.

Birth and death rates mirror the poor harvests. From 1774 on, referring again to table 3.1 and figure 3.1, the death rate began to climb, reaching in 1777 a high of 90.91 per thousand. Again with a temporal lag the birth rate stayed steady during 1774 and 1775 until it fell to a low of 18.07 per thousand in 1776. The whole began to look like the recurrence of disaster.

As early as 1774 the colonists' discontent was marked by those watching the fortunes of the enterprise. To spearhead this discontent a new champion arose in the person of Father Casanovas. He had never been the person to stand by and endure, to wait and hope for better times, as Father Camps had. He complained bitterly first to Turnbull, and failing to get any response there, to the authorities in St. Augustine about the plight of his fellows, of the mistreatment

Photo by Van de Sande; courtesy of Lawrence J. Sweett.

Figure 6.1. One of the Turnbull Canals.

suffered by his countrymen, and about the growing concern as to whether the proprietor was even going to honor his contracts with the workers.

Turnbull, thinking quickly and perceiving the likelihood of another revolt on the plantation, persuaded the governor that it was a plot—a "Spanish Intrigue." The British authorities were apprised of Turnbull's suspicions that the interests of the Cuban fishermen putting in at New Smyrna were less economic and religious than political, that Casanovas was their contact person, in fact, a spy. Given the unsure foothold of the British in East Florida, the story was easily believed and Casanovas was summarily deported. Subsequent entreaties to the governor by Father Camps to recruit a successor to fill the shoes of his assistant were never heeded.

Even without Casanovas to encourage it, agitation gained momentum when it became increasingly known that the contracts, as the settlers understood them, were not to be honored at the end of the set terms. The craftsmen, some of whom were to serve only six or seven years, found their indentures lengthened on the merest pretext or, as they thought, by outright chicanery. One such case was that of Louis Margan, probably of Mediterranean extraction, most likely French, as he is listed in the parish records as "Luis Morgu." He was engaged by contract to work as a blacksmith and

was promised wages of "fifty french crowns" per year for the first
year, to which was to be added ten crowns every year to the wages.
He was to be guaranteed wages as a master blacksmith as good as
any in America were allowed. He was also to be furnished a suit of
clothes every year and "one pound and a half of Bread, one pound of
Meat and eight ounces of Rice, with a pint of Liquor per day (or if
no Liquor were to be had, three pence Per Day in Lieu thereof)."
Instead he received rations no better than that of the other colonists,
and after three or four years his rations were cut down to grits only
(C.O. 5/557:441-442).

Margan bore this with fortitude as he looked forward to being a
free man. However, as he stated later in his deposition in St. Augustine, when he went to get released from his contract "the said Dr.
Turnbull asked this Dep to follow him, which happened to be to the
Gaol, and ordered him fifty lashes, which he received from a Negro,
and then put this Dep. in irons and confined him in Gaol without any
Subsistence except a little Indian corn and water, at the same time
turned his wife to the plantation, and kept his Infant behind at the
age of six months and four days [this baby was Eulalia Margarita,
born April 7, 1775] and allowed the Mother to come only twice a day
to give the Infant the Breast." Margan lasted a couple of weeks, until
finally himself "almost starved" and knowing of the miserable condition of his wife, he capitulated and signed a paper to serve for five
more years. He was then sent to work in the fields as punishment
until Turnbull, about fifteen months later, aware that work was not
going well in the blacksmith shop, reinstated him in his former position (C.0. 5/557:441-442).

News of this kind raced through the settlement. As long as a man
could expect to be released from his work on the plantation and
receive his own property allotment, he could bear a certain amount
of hardship. Even the prospect of death could be faced fatalistically,
as his family, with the help of relatives and godparent connections,
could be counted on to continue to better themselves in the New
World. But if he became aware one fine evening as he looked out
over the land which he thought was to be his, that the chances of
this ever happening were very slim indeed, then his frame of thought
had to shift. If a trained artisan, indentured for seven years, could
have his contract arbitrarily extended for five more years, then what
could he, an ordinary farmer with a longer contract, expect.

A certain amount of desperation had begun to color Turnbull's actions. As early as 1769 his London partners, disaffected by the slow progress of the plantation, had forced the adoption of a revised plan which instead of the original division into three equal parts at the end of seven years substituted a division into five equal parts of which Turnbull was only to receive one.

Not only Turnbull's enterprise, but also his pride, was at stake. He had early turned a deaf ear to Henry Laurens's warning that the soil in Florida was of poor quality and that no laborers but blacks could be expected to endure the climate and turn a profit for land-holders in East Florida. On November 14, 1768, having heard by that time of the revolt on the plantation, Laurens asked Turnbull in a letter politely but in an I-told-you-so vein, "How do you go on, my good Sir, in your Plantation Schemes? Are your new Settlers recon-ciled to their Situation & become more tractable, or do you begin to be convinced that Negroes are the most useful Servants in these Southern Climes?" He then advised him, "Don't spin your thread too fine" and suggested that he get out of the ill-fated venture while he could (Rogers et al. 1978:155-156). Had Turnbull been a less prideful man he might have taken this advice, for with the advent of the lean years occasioned by the drought he was unable to turn a profit for his London partners, who, concerned about this default and with the agreed division time approaching ever nearer, were threatening to force him into an even worse situation.

Just when it seemed that things could not get worse in the prop-rietary endeavor, Turnbull's good friend and defender, James Grant, returned to England. Patrick Tonyn who replaced him, although a Scotsman also, rapidly and surely became Turnbull's worst enemy, so much so that in later years Governor Tonyn was blamed by Turnbull for the breakup of the plantation and the decline of his fortunes, an accusation not entirely without foundation.

The reasons for the instant and continuing animosity between these two men are complex. One simple explanation offered is that Turnbull made an enemy of the new governor at once by not allowing Mrs. Turnbull to return Mrs. Tonyn's call. Later writers have hinted at a prior romance between Turnbull and Mrs. Tonyn, hailing as they did from the same area of Scotland. Given the rigidity of eighteenth-century social structure, and the gossip that circulated about Mrs. Tonyn, it seems more likely that the Turnbulls regarded the Tonyns as beneath them in social station. Since Turnbull and his elegant Greek wife had been important figures around which social life swirled in the province, such shunning had wider repercussions.

Putting aside this woman-spurned explanation of the widening gulf between the two men, the fact must be recognized that whereas Dr. Turnbull and Governor Grant had previously enjoyed favor in London as part of the inner circle of the Earl of Bute, by 1770 the prime minister was Lord North who had no partiality for Buteites. Governor Tonyn, on the other hand, while a Scotsman, was not a part of that earlier cadre of Scots whose influence with George III had been considerable.

In any case, a bitter feud ensued between Turnbull and Tonyn with consequent repercussions in the province, for, given human nature, a feud of this kind, regardless of the original cause, once started, spins on with a life of its own. The situation was almost immediately polarized. Turnbull, as a member of the provincial council, allied himself with William Drayton, the chief justice. On the other hand, Tonyn joining forces with Lt. Governor Moultrie managed to discredit Drayton and Turnbull in the infamous "Bryan Affair," which involved their protection of Jonathan Bryan who had illegally secured a large tract of land from some Creek Indians. And, in fact, it came to the governor's attention that Drayton and Turnbull also had some idea of violating the Indian treaties to secure additional property for themselves (Gallay 1989:138). Tonyn charged both men with disloyalty to the Crown, a particularly serious charge at a time when the colonies in the north were accelerating toward the American Revolution.

Turnbull swiftly retaliated. He and Drayton, escaping the watchful eye of the governor by a trick, sailed for England in February, 1776, where they took their case before the authorities, asking that Tonyn be removed from office. It appeared that those in control in England found it inexpedient to deal with a colonial feud at a time when minds were occupied with much more serious matters. Largely unsuccessful in his efforts, Turnbull did not return to Florida until late in 1777, by which time the New Smyrna colony was shattered, as he always thought, at the hands of the governor. Some credence can be given to Turnbull's viewpoint as, at the very least, Tonyn made little effort to see that the plantation remained intact. Whether he actually added fuel to the already deteriorating situation is difficult to determine from the scanty available evidence.

The years 1774 to 1777 were turbulent times for the loyal colony of Florida, and the uneasy political situation had its repercussions in "Mosquito Town." Rumors of possible rebel invasions of Florida were rampant after the brig *Betsy* was boarded and relieved of her cargo of gunpowder off the St. Augustine bar on August 7, 1775, by a rebel sloop from the Carolinas. After this bold venture, Florida began to mobilize for a possible conflict. Tonyn enlisted Indians for the fight, and organized the East Florida Rangers to supplement the regular British troops. As an interesting aside, Tonyn secured the services of Thomas Brown to organize the rangers, a man whose mistreatment of the colonists he had brought from England to his Georgia plantation was as much of a scandal as the cruelties that were laid at Turnbull's door. Later Turnbull castigated "Bloody Colonel Brown" for his scalping of "rebel" women and children along the Georgia border. Much of this "pot calling the kettle black" took place as divisiveness between Turnbull and the governor increased.

Early in 1776, before the outright break between Turnbull and Tonyn, in an unusually polite letter Governor Tonyn asked Turnbull for a report on his settlers as a potential military force. The proprietor counted 200 males between 16 and 50 years of age, but requested in an equally polite response, fit for review by authorities in London, that they not be mustered:

I do not pretend to be a Judge of their Military Abilities; but can safely vouch for their Loyalty to his Majesty, for their diligent and honest endeavors to fulfill their contracts with me; and for their affectionate care in supplying their Families with the necessaries of Life. And I think that it is a duty incumbent on me to beg Your Excellency would grant such a Protection for these industrious Foreigners, as may prevent their being disturbed from Agriculture, without which they, with their Families must starve (C.O. 5/556:105).

As far as is known, Tonyn never called up the able bodied Minorcan men as a group while they were still on the plantation, but Turnbull claimed reduction of his plantation manpower by enlistments in the rangers (Treasury 77/7, undated), "whereby the profits of our Houses were in great measure lost and the cultivation of the land suspended." This statement, addressed as it was to one of the London partners of the New Smyrna venture, may have been an exaggeration to excuse the economic failures of the plantation.

Nevertheless, the colonists, because of their Mediterranean origins, were suspect, for it was known that Spain hoped to profit from the American Revolution by regaining Florida, which indeed she eventually did. From another quarter it was reported that the Georgia rebels had offered to come to the relief and deliverance of the Minorcans if they would join the cause for independence. Nearby plantation owners were alarmed. One of these proprietors, Capt. Robert Bissett, advised Tonyn that the Minorcans were not to be trusted with firearms and suggested that authorities take the most "turbulent" among them into custody to prevent them from joining the rebels in the event of an invasion (C.O. 5/557:39).

Tonyn, also, was worried about the Minorcans. In September, 1776, he wrote the home office:

Such my Lord has been the state of the settlement since its commencement that it has always been necessary to post a military guard there, to prevent tumult and insurrection, and I am sorry to acquaint your Lordship, that at this critical Juncture it is a thorn in our side, as I am now obliged to reinforce the Guard to preserve internal good order, when the Troops are much wanted to oppose the depredations of the Rebels in our north frontiers (C.O. 5/556:763).

Young Andrew Turnbull, left in charge of the plantation, sounded an even more frantic note in his letter to a friend, Arthur Gordon, in St. Augustine:

I cannot say what might be the consequence regarding the white people as there is a good number of them at present a little discontented, and I am fully persuaded would join the rebels immediately on their landing in New Smyrna [there had been a report of an American privateer headed for New Smyrna to carry off Turnbull's black slaves]. I therefore beg you and Mr. Penman would make application to the Govr. and commanding Officer at St. Augustine to reinforce the party here with a few more men if it is eight or ten only, for it is absolutely necessary, if it was for no other end but keep our own people a little more at awe. If this cannot be done I see plainly that they will grow very insolent and unruly (C.O. 5/556:767).

What of the colonists themselves? Truthfully, their knowledge of

the faraway conflict was limited and their own misery probably made
them apolitical. With crop yields down and the settlers hungry again,
with one priest gone and the other ailing, with their contracts not
likely to be honored, and with Indians pushing past the plantation
boundaries, matters were desperate.

Turnbull's continuing absence exacerbated the problems.
Turnbull's departure was hasty, nor did he plan to be gone for long,
as he left his family at New Smyrna. Later he said (Turnbull
1788:688), "if the doctor [meaning himself] had been conscious of
being a cruel master, he would not have left his wife, with a family
of small children among them, especially"—here his own feelings
creep in—"as they were such foreigners as usually revenge injuries
by murder."

In spite of Turnbull's tyrannies and petty meanness as pictured
in the colonist's depositions, his continuing absence left a leadership
vacuum and hastened the breakup of the plantation. With a quaking
nephew in charge, the overseers and drivers had ample opportunity
to browbeat an already dispirited people. Whether Turnbull did in-
tend to renege entirely on the contracts with the colonists is unknown, but a new rumor began to circulate to the effect that the
proclamation of George III prohibiting granting of lands to any persons except Protestants would invalidate Turnbull's contracts with
them in any case (Beeson 1960:99). There is some hint that Tonyn
might have planted this notion to bring matters to a head. The important point for our purposes is the colonists' belief that they were not
to become landholders, a belief reinforced by the doctor's absence.

The actual events leading up to the exodus from New Smyrna
evidently unfolded in a convoluted scenario. For present purposes
the legendary story now part of the Minorcan heritage is most relev-
ant. As the perhaps apocryphal story would have it, a small event
finally set the exodus in motion. This folk tradition has been most
effectively related by historian Kenneth Beeson, himself a Minorcan
descendant:

> Sometime in the year 1776 a group of gentlemen from St.
> Augustine were visiting Dr. Turnbull's plantation. An act of
> cruelty to one of the laborers was observed by them, and one
> of them remarked that if these people knew their rights they
> could obtain freedom. A young lad named Arnau overheard the
> gentleman's remark and told his mother what he had heard.

Mrs. Arnau was quick to spread the word among their friends. It soon reached the ears of the head carpenter, Mr. Pellicer, and he called a meeting of the colony's leading people. The meeting was held at night under the most secret conditions possible. Mr. Pellicer, Mr. Llambias, and Mr. Genopoly were selected to represent the people of the colony to the governor in St. Augustine, and to ask that their contracts be terminated due to Turnbull's oppression. In order to cover their absence, the three men worked frantically for days to complete all the tasks they were assigned. When the day for their departure arrived, the three men asked that they be allowed to go to the beach and hunt turtles. The overseer gave them his permission, and the three left New Smyrna early in the morning. Going by way of the beach, and swimming part of the way, they reached Matanzas Inlet the following night. Instead of stopping long enough to rest, the men swam the inlet and continued their march to St. Augustine, arriving there the next morning.

Upon arriving in St. Augustine the three men went directly to Governor Tonyn, who fed them and offered them dry clothing. They told him of the cruelty and hunger that existed at New Smyrna, and of the deaths that had occurred over the years. The governor, touched by their sad story, bade them return to New Smyrna and tell their people that the chains of slavery had been broken. This they cheerfully did. (Beeson 1960:103-104).

Pellicer, Llambias, and Genopoly returned to New Smyrna and plans were secretly made to go to St. Augustine. Ninety people gathered one day near the end of April, 1777, and under the leadership of Francisco Pellicer headed up the King's Road to St. Augustine, a road by then broadened and bridged. Turnbull's young nephew followed helplessly, imploring them to return.

In St. Augustine, Governor Tonyn listened to their request for sanctuary in the town, then retained a few to make depositions against Turnbull, sending the rest back to New Smyrna to complete the harvest, since with shipping interrupted by the hostilities food was badly needed in the province. The depositions were taken on May 5, 1777, and within a month about 600 Minorcans had moved from New Smyrna to St. Augustine.

Twenty-one depositions were filed by seventeen deponents (C.O. 5/557:417-480). Presumably after thinking things over, four of the seventeen came back with further grievances to record. Among the deponents were a disproportionate number of Greeks and Italians, a number of craftsmen who had special contracts with Turnbull, and lastly, probably those among the colonists who were the most literate. Ten of the number signed their names and seven signed with an "X."

The depositions were set down by interpreters, one of whom was Joseph Purcell. This was the same Joseph Purcell who had earlier been a draftsman for Bernard Romans, and had related the tales of "horror" concerning the colony which Romans (1775) had published. Romans, certainly no friend of Turnbull's, had said that Purcell "happily withdrew from the yoke," indicating that he was a Minorcan who left the plantation at an early date. Turnbull accused Purcell of misrepresentations in the translation of the depositions from Catalan to English (C.O. 5/558:499-500). Turnbull (1788:686-687) also said that Purcell's father, who had worked as a carpenter on one of Turnbull's ships in Mahón, had requested passage for his family to St. Augustine and that they were never intended to be part of the plantation.

Regardless of some possible distortion by interpreters, and leading questions from the interrogators, the verbal statements of the colonists appear to present the varying experience of each deponent during the plantation years. Granting a degree of reliability to the individual depositions, it still should be recognized that these seventeen individuals are a non-random sample of the colonial group. Minorcan islanders, 80 percent of the population, were represented by only seven deponents, or less than half of those making depositions. Ordinary farmers were also under-represented. However, the mass migration of the colony to St. Augustine confirms accord on the decision to move, but whether the reasons given by the deponents for wanting to move were the same as those of their fellow colonists is an unresolved question.

Some, no one knows how many, of the colonists stayed behind at New Smyrna. Schoepf (1911:285) noted that "only a few remained at New Smyrna, and the whole colony was as good as broke up." Some of the sick and dying were left behind; for the infirm and very young a seventy-five mile walk in the summer heat may have been too rugged an undertaking. Perhaps others stuck it out on the land hoping for eventual ownership of the property. The shaky, or often nonexistent, demographic figures available from 1777 to 1786 permit

no more than an educated guess as to how many chose to remain in
New Smyrna. If as many as 743 were alive in 1778 (the derived
figure in table 3.1), and about 600 migrated to St. Augustine in June,
1777, we can calculate that nearly 150 lagged behind or stayed. In
subsequent parish records individuals from New Smyrna show up
here and there to marry or to baptize their babies, and some later
Spanish land records indicate ownership of property by Minorcans
who either remained or later returned to New Smyrna.

Father Camps remained behind for a few months to minister to
the sick and dying. During this time he was denied use of the sacred
vessels in the church and seems to have been held a virtual prisoner
by Turnbull's men (Gannon 1967:89). After the infirm were taken to
St. Augustine by ship, he was finally permitted to rejoin his
parishioners. On November 9, 1777, the New Smyrna colony ended
with the following entry in "The Golden Book:"

> On the 9th day of November, 1777, the church of San Pedro was
> transferred to the city of St. Augustine, with the same colony
> of Mahonese Minorcans which was established in the said settle-
> ment, and the same Parish Priest and Missionary Apostolic, Dr.
> Pedro Camps
>
> > [Signed] Dr. Pedro Camps
> >   Parish Priest

A contrast between the revolution and attempted flight at the
beginning of the colony in 1768 and the final exodus in 1777 is instruc-
tive of the developing cohesion in the community. Whereas the Italians, aided by some of the Greeks, initiated the earlier abortive
attempt, the final flight came about through the consensus of almost
the whole community. In the latter, however, the Minorcan islanders
and the other ethnic groups were still separate enough that they
played different roles. The written complaints were recorded, as we
have seen, mostly by the Italians and Greeks, with the addition of a
few Minorcans. In contrast, the actual planning and implementation
of the flight itself was carried out by the Minorcan islanders with
men of respect in charge. The one exception in the leadership of this
Minorcan-planned flight was Juan Genopoly, a Greek from Mani,
who it nevertheless appears had turned Roman Catholic and was
closely enmeshed with the Minorcan islanders through godparent
exchanges and who, a year after the removal to St. Augustine, mar-

ried Antonia Rosello, a widow from Mercadal. The agreement on community withdrawal from the plantation, we thus see, was that of a society which had been welded together in one short decade by marriages, godparent exchanges, religion, language accommodation (creolization), and moreover, by the sharing of anxieties and hardships in an isolated and often hostile environment.

II
The St. Augustine Years

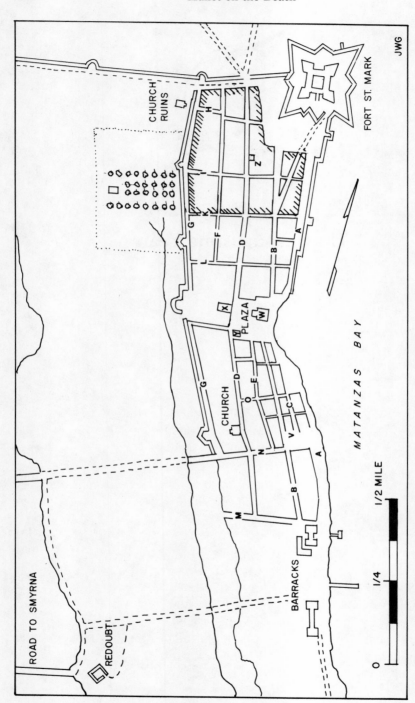

Figure 7.1. St. Augustine in 1777, adapted from Purcell (1777). A. Bay Street; B. Charlotte St.; C. Broad St.; D. George St.; E. Hospital St.; F. Spanish St.; G. Coverd St.; H. Hog Lane; I. Partner's Lane; K. Baker's Lane; L Treasurer's Lane; M. Convent Lane; N. Cunningham's Lane; O. Grogg Lane; V. Little Plaza of the Fig Trees; W. Guardhouse; X. Governor s House; Y. State House; Z. Minorcan Chapel. Minorcan Quarter outlined with hatching.

7. The Minorcans in British St. Augustine

Every night has a day to follow.
Old Minorcan expression

The movement of the colonists into St. Augustine was a dramatic change for the town as well as for the Minorcans, a scene in which one town moved in with another. In the summer of 1777 when the Minorcans first arrived, the population of the St. Augustine was probably not more than 1,000, if that. The arrival of 600 new people, all penniless and speaking almost no English, must have occasioned many changes or, more likely, outright disruptions. Indeed in Turnbull's later account of the matter he pointed out that even if all of the houses in St. Augustine had been vacant there would not be enough housing for the refugees, "for there were more Houses built for them on the Smyrnia Settlement, than are in the whole of St. Augustine, the Barracks excepted" (Turnbull 1777).

Joseph Purcell, translator of the Minorcan depositions, who came to the New World with the Turnbull colony, in the course of his work as a surveyor made a map of St. Augustine in 1777, the very year that the settlers fled to the town. Figure 7.1 is adapted from his map. Hatching has been added to outline the area allotted by Governor Tonyn to the refugees on the north side of town next to the city gate and south of the old Spanish fort. This section was for almost a hundred years referred to variously as the "Minorcan Quarter," or "Quarter of the Mahonese" or "Greek Quarter," or simply as the "The Quarter." As the word quarter implies, it was an ethnic *barrio*, a poorer section of the town. By no means all of the Minorcan community lived there throughout the remainder of the British period and into the second Spanish period, and fewer did so as time went on, but the core of the quarter remained the center of Minorcan life for many years to come.

The main settlement of British St. Augustine when the Minorcans arrived was clustered around and to the south of the plaza. In the area between this concentration of houses and businesses near the plaza and the fort to the north, there were only a few buildings left from the Spanish occupation. Most of these had stood unoccupied since 1763 and consequently were in a state of disrepair. Those of the Minorcans able to lodge their families in these buildings, however, considered themselves lucky, as most found themselves once again forced to construct crude palmetto huts for shelter.

During the first two months in St. Augustine the weather was hot but tolerable. Then heavy rains came, ushering in an unusually stormy fall. While August and September in north Florida have an average rainfall almost the same as that of July, the truth is that the range of fall weather varies greatly from year to year. Some years no more than a few mild blows move the warm season into the cooler weather of winter. Other years, such as that of 1777, storms with high winds and lashing rains hurl up out of the Caribbean in rapid succession. Each interval between storms brings clouds of just-hatched mosquitos bursting forth. The newly arrived Minorcans in their damp hovels situated close by the bay suffered horribly. Many sickened and died.

The descriptions of the first few months of the Minorcan community in St. Augustine by Governor Patrick Tonyn, Lord Germain, then principal secretary of state in England, and by Andrew Turnbull suggest that all had very different views of that critical time.

Governor Tonyn wrote to Lord Germain on July 26, 1777, a first report of the freeing of the Minorcans from their contracts with Turnbull (C.O. 5/557:517). No doubt concerned as to what his superior would think of his allowing the settlers to leave the plantation he proposed, "That these People, my Lord, may not be lost to the Province; it is my intention to direct small lots of Land, to be run out, proportioned to each Family, and I doubt not of their becoming in their state of freedom industrious Settlers, which was impossible to expect from them, under the lash of the Whips and Chains, in the most abject condition of oppression and slavery."

Germain, not easily swayed by Tonyn's eloquence, replied that "The desertion of the Smyrnea settlement by the people, is an unfortunate circumstance for the province, and must occasion a severe loss to the Proprietors." Lord Germain admonished the governor, "If it be in your power to lessen that loss, or give them any assistance in retrieving their Affairs, I must desire you will exert your Endeavors on their behalf" (C.O. 5/558:8). He was here referring to the financial loss which would accrue to Turnbull's partners not to the losses suffered by the plantation laborers. Tonyn, ever one to push things to his own advantage, and using this counsel as a guide, set about spearheading the litigation that would ultimately bring about Turnbull's ruin.

By the beginning of December, Turnbull was back in the province to view the shambles of his dream plantation, having been delayed in New York by a combination of the bad weather and the embargo on shipping. After visiting the plantation, by then devastated in another Indian raid in which several of the settlers who had stayed were threatened with scalping and much of the cherished goods left behind by the refugees had been carried off by the Indians, he repaired to St. Augustine where he wrote to Lord Germain his account of the situation and particularly the condition of the refugees brought about, as he insisted, by the perfidy of Governor Tonyn:

> The Consequences of this strange and destructive Conduct [on the part of the governor] are that these people (having been accustomed for years to a regular and wholesome Diet and to comfortable and dry Habitations with such Exercise by Agriculture as contributed to their Health) on being removed to St. Augustine, they became so sickly, that sixty five of them died in the last two months [October and November 1777] from what I see of their Diseases, Want, and Misery, I think that a few months more will bury the greatest part of them, for as there were not any empty houses in St. Augustine, they were obliged to lay under Trees, and at the sides of old Walls in the rains of August and September, which diseased and dropsied them in such a manner as must end in Death, a few of the young and robust excepted, whose Constitutions have stood the Shock of the complicated Misery, and Wretchedness into which they were deluded; for their want is now so great, that above a hundred of the women and Children went to the Governour's House some Days ago and demanded sustenance in the most clamorous Manner (Turnbull 1777).

Tonyn, on the other hand, obviously still carrying on his feud with Turnbull, insisted in a letter to Lord Germain that the Minor-

cans were being well treated. He blamed their illnesses and deaths
on their poor condition on arrival saying that "Many of them came
to town with dropsies and other disorders, of which several had
died" (C.O. 5/558:104).

So the death rate continued high once the Minorcans reached St.
Augustine; a fact not permitting of quantification as no death records
exist for the period from 1777 to 1784, except Turnbull's perhaps
inflated figure of sixty-five deaths in the first two months of Minorcan residence in town. A look at the baptisms, however, offers in-
sight into continuation of the population decline begun in New
Smyrna. A low of eighteen baptisms were recorded in 1778, followed
by an increase to twenty-seven in 1779 and thirty-seven in 1780 as
matters righted themselves. The next five years saw further
strengthening of this upward trend.

In the meantime, as the tide turned against Britain in the American Revolution, Florida became a loyalist haven. The spirit of rebellion hardly touched Florida; it was too recent an addition to the
empire to have bred an independent colonial identity. In fact, the
news of the signing of the Declaration of Independence was met by
the burning in effigy of John Adams and John Hancock in the plaza
of St. Augustine.

One of Patrick Tonyn's first actions as governor was to promise
protection to loyalists suffering persecution in the other colonies.
Accordingly, a trickle of Tory refugees from the northern colonies
had preceded the Minorcans to St. Augustine, but as the British
fortunes waned that trickle became a stream. By 1783, approximately seventeen thousand people were in East Florida, with a distribution of roughly five blacks to three whites, of which 13,279 were
loyalists from South Carolina and Georgia (Troxler 1989:581-583).
The greatest part of these incoming loyalists settled in or near St.
Augustine. Those unable to find accommodations in a town already
bursting at the seams with people, spilled over into areas in the
north and south parts of the province, even in their extremity occupying some of the still-standing houses abandoned by the Minorcans on the plantation at New Smyrna.

In those last six years of British domain the town of St. Augustine
itself became a conglomerate; multi-ethnic and multilingual. Even
the loyalists were a heterogeneous group including wealthy and poor,
white, free blacks, and slaves; farmers and soldiers and seamen and

men of every trade. The town was further swollen by English troops using Florida as a base. From time to time bands of Indians added to the throng.

The confusion of peoples worked to the advantage of the Minorcan group. Their precarious status as newcomers in the town was brief. They had moved into a town without a farming class at precisely a time when food supplies from the north were cut off. As farmers, fishermen, and hunters they supplied fresh produce for all the hungry mouths. Loyalist farmers arriving in St. Augustine found Minorcans already cultivating the choicest pieces of land near the town, relying on their Old World wisdom and hard-won knowledge of growing conditions in the Florida environment.

A certain amount of opportunism became rampant. Josiah Smith (1932:21), interned in St. Augustine as a rebel, but nevertheless as a reputable Carolina gentleman given the freedom of the town, complained that with all the extra people in the province the Minorcan fishermen were charging an exorbitant price for fish. Minorcan fishermen could charge such prices because they were a near monopoly, but as hunters they competed in the local market with the Indians.

Some Minorcans became craftsmen, often plying the trades they had known in their homelands or on the plantation. Others opened taverns or small wineshops, frequently as a part-time enterprise. Still others shipped out as mariners, and some had even become shipowners before the Spanish returned to claim East Florida.

Despite their contributions to the province, the Minorcans continued to be regarded with ambivalence by the British authorities. They were valued as agriculturalists and fishermen, but their loyalty was always in question, especially after Spain entered the war against Britain in 1779 on the side of the rebelling colonies. In 1780 Governor Tonyn, by then less enchanted with the group than formerly, wrote to Lord Germain, "It is with deep concern that I take this opportunity of signifying to your lordship my apprehension of danger in case of attack by a formidable force. The state of the garrison, although exceedingly healthy, is very inconsiderable. . . Several of the militia are Minorcans, and I have my doubts of their loyalty being of Spanish and French extraction, and of the Roman Catholic Religion" (Forbes 1821:39).

Partly because of this attitude toward them, the colonists continued cohesive as a community during the British period. The group, including the Greeks and Italians, remained almost entirely endogamous, that is, contracting marriage only within their own group. There were a few exceptions, including the marriage of Leonora Genopoly, a daughter of a Greek family from Mani, to Anthony Hinsman, a Britisher, on December 21, 1784. A few others may have married outside the Catholic church and departed with the British, leaving no record.

By 1786, with information now available from Spanish censuses, we find several others married outside the Minorcan group. For example Paula de Torres, a widow from Cuidadela had married Antonio Montes de Oca, a returnee from the first Spanish period and a shoemaker by trade. She and her two New Smyrna-born children, one a crippled boy of sixteen years, lived with him near the heart of the Minorcan quarter. This reluctance to marry out of the group is the more remarkable considering that British St. Augustine was largely male. Leitch Wright (1975:35) believes that "the ratio of men to women may have been two or three to one and possibly higher." Language, religion, and spatial organization unquestionably promoted the group's uninterrupted unity.

Not a little of the cohesiveness was promoted by the reestablishment of the Church of San Pedro. Lacking other space, the downstairs of one of the old residences standing in the heart of the quarter was commandeered for use. Although the parishioners found no fault with this "Chapel of San Pedro," when Father Thomas Hassett, the newly named principal priest, arrived in the fall of 1784 as part of the incoming Spanish regime he thought otherwise. Not in a very good frame of mind after having been injured in a shipwreck in which he lost all of his possessions, he described the church quarters as "wretched," as well as "lacking in all things appropriate for the celebration of the divine liturgy" (Gannon 1967:92). He promptly relocated the parish church to the upstairs of the old bishop's house on the plaza, a masonry building which had been maintained by the British. Thus, as the British vacated the town and the Spanish took over, the Parish of San Pedro officially vanished into history and the Parish of St. Augustine took its place. However, the Minorcans continued to function as an informal parish within a parish until Father Camps' death in 1790.

As the Spanish returned, the change in the status of the Catholic church was only one of the changes in the new regime, changes not altogether to the liking of the Minorcans who had been the only Mediterranean Catholics in the community, able to manage their affairs as they saw fit. Now with the advent of status individuals of Spanish heritage, their lives were certain to change.

This change was gradual, however. When East Florida was re-troceded to Spain under the terms of the Treaty of Paris, all British subjects were allowed up to eighteen months to leave. Most British citizens made plans to go back to the mother country or to another British possession in the New World. But what did this hold for the Minorcans who were nominal British subjects, but whose cultural heritage was much closer to that of the new regime?

In a meeting with Governor Tonyn on this problem, Father Camps expressed a desire to return to Europe. Aware that his was no longer to be an exclusive parish for his flock and tired in body and spirit himself, the prospect of returning to the island of his birth was a congenial one. When they heard of their religious leader's desire, his parishioners decided to leave also. The British were offering them transportation to the Mediterranean or to the Bahamas where they were promised land to settle, but it soon became clear that since Spain had recaptured Minorca in 1782 the British could not return them directly to that island.

In any case, as the new regime began to move into town the Minorcans' plans changed. The two Catholic priests, Fathers Michael O'Reilly and Francisco Traconis, who arrived in June of 1784 per-suaded Father Camps to stay on and to encourage his congregation to do likewise. Tonyn believed that coercion was used by the priests to make the Minorcans change their minds. He wrote to Lord Sydney that "they impressed on the Minorcan women the idea, that their children must be left behind, as the Church was the sole Guardian of the Souls of their children, and it was her duty to prevent their being brought up hereticks, which those that emigrated would be, and would incur eternal damnation" (C.O. 5/561:360-361).

The promise by the Spanish authorities of continued land tenure and eventual ownership of the lands they farmed may have been a real, although less vivid, explanation for the Minorcan change of heart. The older members of the group had already moved twice, and in the case of the Italians at least three times. Why not stay? Their religion was that of the new political regime, and in the case of the Minorcan islanders there was a common cultural heritage and mutual intelligibility between their Catalan language and Spanish. The opportunists among them could see that with the English leaving in such a hurry there was much for the taking or to be bought cheaply.

On July 12, 1784, a final decision had been made. Almost all of the former New Smyrna colonists decided to stay, and Father Camps agreed to stay until another priest could be found who spoke the Minorcan dialect. Accordingly the Greeks and Italians sent a memorial to the new Spanish governor, Vicente Manuel de Zéspedes, saying, "we assure Your Excellency that we rejoice to pass under Spanish dominion, and humbly beg Your Excellency to represent us to His Majesty as desirous of being recognized as natural-born subjects" (Lockey 1949:232). The next day fifty Minorcan islanders likewise signed a memorial assuring His Excellency "that as Catholics and natural-born Spanish subjects we rejoice in finding ourselves restored to the dominion of our legitimate lord and sovereign" (Lockey 1949:233). The separate memorial by the Greeks and Italians was necessary because they were not considered "natural-born Spanish subjects."

Nonetheless, some of the Minorcans did leave the province during the changeover period, if we are to believe departing Governor Tonyn. In April of 1785 he wrote to Lord Sydney, by then principal secretary of state, that "the intentions of the Minorcans were my Lord to emigrate, they had carefully consulted me thereupon, and solicited to send a major part to Gibraltar, others to Dominica and the Bahamas, to the latter of which a considerable number have gone, a few to Dominica, and some to Europe" (Lockey 1949:498).

Soon after his arrival Governor Zéspedes wrote a favorable report on the Minorcans who had remained:

These Minorcans in general are an industrious people. Young and old, they have all retained the Catholic religion, even those reared among the English, and they make use of the mother tongue. Some are traders, others farmers, still others occupy themselves with fishing. There are very few craftsmen among them. Among the traders there are some who have a capital of from one thousand to eight thousand pesos, and some own sloops and schooners. The majority raise crops in the vicinity of the city, few or none owning the land. They rent four or five *fenegas* [a variable measure, usually a third to one acre] of cleared land on which they raise Indian corn and some garden stuff (Lockey 1949:285).

Any discussion of the six or seven years of the Minorcan community in British St. Augustine must rely on flimsy data. No longer pawns in a larger political game, documentary attention shifted away from them. Regardless of the paucity of information, this period of consolidation in yet another new environment must not be underrated. As a group and as individuals they were able in those years to reformulate their lives to conform more closely to the cultural templates they had brought with them from the Mediterranean. In British times these New World settlers were still a distinct community, and becoming more so as time went on. While not by force a social isolate as in plantation days, they were still set apart by their culture, religion, and language and certainly by their separation into an allotted quarter in the town.

8. Population Characteristics: Circa 1786

Every bell has its own ring.
Old Minorcan saying

Governor Zéspedes in a report to his superiors in 1787 described the average Minorcan family in unflattering terms, saying, "a Minorcan with a wife and four or five children (these people are so prolific that one frequently sees a pregnant mother with a baby at the breast and leading another child by the hand) who does not even earn half a *peso fuerte* a day" (Whitaker 1931:57). The picture painted is of large families with babies spaced close together, of extreme poverty, of wage earning as the major means of making a living, and that yielding no more than, as we might put it, a "thin dime" a day.

Yet when the figures are actually tallied of known individuals and their life circumstances something quite different emerges. Then we determine that families were not large even by present standards, that babies came on the average at two year intervals, that most Minorcans were making a living through a varied repertoire of their own inclination and devising, that a few by that time were emerging into outright affluence having good housing and choice lands and owning their own sloops, and a number owned slaves. Even the Minorcans of lesser means had lands, and some owned their habitations. While they were by no means the leading class in town, nor were they prosperous in modern terms, there is evident a measure of contentment.

Choosing one specific time in Minorcan community life will make the figures vivid. The short two-year time period of 1786-1788 was targeted for this purpose, the group by then having been in St. Augustine for a decade and in the New World for two decades. Much had happened in the twenty previous years, individuals had died, babies had been born, but no outsiders had penetrated the population to any degree, that diffusion being left to future decades. Moreover, the late 1780s were a relatively steady time in the colony, or at least as steady as it ever became in the thirty-six years of Spain's second hegemony. Zéspedes was still the governor, the colony of Spanish East Florida was building through securing settlers and making improvements in the capital itself, the Indians were not yet causing serious problems, and most important of all, the threat of frontiersmen from the infant United States pushing down the peninsula to take lands had not yet erupted into outright warfare. Besides, by then three censuses had been conducted, the Spanish being very conscientious in such matters, a map and index of householders had been formulated, lands had been granted, and the parish records had been amplified by the recording of marriages and deaths in addition to baptisms.

The first matter to consider in this glimpse into the life of the Minorcans in one place and at one time is how many they were as well as the sex and age distribution of the population, the kind of basic considerations in any attempt to count heads. After this naturally follows a look at more complex matters such as families, households, occupations, social life, and the approximate relationship to other segments of the populations in the environment.

The three censuses were taken for quite different reasons. The census of 1784, taken by the civil authorities as Spain regained East Florida, was a hurry-up one for the purpose of seeing who remained in the province after the British evacuation and who among them intended to become Spanish (and Catholic) subjects. In 1786 Father Hassett, intending to open a school, conducted a census of those in St. Augustine and within five leagues of the town to see how many children of appropriate ages there might be. Then in 1787 the governor ordered that a count be taken for revenue purposes and also to discover how much land was being farmed, and to entertain more requests for land grants.

Father Hassett's rather full enumeration has commonly been used by historians as the most reliable index of the existing situation at that time, particularly since it names individuals. However, concern has been raised recently as to its reliability in reporting the distribution among subgroups in the city, particularly the issue of underreporting of the Spanish and Floridano segments (Johnson

1989:27-54). Nonetheless, it is the most promising document for present purposes as the proposed education of the Minorcan children was the main reason for which it was conducted in the first place.

Characteristic of the high standards he always lived by, Father Hassett had been appalled by the ignorance he found in Spain's new possession. Not only did this conscientious Irish prelate imperfectly understand the Minorcans speaking their dialect of Catalan (he was barely proficient in Spanish), but he believed them ignorant of proper church doctrine as well, many now having grown almost to adulthood without confirmation since only a bishop or auxiliary bishop can admit communicants to the church. Writing a petition to the Crown he expressed his worry that the children "would grow up useless to Your Majesty and the state" and realized that the cost of such a school must be underwritten since "the greater part of the parents lack the means to pay for the education of their children" (Lockey 1949:540-541). This petition, written in Hassett's poor Spanish was forwarded to the authorities in Cuba on May 13, 1785. A month later as an afterthought, and perhaps by that time having looked into the problem himself, Governor Zéspedes wrote to Bernardo de Gálvez, viceroy of New Spain, describing the "pitiful ignorance of the Minorcans, Italians and Greeks" and asking that "school teachers for the youth of the province" be assigned to St. Augustine (Lockey 1949:554). In point of fact, the school had actually been started, Zéspedes having used funds which he could shift for the purpose, operating no doubt under the principle that the action once taken would be hard for his superiors to reverse.

Thus, when the census was conducted the school had already been in operation for some months and going up and down the streets of the town doubtless gave Father Hassett the chance to ferret out any recalcitrant families who had kept their children home to farm or for other reasons. In any case, as evidenced also by other documents, the individuals listed under the rubric "Minorcans, Italians, and Greeks and the Others Known as Such" were reasonably accurate for those living in town at the time of the enumeration. The other three population categories in the census were "Foreigners," "Floridanos," and "Spaniards." The men in the garrison, estimated from other sources to number about 450, were not counted in the census. The suburban population, which included families too far away to send their children to school, has been estimated at 300 by Lockey (1939:31).

As can be seen in the break-down of the Hassett census in table 8.1, the 469 white persons listed in the Minorcan category represented almost 50 percent of the civilian town population which numbered altogether 943 individuals. Looked at in another way, if the garrison is included, the town is then seen to break out into even thirds—Minorcans (including of course the Italians and Greeks), secondly, the rest of the civilian population and thirdly, the garrison. However, examined through yet another window, that of race distribution, the civilian town was two-thirds white and one third black, slave and free. The number of black individuals in the garrison were not reported in the Hassett census, and free blacks were not separately listed until the census of 1787-1788 (Landers 1988:58).

The whites listed in the "Minorcan, etc." category in Hassett's census are the basis for the construction of the population pyramid in figure 8.1. A pyramid of this kind is a shorthand way of looking at the age and sex distribution of a particular population at any given moment in time. Graphically, the men are on the left hand side of the center line and the women on the right while age groups are in a vertical series with the youngest age group at the bottom. A population in equilibrium will be pyramid shaped, approximating a symmetrical Christmas tree. Any variation from such a model tells a story.

The story here gives us information on the original composition, subsequent history, and status in 1786 of the Minorcan population, that is, those of the original colonists and their descendants. Obvious are the small numbers in the upper age groups; the disproportionately large numbers of men in the 36-40 age group; the population decimations, as reflected for the beginning of the colony and at the time of immigration to St. Augustine; and, lastly the number of children in the 0-5 age group, which gives a broad undergirding to the pyramid. The tale thus told is of a people on an uneven course through time.

We have already dealt with the deaths in the older age group in the initial stage of the colony. The one new factor evident from the pyramid is the better survival rate among women in the 46-50 age group as compared to men in that age group. We can assume that the sexes in this age cohort were roughly equal on arrival at New Smyrna for most of them were married. Then, does the low survival rate of men in the 46-50 age group possibly demonstrate a greater toll from plantation hardships among the men, the well-known high

Table 8.1

Summary of Hassett Census of 1786

	Number		Percent
Foreigners			
Whites, male	48	Whites	40%
Whites, female	38		
Negroes, male	72	Negroes	60%
Negroes, female	55		
Total		213	
Minorcans, Italians, Greeks			
Whites, male	241	Whites	87%
Whites, female	228		
Negroes, male	33	Negroes	13%
Negroes, female	37		
Total		539	
Floridanos			
Whites, male	29	Whites	36%
Whites, female	21		
Negroes, male	42	Negroes	64%
Negroes, female	40		
Total		132	
Spaniards			
Whites, male	27	Whites	78%
Whites, female	19		
Negroes, male	8	Negroes	22%
Negroes, female	4		
Total		59	
Suburban Population			
Whites (estimated)	130		
Negroes (estimated)	170		
Total		300	
Garrison			
Officers and Men (est.)		450	
Grand Total		1693	

Source: Summary of Hassett's census of 1786 by Lockey (1939:31).
Percentages for "Whites" and "Negroes" for each group
added by present researcher.

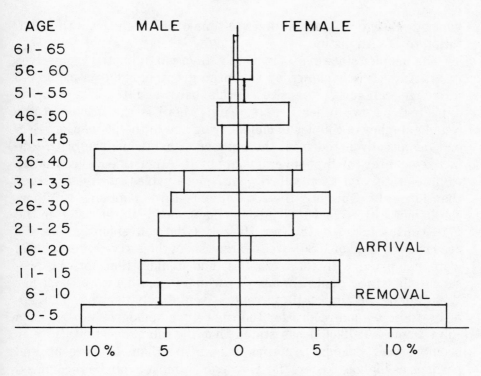

Figure 8.1. Population Pyramid, Minorcans et al., 1786.

death rate from childbirth among women in earlier times not being enough to offset this factor? We can only wonder about this question.

The larger "branch" on the male side of the pyramid in the 36 to 40 year category is not so puzzling, for we already know that young single men outnumbered women in that age group among the original colonial recruits. Likewise, these men would have been between eighteen and twenty-two years old at the colony's inception, the hardiest age group in pre-industrial times, being in physical prime and having survived childhood diseases and not yet suffering from the infirmities of aging.

The pinched-in hourglass look of those in the 16-20 age group, born from two years before the arrival in New Smyrna until two years afterwards, is the most dramatic evidence we have of the low birthrate and the early mortality of children of the first miserable years in New Smyrna. The second population crash, not nearly as spectacular as the first, is evident in the number in the six to ten year age category, born around the time of the flight from the plantation to St. Augustine.

The happier state of affairs as the Minorcans adjusted themselves in St. Augustine is shown by the large group of children in the 0-5 year age category. The size of this baby and toddler group is explained by two other factors. First, there is the matter of the sizable number of couples of childbearing age in the population. Second, as already noted from the number of baptisms, the birth rate increased after the first several years in St. Augustine and continued to accelerate; and as an allied point, more babies survived infancy than formerly. Checking the total of sixty-three baptisms of Minorcan babies in 1785 and 1786 against the named children listed in the 1786 census taken by Father Hassett (who conveniently took his census at the end of 1786), we find that six of the sixty-three children were not listed with their families, and it must therefore be presumed that they died in infancy. An infant death rate of 95.2 per 1,000 births, or almost 10 percent, is tentatively derived. This appears to be a good record for the time since demographer-historian John Demos (1972:561) has stated that the infant mortality rate in preindustrial, colonial America was more than 10 percent and perhaps as high as 20 percent. However, it must again be recognized that our figures are baptism figures and that some babies dying shortly after birth would not appear in the documents. Even taking cognizance of this fact, the number of surviving young children in this era is a strong indication of a group at last experiencing improved conditions.

With about one third of the population below the age of eleven, there must have been children everywhere; the young ones crying and toddling about, the older ones helping their families, attending school or running about the streets as time permitted. Not all of them were models of decorum at all times. Cries of *peekra* and *peek-randina* and *tronya* were uttered by the exasperated adults, judging from the persistence of these words, meaning pest or little pest, in surviving word lists (Rasico 1987a:207-271).

The Hassett census has given us a capsule glimpse of the Minorcans and their descendents in 1786. It is a reasonably accurate document, particularly for the Minorcan population. However, even in that category minor problems arise. The mistakes found, using other documentary sources as a cross check were minor—the inclusion of one family of doubtful ethnicity, one mistake in the age of an individual, and counting one boy twice, once at his own home and again at the home of his aunt. In addition, seven individuals who were clearly not of the original community and their progeny were found in Minorcan households. On the other hand an exact counter-balance of seven clearly Minorcan individuals were by 1786 residing in households outside the Minorcan category. As already mentioned, Leonora Genopoly had married Antonio Hinsman and was counted in the families of "Foreigners" along with her infant daughter Maria Barbara and a baby of unknown parentage, whose name, Inés Ana Antonia, sounds Minorcan. In the same "Foreigners" category we find Jorge Stephanopoly, a Corsican Greek, serving as an overseer for the wealthy family of John Hudson and his wife, Mary Evans. In the Spanish section of the census we find Ignacio Ortagus, Minorcan born, who is a porter in the store of the Spaniard Antonio de Palma and lives in his household. Likewise, in the Floridano enumeration, Paula de Torres, a Minorcan, and her two children by a former marriage were living in the household of Antonio Montes de Oca, Paula's husband. A more accurate recount taken with these problems in mind brings the total of named individuals of the Minorcan community to 476 as enumerated in the Hassett census.

The main problem with the 1786 census document for our present purposes is its failure to count all in the Minorcan community. Several persons at the very bottom of the economic ladder having no permanent housing were not counted, for the same reason that "drifters" or the homeless are missed in any census. Most of the others who were not counted lived more than five leagues from the city, outside the stated area of enumeration.

The 1784 and 1787 censuses and the Cathedral Parish records turned up 127 named individuals not counted by Hassett, bringing the total to 603. The 130 suburban white population, not counted by Hassett but estimated by Lockey (1939:31), certainly included some of these out of town Minorcans. Most of this suburban population, sketchily documented, lived in the North River area, stretching as far as twenty miles north of town. Legal titles, later documented for land in this area, established the North River settlement as heavily Minorcan. Other Minorcans were living on lands south of town and some may still have maintained habitations in the New Smyrna area, or returned there.

In fact, during the 1780s an alternating current of Minorcans moved in and out of town, so that if Hassett had taken his census even six months later he might have turned up the same number of Minorcans living in town, but the people would had been a slightly different mix of individuals. To complicate matters even further, some families maintained houses in town and other homes on their farm lands. Some but not all of this migration was probably seasonal and thus cyclical in nature and did not represent permanent moves.

Gaspar Papi, a Greek who, aside from Andrew Turnbull's wife, was the only one of the original settlement who came from Smyrna in Asia Minor, is an example of that mobile population. In 1783 he was listed as a farmer living in a cottage on four acres of land near the Chapel of the Virgin of La Leche, a half mile north of Castillo de San Marcos, the fort. In 1786 he and his Minorca-born wife, Ana Pons, were listed by Hassett with no location given. In 1787 he was cultivating two-and-one-half acres in an unspecified location and was living (at least some of the time) in the south portion of town in "the same house as Roque Leonardy." A year later the 1788 map of Mariano de la Rocque shows him residing next to Leonardy in a "timber frame house in bad condition" which he, Papi, owned.

However, given all these varied circumstances and the undulations of the Minorcan population, the figure of 603 persons is not as firm a figure as it might seem. Considering several instances, amounting to a dozen or more, of ambiguous name spellings and persons of doubtful ethnicity, it will be obvious that without some arbitrary decisions, it is impossible to come up with a single exact population figure. However, considering the random nature of the errors of inclusion and exclusion, an estimated population figure of 600 can still be stated with some confidence. Of these, 285, or just about one half, were the original Mediterranean-born colonists. Thus, twenty years after 1,403 persons sailed from the Mediterranean only one-fifth of the number were still alive.

The next question to be answered is what other groups were living in the same environment in St. Augustine at that time. Taking them in the order in which they are listed in the Hassett census the "Foreigners of Different Religions and Nations" were listed first. The eighty-six persons enumerated were people left over from the British period with a sprinkling of newcomers to the province perhaps seeking their fortunes. Some of the "Foreigners" had stayed for the very good reason that they owned considerable property or mercantile interests, with such a stake in East Florida that their own interests overrode loyalty to the departing British. One such was John Leslie, listed honorifically as Don Juan Leslie in the census, the wealthy merchant who, under the British along with his partner William Panton in West Florida, had become the principal merchant engaged in trade with the Indians. By 1788 he was well ensconced in the same role under the Spanish regime, Governor Zéspedes having wisely decided not to alter the excellent trading network already in place.

The designation "Floridanos," born in Florida, the next group, included two categories—the few individuals who had been born in the first Spanish period and remained during the British occupation and secondly, persons or families, resident in the first Spanish period but who left at the beginning of the British regime and who had now returned from Cuba to reclaim their property. Francisco Sánchez, a planter, was one of the former. Examples of returned Floridanos were sixty-three year old Don Tomas Cordero, a merchant and his sixty-one year old wife, and her forty-five year old brother, a widower, who brought his two Havana-born children to Florida with him.

The fourth category in the census listed individuals of Spanish birth, numbering forty-six persons. This category had a variety of people ranging from Don Miguel Iznardy, who played a prominent role in the province throughout the second Spanish period, to five poverty-stricken families from the Canary Islands who had recently been brought to St. Augustine. Originally sent to Pensacola as part of a continuing Spanish effort to reduce the poverty and overpopulation of these eastern Atlantic possessions, they were shuttled to St. Augustine. They were the first of a group of 129 individuals who were scheduled to be brought in as settlers to East Florida. The others never came as the governor considered them, from the behavior exhibited by this first contingent, to be useless as workers and shiftless as people, and therefore asked that no more be brought into the province as they would only be a drain on the government coffers (Tanner 1963:147).

The possession of slaves is one index of prosperity and status. In this respect, the ranking from highest to lowest would be from the Floridanos through the "Foreigners," Spaniards, and lastly the

Minorcans. However, there are several problems with this, mostly having to do with the Spaniard category. Included as Hispanics were the low status Canary Islanders and excluded were government officials and some of the officers of the garrison. As an illustration, Governor Zéspedes and his family are nowhere listed in the Hassett census.

What had emerged by 1788 was a cadre of elite including Spaniards, Cubans, several foreigners, and possibly a few of the Minorcan community. In general, however, the Minorcans, the rank and file of the garrison, and the Canary Islanders, formed the bulk of the lower status white population in the town. Below them were the blacks, both slave and free.

A note of caution is in order here. We are dealing with the first years of the Spanish regime, the shakedown period. In later times, even in the next decade following the period of the present study, Minorcan prosperity and status increased, at least for some of the group. Even before that, the Minorcan population was the undergirding of the town in terms of both numbers and continuous residence. Officials came and went, Floridanos, being of an older age group, died or became disenchanted and went back home to Cuba, and the garrison was constantly changing. As Helen Tanner (1963:136) has put it, during this period St. Augustine was a "Minorcan capital."

9. Households

Nobody has ever regretted marrying
or breakfasting early.
Old Minorcan saying

A traveler some years after the time under discussion found that the "cottages [of the Minorcans] which were in the streets nearest the water, were, to a certain degree, picturesque; festooned with nets and roses, shaded by orange-trees; and hung round with cages of nonpareils, and other singing birds" (Latrobe 1835:36). Lacking from this romantic scene are the people who lived in the household.

When we look at the whole matter of household groupings as they were in New Smyrna and in St. Augustine we have a puzzle, part of which can never be unravelled. We have no idea, for example, of who, on the average, lived under one roof on the plantation in New Smyrna. It can be assumed that each family—father, mother, and children—lived together in a separate family dwelling. The documents do reveal that the young single men were dormitoried in the three buildings constructed for the purpose, although, even there, we do not know how many lived together in each of the long houses or whether those of the same national origin lived together. Perhaps there were certain restraints imposed on household structure by plantation requirements and by the wishes of the proprietor. On the other hand, we can guess, as time went on and many people died, that remarriages took place, that relatives or friends moved in with each other, and that orphaned children were cared for by relatives or godparents.

Once in St. Augustine the picture clears. We do indeed find many remarriages, reconstituted or blended families, and people living together in makeshift arrangements. The new factor was their ability to live as they wished, untrammeled by the requirements of the plantation, to set up households, or change living circumstances to whatever advantage they foresaw. Further, we would expect certain Mediterranean features to re-emerge in both settlement pattern and in the household composition. It is to the latter that we look first.

Domestic groupings, domestic production units, households, families all have their own definitions. When it comes to our little community we see an overlap as we look at the constellation of people living under one roof. Part of this is unique to the Minorcans, but other elements are part and parcel of the familial society common in Europe in preindustrial times.

"Domestic groups," Goody (1972:2) has said, "are those basic units which in preindustrial societies revolve around the hearth and the roof, the bed and the farm, that is, around the processes of production and reproduction, of shelter and consumption." Household, used as synonymous with Goody's concept of domestic group, is the unit of analysis in the present study. The categories of family and household show a necessary overlap, often congruence, for the family is nearly always the core of a household. Family indicates kinship usually of a close order, i.e. nuclear, in contrast with household, the cluster of people (or one person) using a common dwelling for purposes of daily living. Any certain family member may be "post" household, and potential household bonding or rebonding is a latent function of close kin ties. Implicit in this is the process of fissioning by which the grown child leaves the parental hearth to establish a household of his own. Not to belabor the issue, family ties are enduring and not always spatially conditioned, whereas a household is the unit of daily living, the spatial and temporal primacy of which is a function of a number of social, economic and demographic variables.

Most of the houses lived in by the Minorcans at this time were simple ones. Albert Manucy (1962:50-54) refers to the customary dwellings of this sort in St. Augustine as the "common Spanish house," or simply as the "the common plan." It was a variation of the limited dwelling type of the European peasantry of the preindustrial world, adapted to New World conditions. "The prototype," as he describes it "is the rectangular one-room cottage of the medieval laborer, a shelter that provided only the necessities — a roof to keep off the rain, walls to stop the wind, a hearth for cooking, and perhaps stairs or a ladder to a sleeping loft. If primitive, it was also practical, especially on the frontier." As time went on and as the household increased in size or affluence another room or two could be added. Even as simple as they were, porches or porticos, balconies, and detached kitchens were often added to them in St. Augustine. Furthermore, the large size of some of these one-room dwellings, the largest being 16x36 feet in St. Augustine, made for more comfort. Also, second stories were added in some cases, although most of the two-story houses were originally built in that fashion.

The roof under which the household lived and worked was not entirely man-made, for in the warm Florida climate the largest living area was open to the sky. Much of daily living took place on the shaded loggia and in the outdoor compound which was commonly walled off by fences or thorny hedges made of Spanish bayonet plants (a species of *Yucca*).

In order to examine the type and composition of Minorcan households occupying such habitations, a total of 152 households were identified. In those households resided 656 individuals—588 white and 68 black. These households were the total number meeting the criteria of (1) dependability of information, and (2) unquestionably of the Minorcan group, including the other ethnics such as Greeks and Italians, who were by 1786-1788 partially assimilated.

The figure of 588 is below the some six hundred Minorcan individuals actually identified. It was necessary to eliminate from the sample the two Anglo-Minorcan households as well as the three men living and working in non-Minorcan households. In several other instances not enough was known of the composition of the households to incorporate them.

Although more than sixty-eight slaves were connected in some way to the 152 households, some were eliminated from consideration for various reasons. A few were rented and therefore not in actual residence, or at least not in continual residence, in the households. Other slaves were found from documentary sources to be living on the slave owner's farm land outside of town. Since the goal was to identify the unit of daily interaction, such individuals were discounted as playing a negligible part in the hearth circle. Minorcan husbands and wives reported absent from their families were for the same reason not included.

The size of the average household was 4.34 persons. As indicated

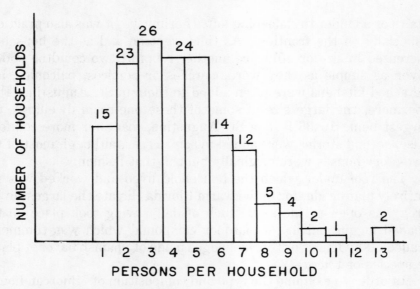

Figure 9.1. Number of Persons per Household.

in figure 9.1, almost an equal number of two, three, four, and five person households existed in the community, lending a flatness to the top of the curve. Two-person households were evenly divided between (1) marital pairs, either old or young, without children and (2) two unrelated or related persons living together. Four-member households commonly contained a couple and two children. Three and five person households were more diverse in composition. Larger households were typically of two types, either affluent families with many children or households where members, family and non-family, served as a work force in the household production unit.

The numerous young under fifteen, 46.6 percent of the total group, lived in 108 (71 percent) of the households (figure 9.2). Commonly, households included no more than two or three children. The age of fifteen is an arbitrary figure chosen for statistical purposes. Actually, thirteen year olds, above the age of confirmation, were considered adult by eighteenth-century standards. As such, the girls were listed as "unmarried" or "wife" and the boys by occupation in Hassett's census.

The families with the largest numbers of children were the wealthier ones in the community. Nutrition, and living conditions in general, as in any group living before the industrial era, had a dramatic

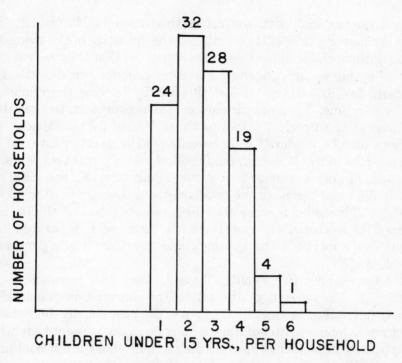

Figure 9.2. Number of Children under 15 years per Household.

effect on the likelihood of children in a family surviving infancy and living to maturity. A direct relationship existed between the number of children in a family and the life sustaining resources in that family household. The household containing the largest sibling group was that of Bernardo Sequí, a trader and the owner of three slaves, who lived in the best section of town. In addition to his six resident children, a seventh, fifteen-year-old Juana, had recently married and lived close by. An eighth child was born to the Seguís on December 19, 1786, a few days too late to be counted in the Hassett census. Although the Seguís were still living in modest quarters at this time, within the next several years they moved into a large coquina house, one of the more sumptuous in town. It was later the birthplace of the Confederate general, Edmund Kirby Smith, and is still standing today.

In addition to resource constraint as a factor in the size of the majority of the Minorcan families at this time, some attempt at family limitation may also be inferred. Two eighteenth-century sources described the natural birth control method used in Minorca at that time. Armstrong (1756:211) mentioned the "practice of the women in suckling their children for two years together, that they may not be starved by numerous progeny." The same practice was described by Cleghorn (1779:60-61), "But lest the Family become too numerous for their Income, it is a practice among the poorer Sort, to keep their Children at the Breast for two or three Years, by this Means, the Mothers may be hindered from breeding." The average interval between births in the Minorcan families under study was two years. In instances of only a year or a year-and-a-half interval, one child had usually died and the next one was conceived soon thereafter.

The 152 households were classified into six types on the basis of common characteristics, and these in turn were separated into twenty-one subtypes. The typology and distribution are presented in table 9.1.

Nuclear family households, Type I, were the commonest, accounting for 55 percent of the total. The designation "nuclear" is slightly misleading as nuclear families in the past usually did not stay intact for as long a period of time as they do at the present time when an extended dependency is the rule. A household often contained father, mother and some of the children, but might not contain progeny old enough to have been launched into the adult world and living elsewhere.

Remarriage families were included in the nuclear category, nearly two-thirds of the households being reconstituted units of this kind. Remarriage because of the death of a spouse occurred with great frequency in the preindustrial world, and in the instance of this community, as we have seen, was especially common because of population plunges.

The centrality of the nuclear family as the heart of most of the Minorcan households is further demonstrated by the fact that we have a number of families either representing way stations to or from the nuclear family ideal, or being breakdowns of the type through absence or death of a key member. Six couples lived in households not yet blessed with children and five older couples were either childless or the children had left or died. Incomplete nuclear families, those with a spouse absent or dead, accounted for the makeup of fifteen households.

Extended families were not the common domestic household ar-

Table 9.1

Type Distribution of Minorcan Households

Type			Number
Type I	Nuclear Families		83
Subtype:	A.	Nuclear family of husband, wife and including children of either spouse by a former marriage	58
	A_s	Subtype A plus slave (s).	19
	B	Same as subtype A plus hired hands, apprentices or extra people	4
	B_s	Same as Subtype B plus slave (s)	2
Type II	Childless Families		12
Subtype:	C	Older couples, childless, or children left or dead	5
	D	Young couples who have not yet had children	6
	D_1	Same as Subtype D plus related and/or unrelated persons	1
Type III	Extended Families		9
Subtype:	E	Nuclear family plus ascending or descending generation kin	2
	E_s	Subtype E plus slave (s)	1
	F	Nuclear family plus lateral kin	4
	F_s	Subtype F plus slave (s)	1
	EF_s	Subtype E plus F plus slave (s)	1
Type IV	Incomplete Families		15
Subtype:	G	Husband away or deceased	9
	G_s	Subtype G plus slave (s)	2
	H	Wife away or deceased	4
Type V	Amicable Arrangements		16
Subtype:	I_s	Two unrelated families living together plus slaves (s)	1
	J	Two or more related persons living together	6
	J_s	Subtype J plus slave (s)	2
	K	Two or more unrelated persons living together	6
	K_s	Subtype K plus slave (s)	1
Type VI	One Person Households		15
Subtype:	L	Living completely alone	12
	M	Living alone but close to kin	3
Total			152

Source: Types adapted from du Toit (1975).

rangement. The nine such households accommodated a widowed parent (although many of those chose to live alone) or the wife's brother. Without exception intact older couples and recently marrieds lived in separate habitations from any other close-kin marital pair, although often nearby.

Several facets of Minorcan life are illustrated by households, which, although designated here as amicable arrangements could just as well be called households of convenience. Many of these were composed of temporary quasi-family clusters. In some instances the only survivors of a previously numerous kin group set up a joint domicile. One household was a "catchall" for stray Greeks. Two Greek widowers first set up a household together. A year after Juan Genopoly's daughter, Leonora, married Anthony Hinsman in 1784, Juan's wife died. After that Genopoly opened his home to his *compadre*, Pedro Drimarachi, a widower with two children. Another unmarried Greek, George Caravach, lived with them. Together they owned three slaves, making a household of eight people. Six households contained two unrelated persons living together. An example was the household of Father Camps; living with him was José Batalini, an unmarried Minorcan islander, who in the mid 1780s in St. Augustine was listed as working in a "shop of drinks."

Many of the households resulted from the way in which young adults customarily left the family circle. Here we come upon a whole area of social structure affecting household composition as well as other matters.

Eighteenth-century Mediterranean girls married at the age of thirteen or fourteen, when they were barely into adolescence. (This is especially documented for the Western Mediterranean; see Brydone 1773, Armstrong 1756, Cleghorn 1779). The same was true for the Minorcan girls in our sample. Of the twenty-nine first marriages contracted by Minorcan girls (including several of Greek ancestry) in the seven-year period from 1784 to 1791, the median and modal ages were fourteen years. The mean average of 14.7 years was somewhat higher than it might otherwise have been because of the four girls married between the ages of sixteen and eighteen. In each of those four instances a reason for late marriage was found, such as the need to stay at home to help a widowed father with younger children in the family.

Boys stayed at home somewhat longer, usually until the age of fifteen or sixteen. In 1786 twice as many boys as girls between the ages of fourteen and sixteen were found living under the parental roof. In only one instance, that of the sixteen-year-old Juan Andreu, did a boy live in the same house as his own father after the age of fifteen, although several did live with a stepfather.

Young men rarely left their own homes in order to marry. An interim period was the general rule. In early adolescence males left the family circle to live alone or with one or more other young men; sometimes with a brother, but just as often with someone completely unrelated. Some moved in with their married sisters, or attached themselves to another household as a worker, most commonly as a farmhand. A few shipped as mariners, later returning to marry and settle down. A few boys, some as young as ten years old, were apprenticed to a trade in a family of the same or slightly higher social station. This was an asymmetrical shift, never a direct exchange, such that a boy might be apprenticed to a family across town and the youth's family might acquire a boy from a third family. One young man, fifteen-year-old Domingo Valls, apprenticed to a carpenter, had lost his whole family in New Smyrna—father, mother and two younger brothers.

This unmarried interim lasted from five to ten years, the age at first marriage for men being somewhere between twenty and twenty-five. Everything points to the existence of a young men's "culture." The complaints of night disturbances were doubtless expressions of this culture.

Thirty-two slave-owning households contained the sixty-eight blacks in the sample. No record exists of the ages of these slaves, but they were almost equally divided by sex. Female slaves were more often attached to town households with small children or to the larger households which functioned as production units. Many, but by no means all, of the male slaves were part of farming households.

Whether slaves actually lived and slept under the same roof as their owners is impossible to document. In some instances this may have been the case, although in the more affluent households they probably occupied subsidiary structures on the property or lean-tos attached to the main house, or simply stretched out on the floor of the detached kitchen to sleep each night.

In summary, the ordinary Minorcan household was at core a nuclear family containing two or three children and perhaps a slave.

Households were mostly medium in size, containing slightly more than four persons on the average, a fact occasioned by the separate living arrangements of older couples and persons recently married and the early exit of young adults from the parental roof. Households not based on nuclear families were either variants of the nuclear core mode or shifting arrangements of convenience.

10. Settlement Pattern

*A fertile almond in the neighborhood
of a road is always bitter.*
Old Minorcan saying

When the Minorcans removed to St. Augustine in 1777 they formed themselves into a "village" within a town. Their original assignment by the British to one section of town, a space without much built environment, allowed them to structure their community in harmony with their own world view. Accordingly their allotted area was not simply adapted for use, but grew naturally, as hastily built huts gave way to more substantial habitations, and a compatible format emerged.

The most striking element coming to the fore here is that the Minorcans, released from the unfamiliar dispersed settlement pattern on the plantation, were able to reassemble themselves in a clustered village layout. This was the familiar one of their homelands where those who worked on farm plots outside of town or fished the estuaries and rivers could group together in the evenings, joining those who had stayed in town. The parish chapel was at the hub of the settlement and the shops or little taverns were dispersed about wherever the families undertaking such endeavors happened to live.

All of this is not to say, however, that the quarter was a strange or unusual part of the existing town pattern, for St. Augustine had been laid out in a Mediterranean plat in the centuries of the first Spanish period of occupation, and had been little altered in the short twenty-year sojourn of the British. The pattern was characteristic of a typical preindustrial city of southern Europe.

Such a city is described by Sjoberg (1967:16-17):

The internal arrangement of the preindustrial city . . . is closely
related to the city's economic and social structure. Most streets
are mere passageways for people and for animals used in trans-
port. Buildings are low and crowded together. . . . significant
is the rigid social segregation which typically has led to the
formation of "quarters" or "wards." . . . The quarters reflect
the sharp local social divisions. Thus ethnic groups live in special
sections. And the occupational groupings, some being at the
same time ethnic in character, typically reside apart from one
another. . . . Despite rigid segregation the evidence suggests
no real specialization of land use such as is functionally necessary in industrial-urban communities. . . . city dwellings often
serve as workshops. . . . Finally, the "business district" does
not hold the position of dominance that it enjoys in the industrial
urban community.

Nonetheless, unlike its European counterpart, St. Augustine was
not the jumble of houses on irregular streets or paths centering on
a small, or even vestigial, plaza. Instead, it was the tidied-up version
dictated by Spain for towns laid out fresh in the New World. Foster
(1960:34) describes how in towns in Spanish America "streets radiate
from a square or oblong central plaza and intersect at right angles
to form rectangular blocks . . . usually the important buildings face
the plaza: church or cathedral, municipal hall, homes of important
business leaders, and other structures central to the life of the inhabitants."

The shape of late eighteenth-century St. Augustine, outlined once
by what had become by that time a crumbling fortified wall, was that
of a long rectangle, conditioned by the shape of the peninsula on
which it was located. This peninsula is a narrow strip, marshy at the
borders, except on the east side facing the tidal river which is in fact
an estuary. The town was given to flooding at times of high tide, but
this disadvantage was offset by its being entirely defensible on three
sides, requiring only watchfulness to the north. East of the town was
the shoal and shifting inlet, very treacherous and long a ship
graveyard. The marshy northern tip of Anastasia Island obscured a
direct view of the inlet from the town, but a watchtower on the
island signaled the arrival of vessels and an approaching mast could
be seen from the town before the craft was fully visible. This barrier
island stretched south a dozen miles to the next tidal inflow, Matan-

zas Inlet, near which, to protect the town's back door, the Spanish had erected a small fort in the early eighteenth century.

The town in the 1780s was flanked by two military facilities, the military barracks to the south and the old Spanish fort (the Castillo de San Marcos) on the north (figure 10.1). In the middle of the populated area a large central plaza divided the town. The governor's house and other public buildings overlooked this plaza. On the east side of the plaza near the water the old Spanish guardhouse, tumbling into ruins, was partially roofed over to serve as the public butcher shop and on designated days the public market was conducted near this building.

Streets extended from the plaza in a modified grid pattern in proper New World Hispanic fashion. The major commercial area, where the prominent citizens lived and conducted their businesses, was concentrated near the bayfront directly north and south of the main plaza, extending south to a small plaza, *La Placita de las Higueras* (The Little Plaza of the Fig Trees), about half way to the military barracks. Present day Charlotte Street provided the most direct route from the Castillo to the barracks, passing by both plazas, and through the concentrated central neighborhoods. At the north end of this route a diagonal path diverged, affording a shortcut to the Castillo entrance. This north-south common passageway went through the eastern edge of the Minorcan quarter. Within the quarter itself a small business hub, mainly serving nearby residents, existed at the corner of present-day St. George and Cuna streets.

The route along Charlotte Street, also called the Street of the Merchants, must have served as the favored avenue for most of the ordinary internal traffic in the town. The streets leading to the exits of the town, in particular the one to the north through the city gate, were important for defense and communication, and for reaching outlying farms and fields, but played minor roles in internal town movement.

The church shown on the north side of the plaza, the present basilica, was not built until five years after the date of the map on which figure 10.1 was based. The old Spanish church in the southwest section of town had also served the English, but was in ruins when they left. The chapel in the quarter which had been established by Father Camps was abandoned as a church facility after the Spanish returned. Father Hassett saw fit to refurbish a building on the plaza

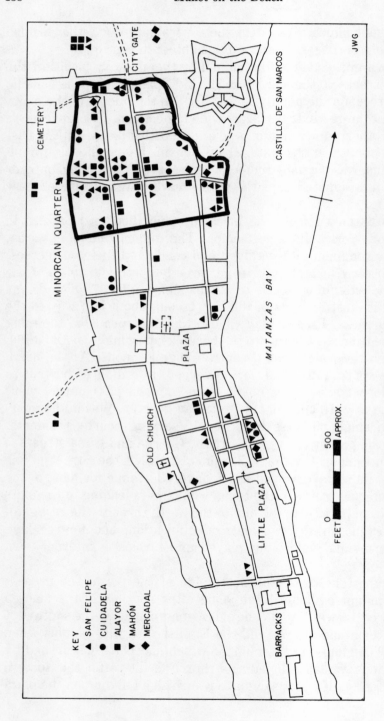

Figure 10.1. Distribution of Minorcans in St. Augustine, circa 1786-1788, based on locale of origin in Minorca. Map adapted from Rocque (1788).

for the parish church. The Catholic cemetery, which Father Camps had been given the use of by the British authorities, was the old Indian mission burial grounds dating from the days of the Franciscan missionaries in the province. This cemetery, called Tolomato, located directly west of the Minorcan quarter, outside the original town boundary, served the church for more than a century (Coomes 1976).

The Minorcan quarter itself occupied the entire northern third of the town as it had in the British period. It was the only "quarter," or ethnic allocation, at the end of the eighteenth century. Indians, once in clusters on the edges of town, were now living in scattered settlements some distance away, in fact beyond the St. Johns River, although they were to be seen in town on market days.

Reconstruction of the actual house placement of individual Minorcan families must remain speculative prior to the time that the engineer, Mariano de la Rocque, platted his map in 1788, with its accompanying index of owners and renters. We know, of course, that during the English period the Minorcan refugees lived primarily in the quarter and worked plots of land to the north and west, outside the bounds of the old city wall. The 1784 census gives vague dwelling locations by association with known landmarks such as "near the single tower" (located at Tolomato cemetery), "by the principal church," or "a musket shot from the line."

The Rocque map, as the most dependable source, was used in the present study as a base for plotting the settlement pattern of the Minorcan community. The 1784 and 1787 censuses yielded some information, and it was possible to fix the position of some families by taking an imaginary tour with Father Hassett as he walked each street to compile his census in 1786. For example, if the locations of families 99 and 101 as recorded by Hassett could be established on the Rocque map and there was a structure between them, it is assumed that Family 100 lived there.

One problem emerged immediately—the transiency of the group, a matter which has already been mentioned. Some families moved as many as four times in the period between 1784 and 1788. As the only white group remaining through the change of political regimes, Minorcans seized the opportunity of moving to more favorable locations, occupying vacated buildings or taking up new vocations which necessitated a move. Even before 1784 much shifting probably took place, due to the building of new houses, through the process of jockeying for a more favorable position, through remarriage, and even because a family or community feud made it necessary.

The rickety board and thatch huts were easy to move, or were simply abandoned when more substantial accommodations could be built in advantageous locations. Lumber was hard to obtain, what with Indians lurking in the pine barrens, and the trees close to town having been heavily depleted by British lumbering activities. Any building falling into disrepair was fair game for those patching their houses or building new ones.

The emergent picture is not unlike that of squatter settlements formed next to towns or cities in present-day Latin America or eastern Europe, with the difference that the Minorcan settlement was a large part of the St. Augustine community. Maj. Gen. Nathanael Greene, commander of the Southern Army during the American Revolution, touring St. Augustine in 1785, wrote to his wife of his surprise that "the town is larger than I expected but the houses are huddled together not unlike one of our winter encampments" (Tanner 1964:17). Like the unknown writer of May, 1774, who described the town as a "heap of ruins" (Fairbanks 1858:163), Greene also noted the "mean appearance" of the buildings.

The relationship of the Minorcan community to the hinterland reveals something of relationships with the larger community of St. Augustine and the province. By 1787, ninety of the 152 households were documented as working land to the north or west of the city. Of these households, seventy-four occupied houses in town but worked their garden plots outside of town, while another sixteen were living in dwellings on their farm land. Seven of these out-of-town habitations were clustered in a hamlet near the location of the old mission of La Leche, a scant half mile north of the fort, and most of the remaining nine were living on their farm land very close to the quarter—near the fort or by the San Sebastian River. Some were farming on what was known as the "government grant," probably working on shares to stock the garrison's larder.

In the preindustrial world, and especially in a pioneer area suffering from constant winds of political change, land ownership was not stable or orderly. A man's right to a piece of land was often a consequence of continued cropping, and tracing a man through the documents often yielded the information that he shifted his farming from one place to another, sometimes joined forces with another farmer in gardening a larger patch, or rented a choice plot from someone else. It was not easy, either, for the Spanish authorities to untangle the confusing rights to farm plots when the British left. Did, for example, a person who had rented or worked on shares on land owned by an Englishman have a right to title of that piece of land when it was vacated by the English owner after the change of flags? In many cases and because of such problems, land ownership was not definitely fixed until well into the second Spanish period, around 1807. A few areas remained common lands somewhat longer.

The mind-set of common lands or understood territory open to all has persisted to the present day. As each traditional hunting or fishing area has been readied for development in modern times objections have been raised. Some protests have amounted to harassment of the interlopers for infringement of these unwritten "laws" by such tactics as strewing the road with nails or tearing down newly-built fences. While the Minorcan community is now no longer the tight group of former days, descendents are still the base of the area's traditional citizenry with their well understood land customs.

In the 1780s the plots farmed by the Minorcans were not large, size varying with the number in the household work force, the few draught animals available and the state of the technology. The newly-arrived Spanish governor, Zéspedes, wrote in 1784 that the "majority [of the Minorcans] raise crops in the vicinity of the city, few or none owning the land. They rent four or five *fanegas* of cleared land on which they raise Indian corn and some garden stuff" (Lockey 1939:285). A *fanega*, Lockey found, was difficult to equate with an English measure, as it seems to have varied from one-third to nearly a whole acre. In the same letter Zéspedes recommended to the Spanish Crown that lands be "divided among these people in proportion to the size of their families." This was eventually done and by the time of the 1787 census forty-seven families had an average of 9.62 acres under cultivation. This figure is based only on those families where land under cultivation is clearly stated, and it should be noted that not all Minorcan men were listed in that census. Also four families with between forty and fifty acres apiece inflated this average figure. One of these, the Greek Pedro Cocifaci, by this time referred to by the honorific "Don," cultivated between forty and fifty acres in addition to his extensive mercantile activities. These larger holdings were definitely the exception, but even they were relatively small at this time compared with the size of the plantations granted some of the Floridanos and Spaniards. The situation was temporary as much larger grants were accorded to Minorcan families in subsequent decades, so that by the time that Florida became a United States territory, many were in possession of sizable acreages.

However, the Minorcan role as small subsistence farmer is clear for the era under scrutiny. Also clear is that a majority of the land farmed was north of the town boundary. For military reasons it was expedient for land to the north of St. Augustine to be kept clear except for agriculture, and huts built on such land could not be more than nine by twelve feet in size or more than ten feet in height. As an added measure these shanties had to be located along the road in order to allow easy torching by one rider in case of attack (Manucy 1962). Given this impermanence, it is not surprising to find that ten or more families living on their land outside of town in 1784 had moved into town by 1787-1788. Doubtless, the easy availability of housing left by the departing British facilitated these moves. Huts on the farmland were mainly, as time went on and as threats of war and actual forays occurred from the north, kept just for housing of slaves or for temporary quarters during the harvest. When border conditions became settled with acquisition of Florida by the United States in 1821, some Minorcan families built better homes for themselves on their farmlands in the area now called North City, thus forming a new Minorcan sector of the town.

Two other hinterland areas existed in the late 1780s, a fact documented by the individuals showing up in the parish records who were absent from any of the censuses. A few people either stayed behind or returned to the New Smyrna area and there was some flow back and forth to St. Augustine. A second area was north of the town, along the Tolomato River and beyond.

As an example, Joseph Manuci and his family must have lived far from town as they showed up for the baptism of their two youngest children, ages three years and six months, in May of 1788, a fact remarkable because of the almost universal practice of infant baptism before the age of six weeks.

Having established the relation to the hinterland, it is important to look at the positioning of subgroups of the Minorcan community within the confines of the town itself.

Of the thirteen Greeks for whom residence sites were established, six were living outside the quarter, mostly scattered around in the south side of town, location apparently being a function of occupation. No clusters of Greek households were found, unless we count the "catchall" Greek household previously mentioned. Godparent exchanges, however, attest to the continuance of close ties among the Greek nationals.

Since most of the Italian men had married Minorcan girls, they were somewhat more integrated into the Minorcan islander group than was the Greek enclave, a fact, however, not substantiated by locale of residence. Only five of the twelve Italians for whom it was possible to fix residence with any degree of accuracy were living in the quarter. A probable explanation for this was the common occupation of these Italians as mariners, and the tendency for mariners to live along the waterfront. Curiously, the twelve households headed by Italian men were found in six pairs. Where one Italian home was found another was close by, functional, perhaps, for the wives while the husbands were away at sea. Godparent exchanges substantiated the quasi-kin bonding of these paired households.

Minorcan islanders were numerous enough to establish patterns of residency in relation to locale of origin in Minorca. Since place of birth was, and still is, a large part of individual identity for Mediterranean peoples, it was probable that persons coming from the same area in Minorca would form clusters in a new locality. As Pitt-Rivers (1961:30) concluded, "A conception of community based on locality runs through the cultural idiom of Southern Europe. . . . The pueblo furnishes a completeness of human relations which makes it the prime concept of all social thought."

Using the sample of the 177 Minorcan islanders for which place of origin was known, as shown in table 2.1, the domicile in St. Augustine was determined for 120 individuals. These individuals were then plotted on a map (figure 10.1) by place of origin in Minorca. It must be borne in mind that these 120 people are about half of the number of surviving Minorcan islanders living in St. Augustine in the middle 1780s. Had origin information been available on the rest, a more conclusive picture might have emerged.

Twelve persons lived just outside the confines of the city. Of the remaining 108, two-thirds of the sample lived inside the boundary of the Minorcan quarter. Men, especially those from Alayor and Cuidadela, lived in the quarter in more instances than women did; a possible result of the marriage of Minorcan women to Greeks, Italians, or Anglos occasioning their move outside the quarter. There was only one contrary case in the 152 households of a Minorcan man married to a Greek girl. Mahónese were the only group of Minorcan islanders who more often lived out of the quarter, with fifteen out of twenty-six individuals choosing to live in other sections of town. Since they came from Mahón, the largest city in Minorca, their urban background perhaps meant a slightly higher level of sophistication, conditioning them to an easier entre into town life south of the quarter.

Place of origin is apparent as an organizing principle although not dramatically so. San Felipe natives formed the most definitive cluster at the western end of Cuna Street. Near Spanish Street they merged into the Cuidadela natives ranging along the rest of Cuna Street. Natives of Alayor commonly lived near the city gate and southward down St. George to Cuna Street. Mahónese were prominent in the western section between the quarter and the plaza. The two Perpal families account for some of this group. Members of the Perpal family were the only ones in the settler group designated by the courtesy titles of *Don* and *Doña* in the early parish records. Because of their higher station, they may never have lived in the quarter, even in the first years after the group moved into town. Lastly, Mercadal natives, being few, showed no special pattern.

A close look at the map reveals an area on the west side of St. George Street where no Minorcan families lived when Mariano de la Rocque platted his map in 1788. How could this be, near as it was to the center of the quarter? From the 1784 census and the 1786 Hassett census it is evident that Minorcan families were living there then. The explanation lies in the return of Floridanos or their heirs who reclaimed their property and ousted Minorcan families from these dwellings. For ten years those living in the quarter had been almost entirely the Minorcan settler group and their descendants, and this incursion of returning American-born Spaniards was the first of many changes sustained by the area in subsequent years, changes which eventually eroded the area as an exclusively Minorcan preserve.

Age groups were fairly evenly distributed throughout the quarter. On the supposition that older couples, being culturally more conservative, might tend to live closer to the center of the quarter than younger couples, a random sample of fifty couples was selected and studied to see if this were so. On the average, these fifty couples lived 204.9 *varas* (the *vara* in use equalled 32.9 inches) from the center of the quarter, already mentioned as the intersection of St. George and Cuna streets. The range was from 8.3 to 658.3 *varas*, with a standard deviation of 44.89. Separated into two classes— young and old couples—with 35.5 years being the mean couple age dividing line, it was found that young couples were slightly more likely to live close to the center of the quarter than old couples, thus sustaining the null hypothesis. It therefore seems that economic constraints, locale of origin, kinship connections, and residence rules were more important determinants of household location than age.

A more penetrating look at family residence patterns leads to a tentative—very tentative—conclusion that the group were uxorilocal (previously designated by anthropologists as matrilocal). Murdock in his classic book *Social Structure* (1949:16) concluded, "If custom requires the groom to leave his parental home and live with the bride, either in the house of her parents or in a dwelling nearby, the rule of residence is called *matrilocal*." Keesing (1975:151) later defined uxorilocal as "residence of a married couple with [or near] the wife's kin (formerly called matrilocal)."

The seven cases examined for possible virilocality—the opposite of uxorilocality, i.e. residence of a couple near the husband's family— yielded only one positive instance, that of Diego Hernández and his son of the same name.

Six cases were found in which there were enough married women and their parents to make some judgement about uxorilocality. In five of the six families married girls were living not in the same dwelling but close to their parents. The sixth, non-conforming, instance was that of the Castell sisters and their mother. Here remarriage on the part of the mother and the marriage of two of the three girls to Italian men evidently disrupted the usual residence rule.

The Vila family, originally from Cuidadela, Minorca, illustrates the usual format. This residential grouping encompassed two parents, three daughters, and two nieces. A kinship chart of the family is presented in figure 10.2, and the location of the cluster is mapped in figure 10.3.

Two brothers, Francisco and Pedro, were the fathers of these girls, Pedro also having sired a boy, Juan. Documentary evidence

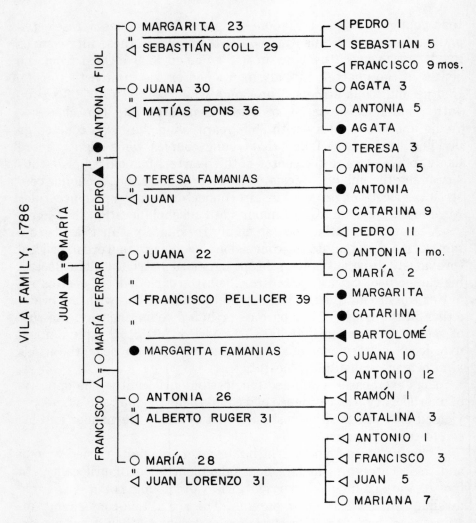

Figure 10.2. Vila Family Kinship Chart

indicates that Francisco and Pedro were the younger sons of Juan and Mara Vila of Cuidadela. Both brothers and their families joined the Turnbull colony leaving their parents behind in the Old World. Even though Pedro and his wife, Antonia Fiol, are known only from being listed as the parents of three children in the parish records, their presence in the New World is inferred from the tender age of

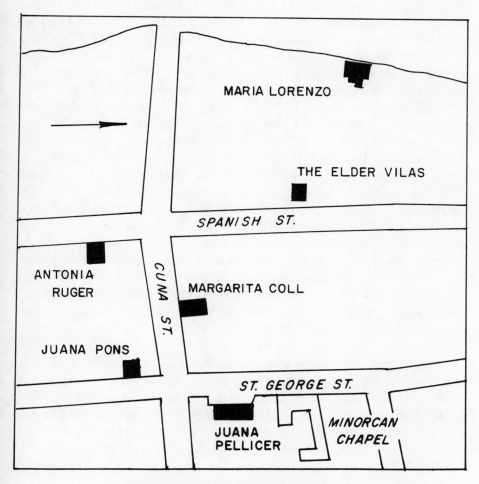

Figure 10.3. Vila Family Settlement Pattern.

their children at the colony's beginning. If, as guessed, Pedro and his wife did die early in the colony's history, their children were probably cared for by Francisco Vila and his wife María Ferrar along with their own three girls. The godparent exchanges between these cousins was much more substantial than was customary for the cousin relationship in the Minorcan group, permitting the conclusion that all six of that generation were raised as siblings after they reached the New World. Pitt-Rivers (1961:105) describes the usual cousin relationship as a vague, inconsequential kin bond in the Iberian tradition, a fact still apparent among St. Augustine Minorcans who often use the term to mean anyone in the Minorcan community on the same generation level as themselves. However, in the Vila family the cousins probably grew up as quasi-siblings under one roof.

By 1786, Francisco, who was a farmer, and his wife lived several doors from the corner of Cuna and Spanish streets, farming at that time four acres outside of town. María, their twenty-eight year old daughter, lived behind them with her husband Juan Lorenzo, a mason and part-time farmer. Antonia, twenty-six years old, lived with her husband, Alberto Ruger, a carpenter, another Cuidadela native, close to the Spanish-Cuna street intersection. The Vila's youngest daughter, twenty-two year old Juana, was the second wife of Francisco Pellicer, famed as the leader of the exodus from New Smyrna. They lived at this time in an early form of duplex house near the corner of Cuna and St. George streets, although shortly afterwards they sold out to Demetrios Fundulakis, one of the original colony hailing from the Greek islands, whereupon the Pellicer family moved to a sizable grant some fifteen miles south of town on what subsequently was named Pellicer Creek.

The nieces, Margarita and Juana, lived in the center of all this family grouping in the Minorcan quarter. Margarita, twenty-three years old, was married to Sebastin Coll, described as a "ship carpenter." Juana, aged thirty, lived with her husband, Marcial Pons, in the wattle and daub house where he ran a tavern at the corner of Cuna and St. George streets. Marcial Pons farmed part time, and the Pons and Pellicer families were the only slaveholders in the extended family group under consideration.

Nephew Juan's place of residence is not clear from the documents, although we can be certain that he and his wife did not live in the family cluster. In 1784 he was farming three acres of land and living in a cabin, perhaps on the farm, close to the fort.

The Vilas are but one vernacular grouping in the community who demonstrate the principle of residence of female progeny after marriage in locations close by the woman's original family. An old Andalusian saying tells of this customary residence change at marriage (Pitt-Rivers 1961:101):

'Tu hijo se casa   'Your son gets married
Y pierdes a tu hijo   And you lose your son
Tu hija se casa   Your daughter married
Y ganas otro.'   And you get another one.'

Given the young age at which a girl married, living near her
family seems a wise decision in any case. The proximity of the young
couple to the wife's family had other implications as well, affecting
relationships between the sexes, age at marriage, and kin and godparent relationships; inheritance and status; and the constitution of
partnerships and work groups as well as other aspects of social organization.

11. Occupations

Mullet on the beach!
Rallying cry of St. Augustine Minorcans

To a closely interacting, traditional community, such as the Minorcans were in the 1780s, it would be a mistake to apply our own concepts of economic life. For one thing, occupational contours were less divorced from the natural world than was true once technology reached a certain level. The rhythms of hot and cold seasons, of rain and drought, of the waxing and waning of tides; all controlled the rhythms of work.

Nor were sole occupations the rule, but, instead, a plurality of activities made up the economic life of a household. While "moonlighting" is known in modern times it is the exception, whereas in earlier times it was a way of life. The very few in the eighteenth century who undertook only one activity were high in status, for even the soldiery or the religious found sidelines to occupy their time, often to the annoyance of their superiors.

John Lee Williams (1837:115) describing the occupations of the Minorcan group when they were under the Spanish regime reported that they "kept little shops, cultivated small groves or gardens, and followed fishing and hunting." He added a profile of their lifestyle: "They were a temperate, quiet and rather indolent people; affectionate and friendly to each other, and kind to the few slaves they held. The even tenor of their way was not often interrupted." Except for failing to mention the mariners in the group, this early eyewitness report checks with the census evidence on occupations.

A distribution of people by occupation was rarely the impetus for a census, although farming and the amount of land under cultivation were certainly prime considerations for the Spanish authorities attempting to resettle the province. Spanish census takers in St. Augustine often listed only one occupation, but collation of these enumerations in different documents yields a picture of seasonality of occupations, many sidelines, and constant change. The time of year and the purpose of a census affected occupational listings also. Hassett, asking occupation in a fallow period, December, found fewer families farming than appear in the 1787 census which was taken to assess farming and land ownership. Through time, work undertaken by Minorcans varied from year to year with changing community needs and individual capacity and inclination. And all of the census takers missed the importance of fishing because it was a subsistence activity for a large number of people in the group, but a full-time occupation for only a few.

Using all available documentary sources, particularly censuses, the occupations of 176 adult Minorcans are listed in table 11.1. These 176 individuals are the only ones whose occupations are known with any certainty. It does not appear that this sample is in any way unrepresentative of the whole. Occupations of women were listed in only three cases, all of them household heads. Nonetheless, in preindustrial society it was a rare woman who was idle, for the wife of the house and the girls took an active part in the work of the establishment. Only the very young and the old and infirm were non-contributors to domestic support.

Farming was at this time the main occupation for household heads, with ninety-six out of the 176 reporting farming as an economic activity. Of these, forty-nine counted it as their only occupation of consequence, while an additional ten listed it as their principal occupation. Another twenty-seventy considered farming as part of their repertoire, while not listing it as a principle activity. Narrative accounts also speak of the Minorcans at this juncture (1784-1788) as the "farming class" of the province. On their small plots of about ten acres or less they raised most of the truck garden produce for the community as well as for themselves, able at last to reactivate their Old World knowledge of subsistence farming and to put into practice the experience and wisdom gained in the nine years on the plantation.

Farming was a household occupation with farm labor provided by the men and boys with an occasional added farm hand or slave, and with the women of the household pressed into service at peak times.

Table 11.1

Occupations

Occupation	Number
Farmer	49
Farmer/Fisherman	6
Farmer/Overseer	1
Farmer/Barber	1
Farmer/Mason	1
Farmer/Carpenter/Fisherman	1
Fisherman	7
Fisherman/Farmer	7
Mariner	37
Mariner/Farmer	4
Mariner/Fisherman	1
Mariner/Tavernkeeper	1
Mariner/Farmer/Fisherman	1
Mariner/Tavernkeeper/Farmer	1
Mariner/Mason	1
Carpenter	15
Carpenter/Farmer	4
Mason (stonecutter)	1
Mason/Farmer	1
Mason/Fisherman/Farmer	1
Merchant/Farmer	3
Merchant/Farmer/Carpenter/Jailer	1
Tavernkeeper	3
Tavernkeeper/Farmer	2
Rum Seller/Carpenter	1
Trader/Farmer/Baker	1
Ropemaker/Fisherman	1
Blacksmith/Mariner	1
Hangman/Farmer/Calker	1
Tailor	5
Shoemaker	4
Seamstress	2
Calker	2
Baker	2
Tiler	1
Weaver	1
Hatter	1
Waiter	1
Sacristan	1
Priest	1
Total	176

By means of partnerships, a common theme in the Mediterranean, several households joined forces, able by this means to diversify crops and better allocate labor resources. This is inferred in a number of instances but documented in only four cases.

The 1787 census, which listed livestock, numbered a total of thirty-one horses, six cows, and one ox owned by the Minorcans. This enumeration of the larger draught animals and dairy stock does not include the small domestic fowl, pigs, and other small animals kept in pens near the houses in town. Partitioning of yards on the Rocque map of St. Augustine indicates the separation of backdoor plots for containment of smaller animals. Neither chickens nor pigs were a problem to feed. Schoepf (1911:246) saw "swine thrive" in the St. Augustine of 1783-84, fed on acorns, chestnuts and roots.

Indian corn was the principal grain crop grown on the out-of-town acreage. Oranges, which became a cash crop for the Minorcan group in the nineteenth century, were not grown in any quantity by them at this time, although orange trees, lending perfume to the air every spring, were planted around many of the habitations. Other vegetables cultivated were the same as those grown in New Smyrna.

Hoe horticulture was common, but so-called "dry farming"—surface plowing of light soils by use of simple plows—increased in time, a readoption of a Mediterranean method. Farm carts were probably diverse and no doubt homemade. Some farmers may have made use of the high, large-wheeled variety, lineal descendant of the Greek country cart of the fourth century B.C. (Singer et al. 1957:545), sometimes modified for pulling by one draught animal or perhaps by a man.

For some households, crops were grown entirely for home consumption; others, larger scale or more ambitious farmers, offered their surplus for sale in the town market or furnished food for the garrison.

Since St. Augustine was a port city and much of the life of the town centered around the waterfront, it is no surprise that mariner was the second most common occupation after farmer. Forty-six of the 176 individuals were mariners with thirty-seven of these men listing it as their only occupation. Aside from the Italians, who often remained in the occupation, the rest seem to have been a shifting group, as young men shipped out for a few years and then married and took up more settled ways of making a living.

While most of these mariners crewed on ships owned by others, some owned their own small boats and a few owned more substantial craft, while still others captained boats taking part in international trade. Domingo Martinely, one of the Italian men, listed himself as "captain of a sloop." Three times during 1787 he left his Minorcan born wife, Mariana Cavedo, to put to sea in the *San Pedro*, sailing in January to the Caribbean, in June to New York, and finally making a short trip to Charleston in September.

An undetermined number of mariners worked harbor pilot boats. The St. Augustine inlet had the justly deserved reputation of being one of the most treacherous on the eastern coast. Wright (1975:45) describing problems encountered by British refugee ships in 1782 and 1783 says, "At least sixteen ships carrying refugees went aground trying to negotiate the channel, resulting in further property loss and suffering. In a single convoy a galley and two provision vessels of the Royal Navy along with six privately owned ships sank with the loss of four lives." Piloting and local knowledge of harbor and inlet conditions were important to the life of the town. Minorcans were the logical choice for this enterprise accustomed as they were to the waterways from St. Augustine to New Smyrna. Antonio Cantar, a native of San Felipe, stated himself as "master of a bark" when Father Hassett took his census, and announced even more grandly to the census taker in 1787 that he was "harbor pilot of all the coast." One of the apocryphal stories told by Minorcan descendants is of a nineteenth-century Minorcan, stricken blind in his youth, but nevertheless so skilled at sailing wherever he wanted in St. Augustine waters that he never ran aground.

Since imported goods and services were scarce and expensive in pioneer St. Augustine, Minorcans readily assumed the roles of craftsmen, tradesmen and shopkeepers. The building trades, as they still are today, were filled with Minorcan workmen. Carpenters were the largest and most affluent group with fifteen listing carpentry as a full-time occupation and seven part-time. When Rocque made his map in 1788 forty-three percent of the buildings were made of wood and another five percent of shakes (Manucy 1962:71). Frame upper stories were not uncommon on the coquina stone houses, which accounted for thirty-six percent of the total number standing. Besides building structures in the town, a large part of carpentry work was boat repair.

The thirteen-member Hernández household situated close to the bayfront south of the plaza was the core of the carpenter's guild. Martín Hernández, is listed as "chief carpenter" and also as a ship carpenter, a useful trade considering the high rate of repair required by wooden boats and the number of ships disabled trying to negotiate the St. Augustine bar. Probably new boats were constructed by the family enterprise as well. He was assisted by his brothers Juan and Joseph, by another, Gaspar, who was a calker, and by two young carpenter apprentices and three slaves.

Perhaps the Hernández household had the major part in planning the float built by the carpenter's guild for the gala fiesta held in 1789 to honor the crowning of the new Spanish king, Carlos IV, as described by Tanner:

> The three day fiesta concluded on the evening of December 4, culminating with a triumphal float drawn through town by six horses. This magnificently decorated construction was the work of a local carpenter's guild, a group with a large representation from the Minorcan population. It was large enough to carry all the guild members, who sported red cockades in their broad hats and carried flaming torches in their hands. At every corner they paused to give cheers for the new rulers, echoed by the little groups of observers (Tanner 1963:207).

In contrast with carpentry, which was an exacting trade, the craft of mason and stonecutter required less skill, and a mason occupied a lower status, lived in a poorer house, owning no slaves at all, and in four out of five cases combining the occupation with another. Carpenters more often came from urban Mahón, while the masons were all from San Felipe—the Ortagus family composing the hub of the mason's group. Their place of origin is not surprising since San Felipe was known as a source of excellent building stone (Armstrong 1756:135). Old World techniques used with the freestone found in Minorca were applicable to the coquina of Florida's east coast.

The garment trade had fourteen workers listed, but doubtless as a home industry the unlisted work force was somewhat larger. Five Minorcans were full-time tailors and four were shoemakers. In addition there was a weaver, a hatter, and two women seamstresses. At that frugal time the bulk of the work of clothing craftspeople involved repairing and remaking rather than the construction of new items.

In the personalistic culture in which they lived, each of these tradespeople had his or her own circle of customers. The best known murder case of the era, one which occupied an inordinate amount of space in the official correspondence with Havana, involved a seamstress and one of her customers. On the evening of November 10, 1785, Lt. Guillermo Delaney, an officer of the Hibernia Regiment stationed in the town, was set upon, stabbed, and beaten by persons he could not identify, an attack from which he later died. He staggered into the house of José Gomila, a Minorcan fisherman. The house was located near the south end of the Minorcan quarter on the main thoroughfare, and since it jutted out into the street provided excellent concealment for the murderer. It seems that Delaney was headed toward that house to visit Catalina Morain, an Anglo-American seamstress who lived there. Although she had been doing some sewing for him, it subsequently appeared that he was also more personally involved with her. After Delaney died, a number of witnesses, including many of the Minorcan neighbors, gave testimony. Although the case was never solved, it was believed that one of Catalina's other suitors had perpetrated the deed (Tanner 1966:136-149). By the time that Hassett took his census the following year José Gomila's wife had died and he had moved in with his daughter, Dorotea, who was married to Martín Hernández, the carpenter, although the Rocque map still shows the Charlotte Street residence owned by José Gomila in 1788. Catalina Morain by the time of the Hassett census had taken up residence in the household of Thomas Cordery, an American Protestant who listed his occupation as butcher.

Other miscellaneous trades were represented in the occupations of Minorcans—waiter, baker, barber, priest, sacristan, jailer, hangman. The hangman, Diego Carreras, not finding enough to occupy him full time, cultivated five acres of land and was also a calker. Other stray facts reveal him as the owner of a horse and living in "a house of his brother [Juan Carreras] next to the Father Parish Priest." Later he took up farming and secured land grants at New Smyrna on the original plantation lands and another plot north of St. Augustine.

Some of the Minorcan men by this time had become merchants, traders, or shopkeepers. Businesses of this kind were the multifunctional ones common to that era, characterized by service to the citizens of the town and, in the case of the larger establishments, deal-ings with the outside world through various trade networks. The five most prosperous Minorcan merchants were Pedro Cocifaci, José Peso de Burgo, Rocque Leonardi, Bernardo Seguí, and Doña Ysabela Perpal (two Greeks, one Italian, and two Minorcan islan-ders). They had competition. Hassett's census listed six non-Minor-can traders in town.

Judging from wills, litigation and other documents, the Minorcan traders were also bankers, in the sense of holding capital and loaning money; they were attorneys-in-fact serving as executors of wills and other legal documents; and in the case of Cocifaci and Peso de Burgo had shipping interests. Better integrated into town life, godparent-ing tied all of these traders to non-Minorcan townspeople, an uncom-mon occurrence for most of their fellows whose godparent ties tended to be within the Minorcan community itself.

Peso de Burgo, who called himself a shopkeeper, was the only one of these businessmen living and conducting his business within the quarter, close to the center of that area in fact. His main patron-age probably came from the Minorcan group. Single at the time, he was living in the other side of the duplex occupied by the Francisco Pellicer family. The two men built a house together and jointly owned a sloop. As Peso de Burgo was prosperous enough to own two slaves, four horses, seven canoes, four cows, and twelve acres of land, he may have furnished the capital while Pellicer undertook the required carpentry for their common-wall building (Ganong 1975:81-99).

The eight spirit purveyors—those listing themselves as wine mer-chant, tavern keeper, rum seller, or as operating a "shop of drinks"—played key roles in the community although their establishments and constituencies varied. Aside from the daily work groups, and often integral with them, the tavern served as the main assemblage place for the men; the same men frequenting the same tavern night after night.

Often these little neighborhood social centers grew quite natur-ally. An extended family and friends might be gravitating each night to one of the houses, likely one of larger dimension although not necessarily. After a while the household head might install a box in the corner and put out wine or other spirits for sale. The business might stay for many years at this level, or alternately develop into a much more formal establishment in which outsiders could imbibe.

Leonardi and Cocifaci probably had more elaborate establishments than the others, and the former, who listed himself as a "wine
merchant," may not have served drinks on the premises at all.
Cocifaci and Marcos Andres, both owners of sloops, were in a prime
location to serve the waterfront crowd, located as they were across
from each other near the water and next to the plaza, and on the
principal passageway through town. We do not know where Juan
Balum had his tavern and he fades out of the documents after 1786.

The other four all served drinks in their homes in the quarter.
Joseph Buchentini's "shop of drinks" was located on the waterfront
side of the quarter and a large part of his trade may have been his
fellows from the pilot launch, since he was also listed as "Mariner of
the tender." The wineshop must have been a minor part of his living
and more a part of his social life, since he also farmed some land.
Pedro Rodríguez's tavern was close to the entrance to the fort,
maybe serving those manning that facility, although the case of rape
of a Minorcan tavern keeper's wife by a soldier during the British
period tells us that military men imbibed closer to the center of the
quarter as well. As we have seen, Marcial Pons, married to one of
the Vila girls, had his tavern near the center of the quarter where
the men in this large and varied family and their friends could gather.
Further up St. George Street, Juan Carreras, the hangman's
brother, sold rum and other goods in one room of his house while his
family lived in the other room. By 1788 the military quarters in the
south end of town were served by Spanish-run taverns near the
barracks.

Fishing was, and continued for many years as, a prominent feature of being a Minorcan; but as it was followed seasonally and in
response to schooling of fish and availability of other sea life, it was
reported as a full-time occupation by only seven of our sample of 176.
The fishing near St. Augustine was fully as rewarding as it had been
in New Smyrna, and now no longer constrained by plantation rules,
the people were able to fit it into their lives as they saw fit. When
Luis Fatio wrote a description of the commerce of East Florida in
1790 he remarked that "the whole sea coast abounds with fish in
sufficient quantities to occupy the families of fishermen, who can find
suitable locations" (Whitaker 1931:137).

Noticeable in the above quote is the mention of "families," and
by this is meant the men in the families although women may have

been partly responsible for helping to dress and market the catch. For the men, participation in fishing groups promoted group solidarity. Men and boys of all ages took part, each step toward greater skill marking another step in a young boy's road to adult status.

Two varieties of cast nets as well as seine nets are still in use today by Minorcan descendants. Both of the cast nets are circular, one depending on bagging for closure (called "Spanish") and the other closed by tuck lines (called "English").

In contrast with the cast net, which was used by one man, the larger seine nets required a group of four to ten men to operate and were mostly used for mullet fishing. Seine nets were of the simple type with floats on the top edge and sinkers at the bottom, and were used on both rivers and beaches. Horses were used on the beach to pull one end of the net along until the catch was judged sufficient for the men to pull it ashore. Even now, when the mullet are running one can see streaks of silver glittering along the tops of the waves, and this form of fishing is still taking place, pickup trucks now substituted for horsepower.

Some fishing took place at night, particularly on the rivers. Canoes or small boats would drift along in the rivers and bays with light from a fat-pine knot torch suspended on an iron grate by which to attract, and see, the fish. A platter-shaped flounder could then be gigged or a school of fish harvested with a net. Sometimes hook and line fishing was called for. Part of the skill was reading the phosphorescent trails in the water to identify the species lurking about. On hot summer nights lights can still be seen floating lazily along in the waterways as fishermen follow their pursuit in time-honored St. Augustine fashion. The difference is that river seining is now illegal, and the lights presently in use are carbide or electric.

Ralph Waldo Emerson, wintering for his health in St. Augustine in 1827, wrote of hook and line fishing:

> The dark Minorcan, sad & separate,
> Wrapt in his cloak, strolls with unsocial eyes
> By day, basks idle in the sun, then seeks his food
> All night upon the waters, stilly plying
> His hook and line in all the moonlit bays.
> (Emerson 1939:90)

Regardless of Emerson's solitary Minorcan of poetic fancy, the size and weight of some of the canoes tell us that fishing often required more than one man. Canoes used were *piraguas* (dugouts), durable and easy, although time-consuming, to manufacture. It was reported by several old-timers that one of these dugouts was still in use in 1920. It was made of cypress, had a beam of two feet, six inches, and was twenty-five feet in overall length (interviews on file, Historic St. Augustine Preservation Board). A vessel of this size was suitable for at least a three man operation, permitting a variety of techniques upon reaching the fishing grounds, including line fishing, seining, and cast netting.

The folk tradition on fishing is clear. The most prevalent story within and about the group will illustrate. It goes something like this: A group of Minorcans is in a structured setting of some kind—church, school, or sporting event—and someone yells "Mullet on the beach!" and the place is forthwith emptied of all Minorcan men. One version has a priest remarking that in case of a fire during mass he could empty the church faster by yelling "Mullet on the beach" than by yelling "Fire!"

The importance of fishing is symbolized by an Eastertide event, continued in observance by Minorcan descendents until the turn of the twentieth century. On Good Friday one of the men went about the town dressed as St. Peter. He carried a net which he tried to throw over the gaggles of little boys who taunted him, a game enjoyed by participants as was well as spectators especially when this "fisher of men" was quick enough to snare a hapless boy.

In addition to fish; crabs, shrimp, oysters, and sea turtles and their eggs were gathered or caught as they had been in New Smyrna. Bird's eggs, particularly those of the Black Skimmer, were harvested for use, while gophers continued to grace the stewpots of Minorcan families.

Although able to maintain a monopoly on supplying fish for the town market, Minorcans had competition from Indians in securing fresh game. Contemporary observers saw Indians striding into town with fresh-killed venison slung over their shoulders. During the mid 1780s hunting at any distance from town was restricted to the fearless or hungry in the Minorcan community.

On the local level much of the trading took place in the plaza on the designated market days. Meat, usually pork or beef, was sold there, the latter being brought in from plantations in the hinterland on "beef carts." The Minorcans sold their fish and vegetables from four-foot-square tables while chickens lay trussed nearby ready for sale. Shrimp, oysters, and stone crabs were added to the display. Fruit was hawked from baskets carried about the streets on the head. The Indians added their venison to the market displays (Smith 1869).

A certain amount of bargaining in the well established Mediterranean tradition doubtless took place, even though some prices, especially for bread, were fixed by governmental decree. This haggling was balanced by the opposite practice of throwing in a little extra for relatives, friends, or for favored customers, a practice that we know occurred because of the lexical survival of the word *countra* (Rasico 1987a:214,238,269). The importance of this practice as part of the exchange pattern of the Minorcans continued for many years. It is reported that as late as the 1960s shopkeepers in small stores in St. Johns County were still saying *"countra"* with a smile as they put an extra turnip or egg in with a buyer's purchase.

Money was in short supply in the town and much of economic life of necessity revolved around the barter system. Within the Minorcan group itself a complicated web of relationships and mutual obligations governed individual exchanges. In a direct exchange an evening glass of wine might be paid for with fish or vegetables needed by the wineshop keeper's household. Other times the transfer of goods might not be so simple. A godparent who was a farmer might furnish food or drink for his goddaughter's wedding festivities, but expect nothing in return until perhaps the day when he suffered a crop failure or other bad luck and could count on those families with whom he had godparent ties to help him out.

Sometimes exchanges were more substantial than just paying for a glass of wine with a plump gopher. For example, shopkeeper José Peso de Burgo allowed the poverty stricken family of Jaime Prats to live in a house on his property and farm part of his land, and in exchange the Prats' fourteen-year-old son, Francisco, was given as an apprentice to the Corsican shopkeeper and lived in his household (Ganong 1975:90).

Distribution and redistribution of goods and services within the complicated web of social and economic obligations therefore served as a safety net. Items exchanged did not have an intrinsic worth. Instead the value given and received was personalized, tinged with many different meanings unknown in the kind of strict money economy that was just then coming to the fore in world markets.

12. Little San Felipe

Bent wood is less brittle; it lasts longer.
Minorcan saying

Residential areas within the Minorcan quarter varied somewhat in status, but having said that it must be acknowledged that aside from the basic distinction between the small upper class and the commoners, status and division into social class as we know them are features of the nineteenth and twentieth centuries. In this earlier time notions of esteem and respect, valuing of individual personality, region of origin, and in the case of blacks the *casta* designation all entered into the regard in which a person was held. Nonetheless, there were poorer and richer people in the St. Augustine of 1786-88 and this applied to the Minorcan group as well. As already mentioned, those Minorcans with less means still lived in the Quarter at this time while those rising in the social scale might reside nearer the center of the town where other people of more affluence lived. The very poorest section of the Quarter itself was the northwest section, Blocks 6 and 11 on the Rocque map of 1788, and this two block area has been chosen for closer study.

The two blocks were separated by Cuna Street (called Partners Lane in the British period), the continuance of which reached the center of the quarter a short block to the east. To the west were farm plots and opposite Block 6 on the west was Tolomato cemetery, the path to it leading off from the north side of the block. A map of these two blocks, based on Rocque (1788), is presented in figure 12.1 with the households designated and with kin and godparent connections mapped.

This little neighborhood, hereinafter referred to as Little San Felipe, after the locale of origin of most of the families, was chosen

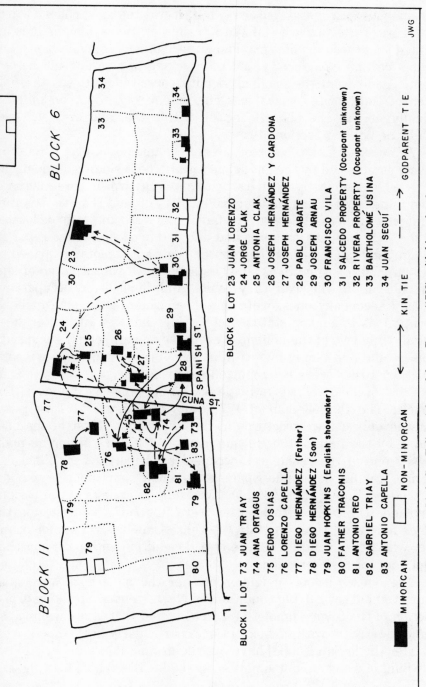

BLOCK 11 LOT 73 JUAN TRIAY
74 ANA ORTAGUS
75 PEDRO OSIAS
76 LORENZO CAPELLA
77 DIEGO HERNÁNDEZ (Father)
78 DIEGO HERNÁNDEZ (Son)
79 JUAN HOPKINS (English shoemaker)
80 FATHER TRACONIS
81 ANTONIO REO
82 GABRIEL TRIAY
83 ANTONIO CAPELLA

BLOCK 6 LOT 23 JUAN LORENZO
24 JORGE CLAK
25 ANTONIA CLAK
26 JOSEPH HERNÁNDEZ Y CARDONA
27 JOSEPH HERNÁNDEZ
28 PABLO SABATE
29 JOSEPH ARNAU
30 FRANCISCO VILA
31 SALCEDO PROPERTY (Occupant unknown)
32 RIVERA PROPERTY (Occupant unknown)
33 BARTHOLOMÉ USINA
34 JUAN SEGUÍ

■ MINORCAN   □ NON-MINORCAN

KIN TIE ◀—▶   GODPARENT TIE ◀---▶

Figure 12.1. Little San Felipe. Adapted from Rocque (1788), with kin and godparent ties added.

for analysis for several reasons. First, it was the most cohesive area
in terms of the town of Old World origin of the residents. It is assumed that these families had known each other for generations, and
that a certain congeniality and interlocking network would be evident. Aside from the original vicinity consistency it was the only
area of the quarter which was almost entirely Minorcan in 1788.
Finally, it was the poorest section within the quarter which was
itself the poorest section of town.

After stating the factor of poverty so unequivocally, it must be
firmly established by the factual material. The residents of the neighborhood were mostly farmers, with plots of two or three acres of
land under cultivation, much smaller plots of land than the average
Minorcan farmer of this era. The farm plots were known to be located
to the west in some instances and inferred in others. None reported
owning any land. Either they rented their small plots or farmed on
Crown land, or sometimes simply staked out a vacant patch of land
for cultivation wherever they could. Additional listed occupations,
usually secondary ones, were mason, mariner, and fisherman. No
occupations of higher status such as merchant or carpenter were
listed. Only two of the families were slave owners, owning one slave
apiece, and one family owned a horse. None owned cows or boats,
or at least they were not reported in any census.

Most of the dwellings in Little San Felipe were hardly more than
hovels. The Purcell map of 1777 (on which figure 10.1 is based)
showed only a few structures in the two blocks. Most of the ones
added by the time of the Rocque map of 1788 were Minorcan-built.
Every one of the residences occupied by Minorcans in Little San
Felipe was of the simple Spanish "common plan" house type, described by Manucy (1962:49-51). According to listings in the Rocque
map index, fifteen of the houses were in "bad" condition and the
other four were rated as "fair." Lorenzo Capella's house, for example, was a "timber frame house in bad condition with palm thatched
roof," a typical description.

The houses in this neighborhood for the most part were little
improvement over living conditions in New Smyrna. Speaking of this
section of the town Vignoles (1823:113) noted that "the dwellings on
the back streets with few exceptions, particularly in the north-west
quarter [little San Felipe] have but the ground floor; and are generally built of wood . . . but almost all are laid with a tabbia flooring."

Little San Felipe was located completely on Crown land, which circled the town on three sides. Those in our little area were thus squatters, people counting on physical occupation of the land and building of houses to give them some claim for a grant of land in the future. Noticeable are some of the houses set back from the street (uncommon in the rest of St. Augustine) as though their occupants hoped to build better houses on the front of their lots at a later time.

As can be seen on the map, the little community centered on Cuna Street, with a web of kin and godparent relationships tieing them together. In contrast, at either end of the two blocks were several non-Minorcan intrusive elements. The south end of Block 11 was occupied by Father Traconis, and next to him was a person referred to as "the English Shoemaker." Father Traconis was the hospital chaplain and the first teacher of the free school. His was the only two-story St. Augustine plan house in the two block area, but even it was in "bad" condition, a structure already on the land when he was granted the property.

Little is known of John Hopkins, the "English Shoemaker," except that his house and lot were both owned by the Crown. He had taken a Minorcan boy as apprentice. perhaps one from a nearby family.

In the middle of the east side of Block 6, Lots 31 and 32 were holdings of a different kind, extensions of the property to the east which had been recently reclaimed by returning Floridanos. Lot 32 contained the only masonry buildings in the block, but they were falling into ruins. Nothing is known as to the possible occupants of the structures on these two lots, although they may have been slaves belonging to the Floridano families in the block to the east.

In the nineteen Little San Felipe Minorcan households lived sixty-eight people. Adding the shoemaker's apprentice brings the total to sixty-nine. The average household size was 3.52, somewhat less than the 4.34 average for the larger sample, a fact which we might expect from the poverty of the neighborhood, since it has already been determined that those with more resources had larger households. Aside from the somewhat larger number of children, a total of thirty (44 percent) twelve years of age or under, the age and sex distribution is approximately the same as in the larger sample of the Minorcan community at this time.

As in the total group, households based on a nuclear family core were the most numerous, accounting for twelve of the nineteen. Next most numerous were the three one-person households. One young man's household had existed in 1784, when brothers Lorenzo and Antonio Carreras and their half-brother Joseph Arnau were domiciled together on Lot 29. After Lorenzo and Joseph married, Antonio continued to live with Lorenzo and his wife for a while, but was living alone in 1788. None had moved from Little San Felipe, however.

Noticeable by their absence were any extended family households, and with only two slaves in the entire nineteen, the households of Little San Felipe were nearly all stripped-down and elementary. At the same time though, extended family complexes, collections of separate family habitations close to each other, were a feature of the area and the neighboring blocks. We already know of the elder Vilas and their extensive family living nearby. They lived on Lot 30 and their daughter María and her husband lived behind them. Both houses were described as in "bad" condition with "palm thatched roof." The social and family life of these two households was somewhat outside the heavy web of relationships along Cuna street which centered in the Ortagus and Clak households.

In the kinship chart of the Ortagus family (figure 12.2) we find that the Ortagus girls were married to Pedro Osias and Pablo Sabate and are found living quite close to Ana, their widowed mother, whose husband Sebastián had died in the summer of 1785. The residence of Sebastián, the son, across town near his wife's family supports our postulated uxorilocal residence rule. Three of the four houses in "fair" condition belonged to the three Ortagus family households in Little San Felipe. The other belonged to Jorge Clak.

Widower Jorge Clak and his sister Antonia lived together before Jorge's marriage to Inés Pablo, a San Felipe native like himself. At first Antonia continued to live in the same household but after the son of Jorge and his new wife reached toddler age and added his noise to that of his half-brothers, Antonia moved to a house on the next lot, perhaps built for her by her brother. The absence of fence separations between these houses assured easy communication and is mute evidence of continuing cordial relations.

Antonia was one of the two spinsters found among the some 600 Minorcans living in St. Augustine. Never-married women were rare indeed in the preindustrial Mediterranean world, and she was well

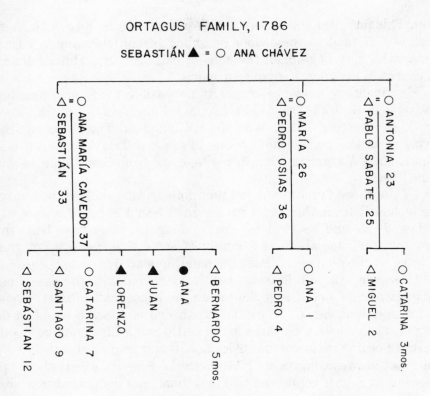

Figure 12.2. Ortagus Family Kinship Chart.

into spinsterhood when she sailed for the New World at the age of thirty-two. As godmother to several Minorcan babies she could not have been severely physically or mentally handicapped, nor would she have survived the rigors of the New Smyrna years had that been the case. It is possible that she was a midwife, a role usually assumed by a mature or older woman who was a widow or single.

Four households with household heads named Hernández lived in Little San Felipe. The son of Diego Hernández, also named Diego, moved from the family home on Lot 77 into a house on Lot 78, one that he may have built for the express purpose of leaving the family hearth. Shortly after the time on which this study concentrates, the younger Diego married a recent widow four years older than himself and presumably brought her and her two children to his new location, making this an instance of virilocal residence. However, her lack of parents in the community may have rendered it the next best solu-

tion. This father and son were not closely related to Joseph Hernández, Lot 27, and his next-door neighbor Joseph Hernández y Cardona, who may have been the sons of half-brothers. Hernández is,
of course, a common Hispanic surname.

Fragmentary evidence makes it impossible to do anything but
guess that Gabriel Triay, Lot 82, and Juan Triay, Lot 73, were
brothers or cousins. Both were from Cuidadela. The choice of Ana
Ortagus as the godmother for one of Gabriel Triay's children was
logical since Margarita Sans, his wife, came from San Felipe, as did
Ana.

Of the three families not yet mentioned, Antonio Reo, who originally hailed from Cuidadela rather than San Felipe, was recently
widowed. He and his twelve-year-old daughter must have been the
two surviving members of a family of some size in New Smyrna,
judging by the number of times the name appeared in early records.

However, Antonio Reo was better connected with the household
complex along Cuna Street than were the households of Bartholomé
Usina and Juan Seguí, at the far north end of Block 6 who had no
godparent ties with the others in the Little San Felipe neighborhood.
Here it becomes evident that block layout and neighborhood clusters
were not always congruent. Entries in the Parish records show the
Usinas and Seguís connected by kin, affinal, and godparent ties with
families to the northeast in the quarter.

Usina's house was built across the foundation of an earlier
Spanish house (Deagan 1974:46), and the family's poverty in the late
eighteenth century gave way to more affluence later, judging by
excavated materials from the house site (McMurray 1975). This lot
is the only one in Little San Felipe on which extensive archaeological
excavations have been conducted.

In 1786 the middle-aged Usinas' fourteen-year-old daughter, Benedita, was living in the Santiago Prats household at the corner of
Cuna and St. George streets, the Prat's own fourteen year old son,
Francisco, as we have seen, was by that time apprenticed to the
shopkeeper, Peso de Burgo, and listed as his dependent. Benedita's
residence away from home runs counter to the usual practice and in
fact she was the only girl of living parents who resided elsewhere
than under the family roof, unless it be with a new spouse. Nearly
a year later she resumed the customary pattern when Antonio Pons
came to claim her as a wife and took her back with him to his farm
in New Smyrna.

Little is known about Juan Seguí except that he was also poor and was part of the large Seguí family. The Seguís accounted for six out of the 152 Minorcan households and hailed from diverse locales in Minorca.

Of the sixty-three Minorcan babies baptized in the years 1785 and 1786, ten were born to Little San Felipe families. Of these ten, two died in infancy, no worse a record than elsewhere in town at that time.

A word about the godparent relationship is necessary because its nature changed under New World conditions. In the Old World tradition the main bond was between godparents and godchild, and only incidentally between the biological parents and the godparents. As the practice was transformed in the Hispanic areas of the New World, and called *compadrazco*, its main locus became the establishment of fictive kinship ties between the parents and the sponsors of their children. The fractures resulting from death, emigration, isolation from extended families, and other factors in a colonial environment made such extra connections crucial for family and community bonding, and even for survival (Mintz and Wolf 1967:174-196). While no complete analysis has been made of the godparent ties in the present case, the parent-to-sponsor relationship seems to have functioned as an important bond in East Florida as in other portions of the Hispanic New World.

We have already talked about the way in which certain names appeared with great frequency in the New World Minorcan group. This was particularly so among the Minorcan islanders and the explanation lies in the fact that they were named according to a definite system. The first of each sex born to a couple were named after the husband's parents, and the second of each sex after the wife's parents. After that, children were named after their own parents if these names had not been used, after another kinsman (particularly aunts or uncles), after a godparent of the same sex, or in honor of a favorite saint, not necessarily in that order of choice. If a family had a large number of children they must have sometimes run out of names, for they started the same naming pattern all over again; and by that time the older children had left the household. If a child died who had one of the grandparent names, the next child of that sex born after the death was usually given that name. The most dramatic example of this is the use of the same name for the next boy born to the Vens family in New Smyrna after their son Guillermo was stoned to death. In the Vila kinship chart (figure 10.2), we see two Antonias in the Juan Vila (the younger) family and two Agatas (Aguedas) in the Matías Pons family, and in both cases the older sibling had died.

This naming pattern often resulted in a long string of the same name for grandfather, father, and son (for example see the Ortagus chart, figure 12.2). On the distaff side, the series of names was always less evident because of the intervening paternal grandmother's name. In total, the use of the same names over and over in a family limited the range of names and this was even more so the higher the death rate in children and the more endogamous the group.

The naming pattern just described is at variance with the other common pattern in the Catholic tradition of naming a child for the saint whose day falls nearest to the child's day of birth. Yet the pattern of so honoring the paternal and maternal grandparents is well documented for parts of Spain even today (See particularly Pitt-Rivers 1961:98, Foster 1960:120) and there can be little question, from the data available, that this custom was imported by the Minorcan islanders.

With so few given names actually in use, and with about the same frequency in 1786 as described in New Smyrna, some confusion between individuals could be expected. This was mitigated in several ways. One of two cousins carrying the grandfather's first name might be designated by his mother's surname also; and thus our Little San Felipe residents Joseph Hernández and Joseph Hernández y Cardona were differentiated.

The use of nicknames was the other method of individualizing. Latter day practice in the St. Augustine Minorcan community and the persistence of nickname usage in present-day Minorca, allow this inference in the absence of documentation. Nicknames picturing some prominent characteristic are even given to whole families, or branches of families, in the Balearic Islands today.

Throughout life, as was the Hispanic way, women used their original family names. All early entries of deaths in the Parish records listed women by their own names and added "wife of" and the husband's name. This was true, but not entirely so, of census enumerations.

Unquestionably, the early age of women at first marriage helps to explain the very few "natural" children as well as those infants born before a decent interval had passed after marriage. In Little

San Felipe, however, Juan Triay did not marry the widow, Juana Ximénes, until after their son, Guillermo, was born, and the Clak baby was born six weeks after his parents marriage.

Before undue immorality can be assumed, we must consider a most curious circumstance. Marriages in St. Augustine in the last half of 1784, and during 1785 and 1786, were all performed in the month of December. The only exception was the marriage of Pedro Salcedo and María Galán on April 20, 1786, whose nuptial vows in Havana, from whence they had recently come to St. Augustine, were evidently questioned by ecclesiastical authorities in Florida.

The last marriage solemnized by Father Camps was in July, 1784. Prior to that time marriages were performed at all times of the year. Although December marriages in 1784, 1785, and 1786 were on different days of that month, and multiple-couple vows therefore cannot be assumed, it may have been easier for the newly arrived priests (Hassett, O'Reilly, and Traconis) to concentrate marriages in a single season.

Faced with a wait of up to a year, many a couple may have decided to contract a secular union until December rolled around and the sacred rite could be performed. After work settled down to a routine in the reorganized parish, marriages were again performed when requested.

In Little San Felipe, Jorge Clak, Juan Triay, Lorenzo Capella, and José Arnau were the newly married men. Being first marriages, Capella and Arnau and their New Smyrna-born brides qualified for the nuptial mass, but like most of their contemporaries probably chose not to take part in the additional sacrament because of the expense.

The marriages of Clak and Triay to widows "qualified" them for an observance of quite a different kind—the *sansarasca*. This word is one of the surviving Catalan words identified, and the durability of this noisy custom was well documented by nineteenth-century observers. Dewhurst (1886:163) explained that "sherivarees [the English word for the custom] are parties of idle people, who dress themselves in grotesque masquerade, whenever a widow or widower is married. They often parade the streets and play buffoon tricks for two or three days, haunting the residence of the new married pair, and disturbing the whole city with noise and riot." The "idle people" were mostly the young men of the Minorcan community hoping that the disguises would protect them from the wrath of their elders. Other surviving words such as *musclamo* and *rabat*, both referring to noise, and particularly *camera doanda*, glossed as "causing noise or confusion in the night," probably refer to this practice. This custom was common, and still is, throughout the Mediterranean and other parts of Europe (Pitt-Rivers 1961:169-170) and endures as the "charivari" or "shivaree" in remote corners of the Anglo-Celtic world as well. Solemnizing marriages in the December festival season in St. Augustine at least confined the noise to a time of the year when the shutters were closed.

Along with Benedita Usina, two other girls in Little San Felipe were of marriageable age, Antonia Reo and Martina Hernández. Minorcan girls anywhere from eleven to sixteen years of age, depending on the age of puberty or confirmation at one end and the age of marriage at the other, had a time of special customs and events. Customs and observances functioned as they do anywhere else to move the girl during this period from the status of child to that of adult woman.

Young women and their ways must have been quite visible in the St. Augustine community, for scarcely a nineteenth-century writer who mentioned the Minorcans failed to speak of the girls of marriageable age. Bemrose (1966:10) typically said, "Their young women are handsome, with black eyes and long black hair, the countenance usually wearing the smile of contentment, through absence of anxiety as to their wants, which are few."

As is generally true in the Latin tradition, young girls were serenaded. A young Minorcan man interested in the girl of the house came with a group of his friends to stand near an appropriate balcony, window, or, one guesses, door in the case of the huts in our small neighborhood, to play their guitars and sing, often songs of their own composition. Before departing, the young man—in Antonia Reo's case he would have been Bartolomé Sintes, her future husband—separated himself from his friends to say a special "good night."

During the carnival seasons more freedom was granted to the young girls than at other times of the year. They were allowed to take part in the masquerading, especially in the daytime. During carnival time the young women held "posey dances" in their homes. Stories of the custom vary, but the description of it by twenty-two-year-old 2nd Lt. Alfred Beckley who actually took part in it himself during his initial tour of duty in St. Augustine in 1824 is probably the most reliable:

> During the carnival season the Minorcan ladies kept up for eleven nights what they called "Posey dances." For the first dance they chose a Posey King and Queen and paid the cost by donations. But on the second night the Posey Queen holding two bouquets of Spanish pinks in her hands, by the presentation of these to any gentleman made him Posey King for the next dance and he chose his Queen by presenting one of the bouquets to any lady made her his Queen and he had to pay the costs of the party. The Minorcan ladies prepared an altar of a number of steps or shelves called a Posey Altar, tastily and profusely decorated with the rich Florida flowers lighted up with wax candles, and it made a splendid spectacle (Eby 1964:318).

But this cycle of dances, as previously mentioned, commenced with another cycle, that of a novena held by the women in one of the homes for nine nights in honor of Santa Elena. In the midst of the joy of youth the shortness of life was never forgotten. This initiation of a joyful celebration with a funereal element, with mature women carrying extensive roles in the first part of the festival, is one close to the heart of Hispanic culture and can still be found at the beginning of some of the patronal fiestas in the Spain of today (Kenny 1969:96-97).

Deaths were somber occasions in St. Augustine, but even there a certain pageantry surrounded the funeral and burial. In Little San Felipe the funerals for the two infants who died, and especially for Sebastián Ortagus (the older) who died on July 8, 1785, were probably not much different from the Minorcan funeral practices observed in 1831 by Bemrose (1966:11). He found that "even death for the people seems to have lost his terrors! When death happens, the deceased is laid out and decked in finery. The body is surrounded by eight large silver candles, during day and night. Some are even laid out upon the side walk, so that the passer-by may show his respect by examining the spectacle."

Just as births, marriages and deaths—markers along the course of each person's life—were ceremonial occasions, the many holidays and celebrations formed an annually recurring cycle closely nested

Harper's New Monthly Magazine, January, 1875.

Figure 12.3. A Fromajardis Serenade.

in the culture of the community. The festival round, including the Fromajardis (figure 12.3), partly obliterated on the plantation, could burst forth in full flower again once the Minorcans had come to St. Augustine and readjusted their lives. A slave who first came to St.

Augustine in the second Spanish period writing his memoirs some years later remarked that "many were the days in the calendar for celebration and public festivity," and added that "the people are the gayest I can imagine. Serenades, processions, balls, picnics that they call 'convites,' masquerades, came the year round in constant procession" (Smith 1869). He especially remarked on St. Johns Day when "three days preceded by many evenings of carnival were passed in masking in the streets." Another contemporary observer, Ambrose Hull, a new settler, writing a letter to his sister in the north from New Smyrna where he had built a house atop the massive foundation ruins on the old Turnbull plantation, told her that he expected to make a visit into St. Augustine for "this is the season for dancing there" (Rutherford 1952:33). The letter was dated June 27, 1805 and thus refers to the midsummer festivities of St. Johns Eve.

These days and even weeks of high excitement which punctuated the lives of the Minorcans were times when those living in the neighborhood of Little San Felipe could forget for a time how close they still were to a subsistence level. The monotony of their routine days was somewhat different.

Most of daily domestic life took place in the family compound within the high fences. House entries, when Rocque mapped the town, were generally offstreet, providing some measure of seclusion; taverns and shops with doors on the street side were the major exception. The practice of facing the loggias (arbors were probably the rule in this poorer section of town) to the south and east to catch the prevailing winds in the summer and to protect against the winds of the winter season (Manucy 1962:61) prevented the opening of one dwelling from facing that of another household. With little privacy in a family house or compound, at least there was some privacy from the neighbors, although the location of fence lines show this to be less true of closely related families living near each other. However, caution must be used when speaking of privacy, for it is a relative term. In the era under discussion, there was little privacy as we know it today, either within the household or in the community. Life was lived in a very public arena.

Kitchens were either a part of the only room or in a smaller second room, as those which can be seen on the map (figure 12.1) attached to the Vila, Arnau, Usina and Capella dwellings. Some houses had smoke holes but Manucy (1962:123) believes "the mosquitoes were worse in these ventilated ones." Cooking by the poor was done in open pots or braziers, easily moved outdoors in the warm months, perhaps to a palm thatched lean-to protected from the rain. The small structures two or three *varas* from the houses, and more prominent in Little San Felipe than in other sections of town, may have been kitchens for they were mostly found near one-room houses. If not kitchens or sheds for livestock, they were probably privies.

Each household had its own shallow-water well, useful for other purposes as well as supplying water. On hot, still summer nights, so the folk tradition goes, it was the practice to put one's head down in a well, the nearer the well to the bayfront the better, to listen for the distinctive croaking, throbbing sounds of the black drum, a common fish in local waters.

We can picture a typical summer day with most of the men, often accompanied by other members of the household as well, heading for the farm plots with farm tools slung over their shoulders, perhaps some of them pulling carts behind them. The men would have been dressed in blouse and breeches and the women in the more traditional Minorcan garb of shift, full skirt, an apron over all, their hair hanging down their backs in one long plait nearly to the heels, and perhaps a *rebozilla* (*rebocillo*) on their heads.

The *rebozilla* is a distinctly Minorcan head covering. It is a semicircular cloth, 1.30 meters in diameter, fastened tightly under the chin so that it frames the face, the extra cloth falling down the back almost to the waist (Foster 1960:98). When made of white cloth it makes the face look fuller, as does the old-fashioned headdress of the nun's habit which it resembles.

If the fish were running, farming or other activities might be suspended for the day, to the delight of the small boys who could then go along with their fathers, grandfathers, and uncles.

The usual breakfast of bread dressed with oil was eaten early; this traditional Minorcan way of starting the day was in later years adapted with the addition of vinegar and salt and pepper into what Minorcan descendents now call "bread salad." Later in the morning in this earlier time, those who remained at home would start the customary vegetable stew, enhanced by fortuitous additions of fish or meat, or perhaps a gopher, left to simmer while the women and girls went about their other work, those like the Ortagus women

Gift of Fernando A. Rubió.
St. Augustine Historical Society.
Figure 12.4. Old World Female Minorcan Dress.

perhaps sharing common chores. Judging from the ordinary practice in Minorca, if the men did not expect to return in time for the midday meal, they took along ingredients and made up a stew for themselves at their work site.

Gift of Fernando A. Rubió.
St. Augustine Historical Society.
Figure 12.5. Old World Male Minorcan Dress.

Keeping clean was easier than in New Smyrna. Even the poorest family could obtain whitewash to apply to the house inside and out, as much for the discouragement of the ubiquitous insects as for appearances sake. The fences, made of odd collections of boards, or poles, or Spanish bayonet plants rather than masonry in this poor neighborhood, probably also served as clotheslines for the few clothes and other linens when they were washed.

Time had to be spent in mending the clothes and making new ones, in collecting Spanish moss to freshen the mattress pallets, in attending to the babies, the pigs and chickens, and the small kitchen gardens; time which left a woman little leisure.

The middle of the day was a welcome interlude in a hot climate; then the main meal was eaten, followed by the afternoon siesta, a practice resumed after the New Smyrna years.

Men and women spent their evenings quite differently. If they were not engaged in night fishing, the men's evenings were spent in the taverns. Using kin and godparent relationships as indicators we can be almost certain that those in Little San Felipe assembled either in the wineshop run by Marcial Pons a short block away or in Juan Carreras's establishment further up St. George Street. Women and children spent their evenings closer to home, maybe turning in early, especially in winter, to save the few homemade candles or the supply of lamp oil.

The sounds of an ordinary day we can guess at, but the smells must have been a rare blend. The perfume of the flowering plants and trees and the pungent onion-garlic-pepper fragrance of the stews could not overcome the latrine and animal odors, the bits of rotting fish clinging to the fishnets and the wafting vapors of corpses in the nearby cemetery, the last described by Father O'Reilly as "harmful to the health" (Coomes 1976). Situated close to the burial ground, Block 6 residents must have been all too aware of the last, especially when the breeze came from the west.

The church and the people's religion permeated life, binding all together in the present and giving promise of an afterlife. Daily mass was attended by some, especially the women, and on Holy days and Sunday it was obligatory. The women could often be seen hurrying to mass before their daily chores began, their heads covered with their *rebozillas*, usually white, and wearing slippers of their own manufacture. Dark veils were worn to church later in the day or at certain times of the Lenten season and assuredly by those in mourning.

The women sat on the floor in the middle of the sanctuary on whatever they had brought from home to ease themselves, while the

men sat around the edges. After mass on Sunday, merrymaking and
a certain amount of trading went on in the plaza.

By this time, those in Little San Felipe no longer attended mass
at the nearby chapel on St. George Street, but walked to the building
on the plaza where they mingled with the rest of the townsfolk.
While they still had the comfort of their own priest, Father Camps,
more feeble all the time, had cut back on his parish work. He continued to minister to the sick and dying among his flock, soothing
them in their familiar language, but he preached less sermons than
formerly. One of the delights of his declining years was the visit of
a bishop who could speak the Catalan language with the Minorcan
people.

It was in July of 1788 that a bishop first visited the newly regained province of East Florida to investigate religious life. This was
the first time that any of the original colonists of the Minorcan community had seen a bishop since they had arrived in Florida twenty
years before. In fact, those born in the New World had never been
confirmed. The way in which this visit came about involved a Minorcan woman, so it is appropriate to tell of it here.

Sometime during the British period Antonia Garriga, born in
Alayor, Minorca, married an Englishman. Her husband had a
mulatto daughter who lived with them. This husband died, and when
given the opportunity, Antonia decided to take her stepdaughter and
emigrate to the Bahamas with the departing British. She was, however, shipped back and forth between British and Spanish ships before leaving from Fernandina and finally sent back to St. Augustine
for the governor to handle since it had become apparent that she was
engaging in prostitution. She then married Francisco Selort, a
Minorcan islander with whom she lived in the "Greek Quarter" along
with the stepdaughter whom Francisco listed as a "mulatto slave."
Antonia's reputation became even worse, and it also came to the
attention of the authorities that she was a bad influence on her stepdaughter. After severe warnings from Father Hassett and a bout in
jail she was ultimately deported to Havana, while Father Hassett
had the stepdaughter baptized and placed with a respectable family
in St. Augustine. In Havana, Antonia complained of Father Hassett's
treatment of her, and claimed that she had been illegally deported.
It was this incident in addition to certain moral irregularities on the
part of the garrison recently come to the attention of the authorities,

that brought about the visit to East Florida of Fray Cyril de Barcelona, Auxiliary Bishop and Vicar of the Joint Province of Louisiana-West Florida.

The bishop soon learned the truth about Antonia's complaints and went about more important business. His investigations yielded the conclusion that the ecclesiastical work of Father Camps was commendable. He found that the other priests were in general conducting themselves properly, but in response to some complaints he urged Fathers Hassett and O'Reilly to preach more instead of leaving the bulk of this job to Father Camps and Father Traconis. It seems that Father Hassett's difficulty with languages also made him a very poor speaker. Father Hassett was further faulted, probably by one of the Minorcans, for not holding proper rogation processions to insure bountiful crops. Otherwise the bishop found things more or less in order in the parish except for the number of slaves who needed the sacrament of baptism. Any slave owner, he decreed, could suffer excommunication from the Church if household slaves were not baptized. Of the fifty-eight slaves held by the Minorcans as recorded in the 1786 census only twelve (21 percent) were baptized. This was no worse a record than for the other households in the town and province. The two slaves in the Little San Felipe area, those belonging to Juan Triay and Pablo Sabate, were neither one baptized.

The bishop was particularly impressed with the way that the free school for boys was operating. Father Hassett had previous experience organizing schools in his prior parish in Philadelphia, and Father Traconis, who was responsible for the lower grades, was an excellent teacher. A layman, José Iguíñez, taught the higher grades. One church historian concluded that "the rules under which the school was conducted are still striking for their high standards, respect for discipline, and practical good sense" (Gannon 1967:93). Reading, writing, and arithmetic were the subjects taught in addition to church doctrine and befitting behavior. The capacity of each individual student was to be assessed so that he could advance properly in his subjects, and standards were set for the teachers. No boy could advance until the material had been thoroughly learned. The rules were strict and the children helped to keep up the building. School hours were long—seven o'clock in the morning until sunset, with two hours off in the middle of the day for the boys who lived near enough to go home for dinner and siesta. The requirement that only Spanish

St. Augustine Historical Society.

Figure 12.6. The Juan Triay House, built about 1806.

be spoken in the school must have been difficult to enforce at first, but a knowledge of spoken and written Spanish put these youngsters ahead of their illiterate, Catalan-speaking elders. Far-reaching changes that always occur when an institution replaces the tutorial function of the family began to alter the way of life in Little San Felipe and in the rest of the Minorcan community.

During weekdays those boys in Little San Felipe walked south past the plaza joining boys from all over town and the outlying areas to arrive at the school on time. There was to be no fooling around on the way and if they met an adult they were to salute with proper courtesy. School, obligatory for the white boys, was allowed, but not required, for the black boys, who could sit only in the back. They could attend if their parents, in the case of the free blacks, or their masters, in the case of the slaves, would release them from their duties.

The shantytown area that we have been discussing, although considered separately here, was well integrated into the rest of the Minorcan community through kinship, economic, and religious ties. Nor does the expression "culture of poverty" fit, because the people in the neighborhood lived very much as their fellows did elsewhere in town, just a little more precariously. The way up the social and economic ladder was through effort and ingenuity, and his friends and family did not think less of a man if he did not or could not choose that course. Almost all of the Little San Felipe households had connections with better-off relatives, and godparenting patterns show few discernable status determinants at this time. Sebastián Ortagus the younger had married into the Cavedo family, Jorge and Antonia Clak's sister had married one of the Perpals, and Juan Seguí counted Bernardo Seguí, the trader, as one of his relatives.

Juan Triay and Pablo Sabate, the slave owners, showed more upward mobility than their neighobrs. By 1787 Sabate had increased the one and a half acres reported in 1784 to a total of twenty acres, and was asking for more. Triay's landholdings also increased, and soon after the turn of the century he was able to build a substantial two-story coquina house where his *barraca* had once been (figure 12.6). It is the only house built by one of the Minorcan families in this two block area which is still standing today. It illustrates the fact that a gain in affluence did not necessarily mean a move across town; many families chose to continue living on the same property, making thereon any needed improvements.

13. An Upwardly Mobile Family

A brother's love is a dog's love.
Old Minorcan saying

Despite the description of the Minorcans by George Fairbanks, a nineteenth-century historian, as an "unambitious class of inhabitants, with their strong attachments, and local ties" (1858:191), upwardly mobile trends in some families were discernible as early as 1784 when Spain regained East Florida. Land, slaves and livestock had been acquired and a few traders and merchants were doing well. Individual entrepreneurship was only one way of getting ahead. A fortunate marriage, rather than sweat of the brow, boosted some families. The Cavedos (figure 13.1) were such a family.

The original spelling, Quevedo, gave way in the later documents to Cavedo, indicating a lowering of the first vowel. Such pronunciation shifts often took place in the names of the colonists under the influence of the English, Spanish, and later, American languages. Cavedo is used in the following material in the interest of clarity.

The Cavedos, like their compatriots discussed in the previous chapter, were from San Felipe. Santiago Cavedo and his wife, Inés Victori, came with the original colony. With them were at least four children: Ana María, nineteen years; Inés, eighteen years; Juan, six years, and Mariana, three years. Ana María and Inés were both above the usual marriage age upon arrival at New Smyrna, and although we cannot be absolutely certain that they were unmarried at that time, the lack of any documented children for either at this period indicates that they were single in the early years on the plantation. Perhaps the family suffered from starvation in Minorca and the girls were discouraged from bringing home husbands to share in the diminishing food supply.

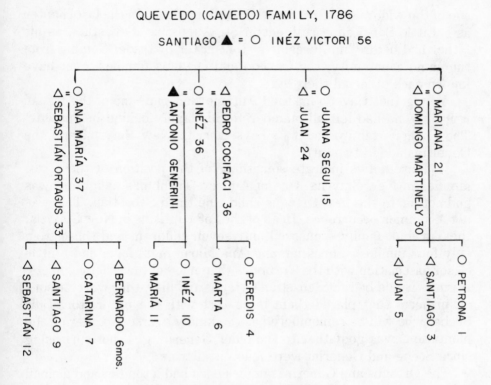

Figure 13.1. Cavedo Family Kinship Chart.

Whether Santiago ever lived to see the New World is questionable. His name did not appear in any of the documents, and no further children were listed among the baptisms. His name is inferred from the names of his grandsons, and his presence assumed because no documented case can be found of a widow and children being permitted to sail with Turnbull. In any case, Inés was listed as a widow by the time she reached St. Augustine.

The life of the family in New Smyrna was probably an average one, the three women working together in the fields, taking the younger two children along. Within four years after arrival, little Juan was ten years old, old enough to work in the boys' special work crew.

The marriages of the two girls in the middle years of the colony, probably about 1773 and 1774, must have brought a welcome male element into the family. Ana María married Sebastián Ortagus, the

son of the widow Ana Ortagus who was introduced in the last chapter
as a Little San Felipe resident in St. Augustine. Sebastián, as his
father had before him, became a stonecutter by trade. Coming from
the same community, the Cavedo and Ortagus families must have
known each other all their lives.

Young Inés Cavedo married Antonio Generini, one of the Italian
recruits who had left all members of his family behind in Tuscany.
The Ortagus family had two boys born in New Smyrna and the
Generinis added two girls.

Godparent ties indicate something of the position of these two
families in New Smyrna. One of Andrew Turnbull's daughters was
godmother to the first Ortagus child, the third Sebastián. This was
not a common occurrence. In all of the 258 baptisms in New Smyrna,
the Turnbull family sponsored only seven children, and those from
only four families. Sebastián and Ana María must have had a little
closer association with the Turnbulls than most of the other colonists.
A guess would be that Sebastián Ortagus and his father were masons
on projects that placed them in contact with the proprietor. Luis
Soche, who will be remembered as the kindly overseer/driver on the
plantation, was godfather to the older Generini girl, not surprising
since Soche and Generini were fellow Italians.

The Ortagus and Generini families each had a toddler and a small
baby at the time of the flight to St. Augustine. At about that same
time Antonio Generini died. Inés did not remain a widow very long
before she married Pedro Cocifaci, the Corsican Greek, who as we
have already hinted, became and remained during his lifetime a very
substantial, if colorful, citizen.

In St. Augustine, Inés Victori (Cavedo), like the others in the
colony, probably initially occupied a hastily constructed hut in the
quarter, perhaps near her fellow townspeople from San Felipe. However, by the middle 1780s the fortunes of the family had improved.
In addition to the favorable Cocifaci marriage of daughter Inés, the
son Juan had married Juana Seguí, the daughter of the successful
merchant, Bernardo Seguí. In 1786 Inés Victori was living with the
newlyweds. Juan had set himself up as a tailor, and in addition to his
wife and mother, he had a fourteen-year-old apprentice and a female
slave. It is not clear where the household was located in 1786, but in
the 1787 census Cavedo is listed as living "in front of the treasury,"
at that time by the bayfront north of the plaza. In the following year

St. Augustine Historical Society.

Figure 13.2. The Cavedo House (foreground): Andres Ximénes and Bernardo Seguí houses immediately beyond.

when Rocque platted his map, the household was located south of the plaza on Hospital (now Aviles) street, just down the block from Bernardo Seguí and immediately next door to another of Bernardo's properties. The land and house may have been given to the young couple by the bride's father. The house was described as having a thin wall of tabby and being in "fair" condition on the Rocque map index. A photograph of the house which was still standing in the late nineteenth century (figure 13.2) shows it to be one of the older styles built in the first Spanish period, or at least the street-fronting wall appears to be a facade which might once have been a part of a flat-roofed house. The southern portico, or perhaps room, shown on the Rocque map was gone by the time that the picture was taken. A smaller structure, probably the kitchen, was on the lot, near the southern boundary. The filled door and window openings of this house are still visible today as part of the wall at the corner of Aviles and Cádiz streets, property now owned by the Sisters of St. Joseph.

Earlier, in 1778, soon after reaching St. Augustine, when she was thirteen years old, the youngest Cavedo girl, Mariana, married Domingo Martinelli, a native of Venice, the same Martinelli who carved out a place for himself by captaining a ship to international ports. According to the age given in the Hassett census, thirty years, he would have been a young lad of twelve years when he embarked for the New World from the port of Mahón. We know that he is one of the original colonists because he is listed in the parish records in New Smyrna, and also his is the third signature on the Italian-Greek memorial swearing allegiance to the Spanish Crown at the beginning of the second Spanish period. A youth of tender years could be set early upon the course of manhood in the troubled times of the eighteenth-century Mediterranean.

In St. Augustine the Martinelli family lived in the southeast corner of the Minorcan quarter, by the waterfront, near the other mariners in town. Their house was one of the best and largest in the quarter. It was described as a timber frame house in "good" condition in the Rocque index and is shown on the map as having three long, narrow rooms. The house was probably constructed in the British period. The household also included an unbaptized male slave and a baptized female slave, and by 1786 there were three Martinelli children. Martinelli owned another house and lot on St. George Street, a block north of the plaza.

Meanwhile, Sebastián Ortagus and his wife, the oldest Cavedo girl, were living in a house, exact location unknown, owned by him and his three brothers-in-law—Martinelli, Cocifaci, and Juan Cavedo. The 1784 census entry for Ortagus described a "house and its grounds in community with three brothers-in-law . . . he lives in said house near the Principal Church." Fixing the exact location is a little difficult, but it is presumed that the family lived near the plaza where Hassett established the church when he reached town that same year.

The connection of these four men for economic purposes was a function of the matrifocal (woman-centered) connection through the Cavedo family, or conversely, the marriage ties may have resulted from mutual business interests. However, where uxorilocal residence is the rule, the brother-in-law relationship becomes an important one, and the relationship with the blood brother less important, since a brother may live across town or even in another community near his own wife's people. Structurally, then, the husbands of a closely related group of women were automatically welded into a unit for certain joint ventures. Cocifaci, the oldest and most affluent, was in a prime position to be the hub or center of this developing cartel.

Pedro Cocifaci's stubborn opportunism threaded through all of his life activities. As a single man in Corsica he had bound himself to Turnbull for a period of six years service. In his deposition against Turnbull he documented his part in the rebellion at the colony's beginning. He boarded a schooner in the river because he was afraid of being shot if identified as one of the rebels. When the ship was captured and taken back to the plantation, one of the clerks told Turnbull that Cocifaci intended to kill him (Turnbull), which Pedro claimed was not true. Nonetheless, he received a lashing. He tried to escape again, was caught and given fifty more lashes and required to wear a twenty-eight pound chain for a month.

After six years Cocifaci asked Turnbull for his discharge and for the land promised him. Turnbull refused, so Pedro again decided to run away; whereupon Turnbull discovered the plot and told him that he must work four more years with security and six without. Presumably this meant that he had to start all over to earn his passage to the New World and then work toward his land claim during the last six years.

By 1777 Pedro Cocifaci was understandably bitter. He claimed that he had seen people forced to eat alligators and even cowhide that was given to them to make moccasins. He ended his deposition saying that he "verily believes if he was to relate everything that was done on the Plantation, there would be no end to it" (C.O. 5/ 557:473).

In St. Augustine, Cocifaci prospered. By the time of Florida's return to Spain, he and his family lived in a house located on St. George Street, described as "on the way to the Minorcan chapel." The house was just south of the quarter proper and on the north edge of where the "better" citizens lived. He owned three slaves, conducted his business from buildings on the waterfront, owned a schooner and ran his wineshop on the side.

Having much to lose, Cocifaci was not happy about casting his lot with the Spanish. Rather than stay after the British evacuated, he decided to sail to Dominica. For the third time in his life he boarded a ship to avoid an unpleasant situation, or perhaps this might be counted the fourth time since we know nothing of what circumstances caused his exit from Corsica. Again he was thwarted. According to a contemporary English account he was "an industrious man, who after being on board a Vessel in order to settle under a British Government at Domenica [*sic*] was detained by Authority . . . until falling sick" (Statement made by George Miller, Charlestown, S.C., November 15, 1787, Treasury 77/7:204).

This episode did not prevent Cocifaci from signing the memorial of the Greeks and Italians swearing eternal allegiance to Spain and declaring "readiness as such to sacrifice our lives in royal service" (Lockey 1949:232). His was the first signature affixed to the document; fitting, as he was the one of the most stature in the group and the signators appear to be in rank order.

Contrary to his fears, Pedro Cocifaci and his family prospered under the Spanish. He had added one more slave, for a total of four, by 1786, making him one of the largest slaveholders of the original colonial group. By 1788 he owned a large two-story stone house in good condition, located next door to the Spanish treasury near the bayfront, which served as home and business quarters.

Cocifaci still owned the property on St. George street, and as was sometimes the custom, allowed Joaquín Matoste (variously spelled Macheochi, Macoqui and Madsoqui), another member of the original colony, to build his house on other land that he owned in the same block. Matoste, a mariner from Tuscany, was sometimes listed in the documents as master of the *San Pedro* on its various voyages (Lockey papers: document dated March 14,1786) attesting to his role in the Cocifaci-Martinelli-Cavedo-Ortagus trading complex.

By 1787, Cocifaci, in addition to his "shop of dry goods and drinks," found time to oversee the cultivation of his forty to fifty acres of land, as well as his other enterprises.

The business interests of this enterprising Greek were quite diversified. When Father Camps died in 1790, Pedro Cocifaci and Bernardo Seguí became the executors of the priest's will. The settlement of the estate was slow, and when there was a hint that the accounts rendered by Cocifaci were questionable, Seguí, in a huff, asked to be relieved of his duties as executor. This whole affair may have caused some hard feelings in the family, given the connection of the two men through the Cavedo family.

Cocifaci undertook obligations as counsel or lawyer-in-fact with families outside the Minorcan community as well. He and Francisco Fatio became counsel for John Hudson and his wife, Mary Evans, in some complex litigation involving sizable debts incurred by Hudson as he systematically went through his wife's fortune (left to her by another husband), and which later included criminal charges also. An association with Fatio, one of the wealthiest and most influential citizens in both the British and second Spanish regimes (Parker 1988), is an indication of Cocifaci's increasing prominence in the town. In the Hudson matter, however, it was Cocifaci who bowed out when the case dragged on, leaving Fatio to cope with what he termed "this disgusting case" (Griffin 1977b:57-76).

In spite of his marriage into and heavy involvement with the Minorcan community, Cocifaci remembered his Greek heritage enough to insist on the Greek names, Marta and Peredis, for his two daughters.

How closely the brothers-in-law were involved in economic activities is not totally known. That they owned land together is certain, and it appears that Martinelli may have been the sea arm of the enterprise. He was prominent enough in the second Spanish period to be mentioned frequently in the official correspondence particularly as the captain of the *San Pedro*, which it seems was the schooner owned by Cocifaci. Several times when food, particularly wheat flour, was needed in the province Martinelli was dispatched to New York with a letter from Governor Zéspedes to the Spanish chargé d'affaires, Diego de Gardoqui, to secure provisions (Lockey papers: documents dated 6/30/1786, 7/1/1786, 8/20/1786).

Sebastián Ortagus had changed his occupation from stonecutter to mariner by 1787. The unlikelihood of a Minorcan family man becoming a mariner at the age of more than thirty years may give a hint that he was working more closely in the family trading complex by then. One can guess that goods for manufacture into clothing were brought by Martinelli in the *San Pedro*, to be distributed by either Bernardo Seguí or Pedro Cocifaci. Eventually some of these goods reached young Juan Cavedo for manufacture into clothes for his customers. The best evidence that we have of the close social and business relationship among the four men is the godparent web growing denser with time and with the new births in the family. The social life probably revolved around Cocifaci's wineshop.

What of the women in the family? Their lives would have centered around their homes and church, for the church was the only place where women met in large assemblages. Unlike their poorer relatives in the quarter they were able to wear white satin slippers to church for special occasions and may have forsaken their traditional Minorcan *rebozilla* for the more fashionable lace *mantilla*. For the women of the Cavedo and Ortagus families, the nearby *Placita de las Higueras* afforded an opportunity to mix with the higher status women of the town.

Inés Cavedo, as the matriarch of the family, was well respected in the community, for she, like her son-in-law Pedro Cocifaci, was godparent to a number of children, and her age, fifty-six years in 1786, perhaps qualified her to be a midwife for the Minorcan group. One entry in the baptismal records supports this notion. She was godmother to the child, Inés Ana Antonia, whose parents are described as "unknown" and who was taken in by Leonora Genopoly to nurse along with her own new baby. The godfather of baby Inés, who was baptized on the day of her birth, November 17, 1786, was Lorenzo Capó, the sacristan. In this instance Inés Cavedo may have served as the midwife for some unfortunate girl delivered of a "natural child."

The Cavedo family, as a feature of their social standing, enjoyed a closer connection with the wider community than did their fellows from the Turnbull colony. At least two of the three girls and the son had married well. The family counted two Italians and one Greek as sons-in-law—from ethnic groups better integrated with the town than were the Minorcan islanders. Then, as various of the households reached a position of greater prominence they began to act as godparents to Catholic families outside the original settler group. At the same time they did not neglect the ties with their own community, including their own less prosperous kinfolk and those from their hometown of San Felipe.

14. Afterword

Good and evil are all the same when they are past.
Old Minorcan saying

In this twenty-year glimpse of the Florida Minorcan community in the making, we have seen how an aggregate of people—a diverse collection of individuals and families from traditional Mediterranean cultures—full of hope, set out on a disorienting voyage to the New World, how they experienced a death-camp like existence on an indigo plantation, and how, in desperation, they fled, like the exodus from Egypt, to the sanctuary of St. Augustine where they reordered their familiar way of life.

During this period (1768-1788), unfolding world events outside their own isolated world altered the course of their fortunes. That they came together in the first place was set about by the need to populate a newly acquired British province and the consequent grandiose dream of a Scottish physician bent on an empire in the New World, a not unusual dream for an upperclass man of those expansive times in Great Britain. These prospects turned to desperation in the Florida wilderness as the proprietor tried to turn Mediterranean colonists, long accustomed to independence, into slaves on his plantation. Then the burgeoning American Revolution, as well as a change of the power axis in England by which a new governor was assigned to East Florida and through which the proprietor fell out of favor, afforded the Minorcans a chance to escape. By then the Minorcan community, including the Greeks, Italians, and other nationals, was welded into unity by language, similarity of cultures, intermarriage, isolation on the Florida frontier, and oppression jointly suffered. Soon the American Revolution itself with the resultant influx of Tories into Florida gave the Minorcans a chance to better themselves

in the boomtown that British St. Augustine became. At last, the
fortuitous return of East Florida to Spain by the Treaty of Paris
allowed the community to become the core population of an Hispanic
capital.

    While the course of events on the world stage altered their for-
tunes from without, other things were happening on the micro-level
of the community itself. The settlers experienced constant sickliness
and the deaths of loved ones and friends, even murders at the hands
of the overseers and drivers on the plantation, all the while building
rustic shelters in a wilderness where they tried valiantly to sustain
life. Low level irritants, but none the less important on the plantation, were the unfamiliar dispersed settlement pattern imposed upon
them, the unaccustomed work group format necessary for monocul-
ture, and the interruption of the work-holiday rhythms to which they
were accustomed in the Mediterranean.

    In St. Augustine, the survivors of this devastating experience
were able to put the pieces of their cultural mosaic back together.
They regrouped in the village format and hinterland relationship
comfortable for them. Former subsistence patterns incorporating
several occupations and sidelines re-emerged for each family, that
repertoire by then enhanced and shifted by more than a decade's
knowledge of the Florida environment. Similarly, the customary
church and folk holidays were reestablished in harmony with these
working patterns. The population stabilized in St. Augustine and the
community began to grow in numbers. A few of the group had risen
in the town, but family and kin networks still kept them close to their
less affluent fellows.

    The next few years after the close of the present story were
times of change for the Minorcan community, times which both altered and at the same time solidified them as a group. Father Camps
died in 1790 and the "sub-parish" of San Pedro disappeared with him,
so that henceforth they were part, but especially at first, a principal
part, of the St. Augustine parish. Indian hostilities increased causing
the abandonment of many of the outlying farms and plantations.
Then when tensions with the new United States to the north erupted
into border warfare, the Minorcan men fought valiantly in the militia,
and even the women played their part. We know of the women's role
from a letter written by an American soldier to his mother in the
north in 1812 when "patriot" troops had St. Augustine under siege.

He described how Minorcan girls along the North River enticed his comrades to their deaths (Patrick 1954:171).

Once Florida became a United States territory loyalties shifted. They then knew Americans as individuals, and intermarriages were taking place between Minorcan girls and men from the southern frontier. By the time of the Civil War the Minorcans were almost all southern sympathizers. A majority of the names on the Confederate monument in the plaza of St. Augustine are Minorcan, and the women, again using beauty as their weapon, acted as spies among the Union troops stationed in the town, promptly relaying information to the Confederates encamped inland on the St. Johns River.

Under the influence of the English language in the years after the Spanish left, the *menorquin* dialect of Catalan began to fade as a hearth language, although a few words, largely expletives, have survived to the present day. In the same fashion, the impact of another culture took its toll on Minorcan celebrations and customs, although like the language, certain ones, notably the Fromajardis serenade, continued into the early twentieth century.

The Catholic church as a center of community life and the cohesiveness of the families are two aspects which remain important in the modern community, as does also an intimate relationship with the natural environment. In certain more indigenous sectors the cry "mullet on the beach!" still brings pickup trucks trundling down the highway to the beach, hauling wooden dories behind them. An independence and resiliency is still characteristic of those who call themselves Minorcans. The attachment of the people to St. Augustine is marked, leading to a belief held by some that it is unhealthy to leave St. Augustine, that it might even cause a person to sicken or die.

What of those singled out in this work for consideration? Pablo Sabate, the records tell us, continued to rise from his humble beginnings in the Little San Felipe neighborhood, as it has been called here, securing in subsequent years large land holdings, later inherited by his daughter who married Antonio Alvarez, a several-term mayor of St. Augustine. Likewise, Francisco Pellicer, the leader of the exodus from New Smyrna, added to his extensive holdings and played an important part in the Indian wars. Among his descendents, Anthony Domingo Pellicer became the first bishop of San Antonio, Texas, and Dominic Matthew Manucy (also descended from José Manuci) became bishop of Mobile, Alabama.

Photo by Griffin.

Figure 14.1. A Pickup Load of Fish.

In 1795 natives of San Felipe were surprised when a fellow townsman, Esteban Benét, sailed into St. Augustine. His family was well known in San Felipe and even in the New World where his uncle was an important officer in the Spanish navy, stationed in Havana. After reaching St. Augustine, Esteban married Catalina Hernández, and their child, Pedro Benét became an informal leader of the Minorcans in the town, often called "the king of the Minorcans." Their best known descendant came several generations later, however, in the person of the novelist-poet Stephen Vincent Benét.

A well-remembered Minorcan of the second generation is José Mariano Hernández, born in 1788, just as this part of the story closes, to Martin Hernández, mentioned as the principal figure in the carpenter's guild, and his wife Dorotea Gomila. Joseph M. Hernández, as he is called in later documents, became a member of the first territorial legislature in Florida and was Florida's first delegate to the United States Congress, but he is best remembered for his prom-

Photo by Ken Barrett, Jr.
St. Augustine Historical Society.

Figure 14.2. Minorcan Monument, St. Augustine.

inent role in the Seminole war as brigadier general of the Florida
militia and for his capture of Osceola (Griffin 1987).

Other names—Andreu, Arnau, Canova, Capo, Genovar, Llambias, Leonardi, Lopez, Masters, Oliveros, Ortagus, Pacetti, Papy, Perpal, Pomar, Ponce, Reyes, Rogero, Seguí, Triay, Usina—are still a part of the St. Augustine scene, while many names—Cocifaci, Martinely, Gomila, Genopoly, Stephenopoly, Generini, Soche, Cavedo, Famanias, and others, have vanished. Because a name is not in the telephone book, however, does not mean that descendents no longer live in St. Augustine, only perhaps that the name has daughtered out.

When Latrobe visited the town in 1832 he found that "about ten of the original stock were still alive." He gives us a good picture of these last remaining pioneers and their descendents calling them "the most interesting portion of the present population" and mentioning their "quiet demeanor and inoffensive habits." He found them still forming "a distinct community retaining their national features, language, religion and manners" and further described them as "honest, simple, and laborious in their occupations as fishermen and farmers" (Latrobe 1835:36).

These last ten remaining survivors of the Mediterranean-born colonists must have been young children on the plantation, and as such may not have suffered as their elders did from the flashbacks and recurring nightmares which modern psychology tells us are so common among those who have gone through catastrophic experiences.

Within a few short years even they, with their hazy memory of the Old World and New Smyrna days, had passed into history. Two descendents (Benét and Benét 1933:26, as adapted by Woodland 1989:9), speaking of their forbears, said in spare verse:

> They came here, they toiled here,
> They suffered many pains.
> They lived here, they died here,
> They left singing names.

Bibliography

Records from the British Public Records Office are cited as C.O. (Colonial Office) and T (Treasury) followed by volume and page numbers. Microfilm copies are at the St. Augustine Historical Society and P. K. Yonge Library of Florida History, University of Florida, Gainesville.

The Lansdowne manuscripts are available in the Clements Library, University of Michigan. Some copies are in the library of the St. Augustine Historical Society.

The Lockey collection of transcripts and translations is available at the P. K. Yonge Library of Florida History, University of Florida, Gainesville.

The Connor Collection is on microfilm at the P. K. Yonge Library of Florida History, University of Florida.

The East Florida Papers (EFP) are in the Library of Congress. Microfilm is at the P.K. Yonge Library and the library of the St. Augustine Historical Society. A card calendar of these papers has been prepared by the P. K. Yonge Library, and is also available on microfilm at the same libraries in Gainesville and St. Augustine.

Adam, Leonard
   1947 Virilocal and Uxorilocal. American Anthropologist 49:678.
Anderson, M. S.
   1961 Europe in the Eighteenth Century. New York: Holt, Rinehart and Winston.
Arensberg, Conrad, and Solon T. Kimball
   1965 Culture and Community. New York: Harcourt, Brace and World.

Armstrong, John
  1756 The History of the Island of Minorca. London: Printers to
    the Royal Society.
Aschmann, Homer
  1959 The Central Desert of Baja California: Demography and Ecol-
    ogy. Berkeley: University of California Press.
Bailyn, Bernard
  1986a The Peopling of British North America, An Introduction.
    Madison: University of Wisconsin Press.
  1986b Voyagers to the West: A Passage in the Peopling of America
    on the Eve of the Revolution. New York: Random House.
Bartram, John
  1942 Diary of a Journey Through the Carolinas, Georgia and
    Florida from July 1, 1765 to April 10, 1766. Transactions of the
    American Philosophical Society 33: Part 1.
Bartram, William
  1958 The Travels of William Bartram. Edited by Francis Harper.
    New Haven: Yale University Press.
Beeson, Kenneth H., Jr.
  1960 Fromajadas and Indigo: The Minorcan Colony in Florida.
    Unpublished M.A. thesis in history. Gainesville: University of
    Florida.
  1966 Janas in British East Florida. Florida Historical Quarterly
    44:121-132.
Bemrose, John
  1966 Reminiscences of the Second Seminole War. John K. Mahon,
    ed. Gainesville: University of Florida Press.
Benét, Rosemary, and Stephen Vincent Benét
  1933 A Book of Americans. New York: Holt, Rinehart and
    Winston.
Bennett, John W.
  1976 Anticipation, Adaptation and the Concept of Culture in An-
    throplogy. Science 192:4242.
Bond, Stanley C., Jr., Susan R. Parker, and Susan N. Smith
  1990 The Sabate Plantation: The History and Archaeology of a
    Minorcan Farmstead. Manuscript. St. Augustine: Historic St.
    Augustine Preservation Board.
Braudel, Fernand
  1972 The Mediterranean and the Mediterranean World in the Age
    of Philip II. 2 vols. New York: Harper and Row.

Brooks, C. E. P.
  1970 Climate Through the Ages: A Study of Climatic Factors and
    their Variations. New York: Dover.
Bryant, William Cullen
  1850 Letters of a Traveler. New York: George Putnam.
Brydone, Patrick
  1773 A Tour Through Sicily and Malta, in a Series of Letters to
    Wm. Beckford, Esq. 2 vol. London: W. Strahan.
Calvert, A. F.
  1910 Catalonia and the Balearic Isles. London: John Lane.
Campbell, J. K.
  1964 Honour, Family and Patronage: A Study of Institutions and
    Moral Values in a Greek Mountain Community. New York and
    London: Oxford University Press.
Camps, Pedro
  1768-84 The Golden Book of the Minorcans. Parish Records, Dio-
    cese of St. Augustine. Microfilm. St. Augustine Historical Soci-
    ety.
Caro Baroja, Julio
  1963 The City and the Country: Reflections on Some Ancient Com-
    monplaces. *In* Mediterranean Countrymen. Julian Pitt-Rivers,
    ed. Pp. 27-40. Paris: Mouton.
Casselberry, Samuel E., and Nancy Valavanes
  1976 Matrilocal Greek Peasants and Reconsideration of Residence
    Terminology. American Ethnologist 3:215-226.
Chamberlain, Frederick
  1927 The Balearics and Their Peoples. London: John Lane.
Cleghorn, George
  1779 Observations on the Epidemical Diseases in Minorca, from
    the Year 1744-1749, to which is Prefixed a Short Account of the
    Climate, Productions, and Inhabitants and Endemical Distem-
    pers of that Island. 4th ed. London.
Coomes, Charles S.
  1975 The Old King's Road of British East Florida. El Escribano
    12:35-74. St. Augustine Historical Society.
  1976 Tolomato Cemetery. El Escribano 13:107-138. St. Augustine
    Historical Society.
Corse, Carita Doggett
  1919 Dr. Andrew Turnbull and the New Smyrna Colony of

Florida. Jacksonville FL: The Drew Press. (Revised edition, St. Petersburg: Great Outdoors Publishing Co., 1967)

Curley, Michael
  1940 Church and State in the Spanish Floridas (1783-1822). Washington: Catholic University of America.

Deagan, Kathleen A.
  1974 Sex, Status and Role in the Mestizaje of Spanish Colonial Florida. Unpublished Ph.D. dissertation in anthropology. Gainesville: University of Florida.

Demos, John
  1970 A Little Commonwealth: Family Life in Plymouth Colony. New York: Oxford University Press.
  1972 Demography and Psychology in the Historical Study of Family Life; A Personal Report. *In* Household and Family in Past Time. Peter Laslett, ed. Pp. 561-569. Cambridge: Cambridge University Press.

DeNevi, Don, and Noel Francis Moboly
  1985 Junipero Serra: The Illustrated Story of the Franciscan Founder of California's Missions. New York: Harper and Row.

Dewhurst, William W.
  1886 The History of St. Augustine, Florida. New York: G. P. Putnam Sons.

De Vorsey, Louis, Jr.
  1966 The Indian Boundary in the Southern Colonies, 1763-1775. Chapel Hill: University of North Carolina Press.
  1971 De Brahm's Report of the General Survey in the Southern District of North America. Columbia: University of South Carolina Press.

du Toit, Brian M.
  1975 Akuna: A New Guinea Village Community. Rotterdam: A. A. Balkema.

Eby, Cecil D., Jr.
  1964 Memoir of a West Pointer in St. Augustine: 1824-1826. Florida Historical Quarterly 42:307-320.

Emerson, Ralph Waldo
  1939 Emerson's Little Journal at St. Augustine, March 1827. Florida Historical Quarterly 18:84-93.

Fairbanks, George R.
  1858 The History and Antiquities of the City of St. Augustine,

Florida. New York: Charles B. Norton. [Facsimile edition, University Presses of Florida, 1975].

Forbes, James Grant

1821 Sketches, Historical and Topographical of the Floridas: More Particularly of East Florida. New York: C. S. Van Winkle. [Facsimile edition University of Florida Press, 1964].

Foster, George M.

1951 Report on the Ethnological Reconnaissance of Spain. American Anthropologist 53:311-325.

1960 Culture and Conquest: America's Spanish Heritage. New York: Viking Fund Publications in Anthropology 27.

Gallay, Alan

1989 The Formation of a Planter Elite: Jonathan Bryan and the Southern Colonial Frontier. Athens: University of Georgia Press.

Gannon, Michael V.

1967 The Cross in the Sand. Gainesville: University of Florida Press.

Ganong, Overton G.

1975 The Peso de Burgo-Pellicer Houses. El Escribano 12:81-99. St. Augustine Historical Society.

Gillispie, Charles Couston

1954 A Diderot Pictorial Encyclopedia of Trades and Industries. 2 vol. New York: Dover.

Gilmore, David D.

1987 Aggression and Community: Paradoxes of Andalusian Culture. New Haven: Yale University Press.

Goody, Jack

1972 Domestic Groups. Module in Anthropology 28. Reading, Mass.: Addison-Wesley.

Gough, Kathleen

1961 Variation in Residence. In Matrilineal Kinship. David M. Schneider and Kathleen Gough, eds. Pp. 545-576. Berkeley: University of California Press.

Gray, L. C.

1941 History of Agriculture in the Southern United States to 1860. 2 vol. New York: P. Smith.

Gregg, William H.

1902 Where, When, and How to Catch Fish on the East Coast of Florida. Buffalo and New York: Matthews-Northrup.

Griffin, Elizabeth
    1987 Joseph M. Hernández: Planter, Soldier, and Politician. Un-
        published senior paper, department of history, University of
        Florida. Copy at St. Augustine Historical Society.
Griffin, John W., and Robert H. Steinbach
    1990 Old Fort Park and Turnbull Canal System Archaeological
        Survey Project. St. Augustine: Historic Property Associates
        (under contract for City of New Smyrna Beach).
Griffin, Patricia C.
    1976 Thalassemia: A Case Study of the Minorcans of Florida. Un-
        published manuscript, St. Augustine Historical Society.
    1977a Mullet on the Beach: The Minorcans of Florida, 1768-1788.
        Unpublished M.A. thesis in anthropology. Gainesville: Univer-
        sity of Florida.
    1977b Mary Evans: A Woman of Substance. El Escribano 14:57-76.
    1983 The Spanish Return: The People-Mix Period, 1784-1821. *In*
        The Oldest City: St. Augustine, Saga of Survival. Jean Parker
        Waterbury, ed. Pp. 125-150. St. Augustine: St. Augustine His-
        torical Society.
    1988a The Minorcans. *In* Clash Between Cultures: Spanish East
        Florida, 1784-1821. Jacqueline K. Fretwell and Susan R.
        Parker, eds. St. Augustine: El Escribano 25:63-83.
    1988b The Impact of Tourism and Development on Public Ritual
        and Festival: St. Augustine, Florida, 1821-1987. Unpublished
        Ph.D. dissertation in anthropology. Gainesville: University of
        Florida.
Harlow, Richard F., and F. K. Jones
    1965 The White-Tailed Deer in Florida. Technical Bulletin 9. Tal-
        lahassee: Florida Game and Fresh Water Fish Commission.
Harrison, G. A., J. S. Weiner, J. M. Tanner, and N. A. Barnicot
    1964 Human Biology. London: Oxford University Press.
Homans, George C.
    1941 English Villagers of the Thirteenth Century. Cambridge:
        Harvard University Press.
Hulse, Frederick S.
    1971 The Human Species. 2nd Ed. New York: Random House.
Johnson, Joseph, M.D.
    1851 Traditions and Reminiscences. Chiefly of the American Rev-
        olution in the South, including Biographical Sketches, Incidents

and Anecdotes—a few of which have been published, Particularly of Residents in the Upper Country. Charleston: Walker and James.

Johnson, Sherry
1989 The Spanish St. Augustine Community, 1784-1795: A Reevaluation. Florida Historical Quarterly 68:27-54.

Keesing, Roger M.
1975 Kin Groups and Social Structure. New York: Holt, Rinehart and Winston.

Kenny, Michael
1969 A Spanish Tapestry: Town and Country in Castile. Gloucester, Mass.: Peter Smith.

Landers, Jane
1988 Black Society in Spanish St. Augustine, 1784-1821. Unpublished Ph.D. dissertation in history. Gainesville: University of Florida.

Latrobe, Charles J.
1835 The Rambler in North America: 1832-1833. New York: Harper and Bros.

Leland, Jack
1976?. Research reported *in* Indigo in America. Parsippy, New Jersey: BASF Wyandotte Corporation.

Lockey, Joseph B.
1939 The St. Augustine Census of 1786. Florida Historical Quarterly 18(1):11-31.
1949 East Florida 1783-1785: A File of Documents Assembled and Many of Them Translated. Berkeley: University of California Press.

Lockridge, Kenneth A.
1970 A New England Town: The First Hundred Years. New York: W. W. Norton.

Lopreato, Joseph
1967 Peasants No More. San Francisco: Chandler.

Ludlum, David M.
1984 The Weather Factor. Boston: Houghton Mifflin.

Luther, Gary
1987 History of New Smyrna. New Smyrna FL: Gary Luther.

Manucy, Albert
1962 The Houses of St. Augustine: 1565-1821. St. Augustine: St. Augustine Historical Society.

Manucy, Will
  1975 Oral History Tape. St. Augustine Historical Society.
Markham, Sir Clements R.
  1908 The Story of Majorca and Minorca. London: Smith, Elder & Co.
McMurray, Carl Dempsey, Jr.
  1975 The Archaeology of a Mestizo House. Unpublished M.A. thesis in anthropology. Gainesville: University of Florida.
Menzies, Archibald
  1763 Proposal for Peopling His Majesty's Southern Colonies in the Continent of America. Megerly Castle, Pethshire. Photostatic copy, St. Augustine Historical Society.
Mintz, Sidney W., and Eric R. Wolf
  1967 An Analysis of Ritual Co-Parenthood (Compadrazgo). *In* Peasant Society. Jack M. Potter, May N. Diaz, and George M. Foster, eds. Pp.174-199. Boston: Little, Brown and Co.
Mowat, Charles Loch
  1943 East Florida as a British Province, 1763-1784. Berkeley: University of California Press. [Facsimile edition, University of Florida Press, 1964].
Murdock, George Peter
  1949 Social Structure. New York: Macmillan.
Neville, Gwen Kennedy
  1979 Community Form and Ceremonial Life in Three Regions of Scotland. American Ethnologist 6:93-109.
Panagopoulos, E. P.
  1956 The Background of the Greek Settlers in the New Smyrna Colony. Florida Historical Quarterly 35:95-115.
  1966 New Smyrna: An Eighteenth Century Greek Odyssey. Gainesville: University of Florida Press.
Parker, Susan R.
  1988 "I am neither your subject nor your subordinate." *In* Clash Between Cultures: Spanish East Florida, 1784-1821. Jacqueline K. Fretwell and Susan R. Parker, eds. St. Augustine: El Escribano 25:45-60.
Patrick, Rembert W.
  1954 Florida Fiasco: Rampant Rebels on the Georgia-Florida Border, 1810-1815. Athens: University of Georgia Press.

Paul, Elliot
1937 The Life and Death of a Spanish Town. New York: Random House.
Pennington, Edgar Lee
1927 The Rev. James Seymour S.P.G. Missionary in Florida. Florida Historical Quarterly 5(4):199-201.
Pitt-Rivers, Julian
1961 The People of the Sierra. Chicago: University of Chicago Press.
1963 Mediterranean Countrymen. Paris: Mouton.
Postlethwayt, Malachy
1757 The Universal Dictionary of Trade and Commerce. 2d ed. London: John Knapton.
Proby, Kathryn Hall
1974 Audubon in Florida. Coral Gables: University of Miami Press.
Purcell, Joseph
1777 A Plan of St. Augustine Town and its Environs in East Florida, from an Actual Survey made in 1777 by J. Purcell, Surveyor. Original in National Archives; copy at St. Augustine Historical Society.
Quinn, Jane
1975 The Minorcans in Florida: Their History and Heritage. St. Augustine: Mission Press.
Rasico, Philip D.
1983 The Spanish and Minorcan Linguistic Heritage of St. Augustine, Florida. El Escribano 20:1-25. St. Augustine: St. Augustine Historical Society.
1985 A Complementary, Annotated Lexicon of the St. Augustine Minorcan Dialect. El Escribano 22:3-41. St. Augustine: St. Augustine Historical Society.
1987a Els menorquins de la florida: historia, llengua i cultura. Mahon, Menorca: Publicacions de L'Abadia de Montserrat
1987b Minorcan Population of St. Augustine in the Spanish Census of 1786. Florida Historical Quarterly 66:160-184.
Rogers, George C., Jr.
1976 The East Florida Society of London, 1766-1767. Florida Historical Quarterly 54:479-496.

Rogers, George C., Jr., David R. Chesnutt, and Peggy J. Clark, eds.
    1978 The Papers of Henry Laurens. vol. VI. Columbia: University
    of South Carolina Press.
Rolle, Denys
    1765 The Humble Petition of Denys Rolle, Esq. [Facsimile edition,
    University Presses of Florida, 1977].
Romans, Bernard
    1775 A Concise Natural History of East and West Florida. New
    York: the author. [Facsimile edition, University of Florida
    Press, 1962].
Rocque, Mariano de la
    1788 Plano Particular de la Ciudad de S^n Agustin de la Florida.
    Original in Bureau of State Lands, Department of Natural Re-
    sources, Tallahassee, Florida.
Roselli, Bruno
    1940 The Italians in Colonial Florida. Jacksonville FL: Drew
    Press.
Ruidavets y Tudury, Pedro
    1887 Historia de la Isla de Menorca. Vol. II. Mahón.
Rutherford, Robert E.
    1952 Settlers from Connecticut in Spanish Florida: Letters of Am-
    brose Hull and Stella Hall, 1804-1806. Florida Historical Quar-
    terly 30:324-340.
Santo Domingo
    1777 Copy of royal cedula to bishop of Cuba, Aug. 16, 1771, en-
    closed in Echevarría to José Gálvez, April 4, 1777. Santo
    Domingo 2594.
Schafer, Daniel L.
    1983 . . . not so gay a Town in America as this . . . In The Oldest
    City: St. Augustine, Saga of Survival. Jean Parker Waterbury,
    ed. Pp. 91-123. St. Augustine: St. Augustine Historical Society.
Schery, Robert W.
    1972 Plants for Man. 2d edition. Englewood Cliffs NJ: Prentice-
    Hall.
Schoepf, Johann David
    1911 Travels in the Confederation, 1783-1784. Alfred J. Morrison,
    trans. and ed. Philadelphia: Wm. J. Campbell.
Selye, Hans
    1956 The Stress of Life. New York: McGraw Hill.

Siebert, Wilbur Henry
  1929 Loyalists in East Florida, 1774 to 1785. 2 vols. DeLand FL: Florida State Historical Society.
Singer, Charles, E. J. Holmyard, A. R. Hall, and Trevor I. Williams, eds.
  1957 A History of Technology. Vol.II. New York and London: Oxford University Press.
Sjoberg, Gideon
  1967 The Preindustrial City. *In* Peasant Society. Jack Potter, May N. Diaz, and George M. Foster, eds. Pp.15-24. Boston: Little Brown.
Smith, Jack
  1869 The Story of Uncle Jack. Unpublished manuscript in the Buckingham Smith collection. New York: New-York Historical Society.
Smith Josiah
  1932 Josiah Smith's Diary, 1780-1781. South Carolina Historical and Genealogical Magazine 33(1):1-28.
Stork, William
  1766 An Account of East Florida, with a Journal kept by John Bartram, Botanist to His Majesty for the Floridas; upon a Journey from St. Augustine up the River St. John's. London: Nicoll and Woodfall.
Swanton, John R.
  1922 Early History of the Creek Indians and Their Neighbors. Bureau of American Ethnology Bulletin 73. Washington: Smithsonian Institution.
  1946 Indians of the Southeastern United States. Bureau of American Ethnology Bulletin 137. Washington: Smithsoniam Institution.
Tannahill, Reay
  1973 Food in History. New York: Stein and Day.
Tanner, Helen Hornbeck
  1963 Zéspedes in East Florida, 1784-1790. Coral Gables: University of Miami Press. [Reprint, Jacksonville: University of North Florida Press, 1989].
  1964 General Greene's Visit to St. Augustine in 1785. Ann Arbor: William L. Clements Library.
  1965 The Delaney Murder Case. Florida Historical Quarterly 44:136-147.

Taylor, Matilda D.
 1916 Odd Customs of the Early Days. St. Augustine Record, February 2.
Taylor, Thomas W.
 1984 "Settling a Colony over a Bottle of Claret": Richard Oswald and the British Settlement of Florida. Unpublished M.A. thesis in history, University of North Carolina at Greensboro.
Thompson, Edgar T.
 1959 The Plantation as a Social System. *In* Plantation Systems of the New World. Social Science Monograph 7. Pp. 26-37. Washington: Pan American Union.
Troxler, Carole Watterson
 1989 Refuge, Resistance, and Reward: The Southern Loyalists' Claim on East Florida. Journal of Southern History 55:563-596.
Turnbull, Andrew
 1777 Letter to Lord Germain, St. Augustine, December 8. Transcript, St. Augustine Historical Society.
 1788 A Refutation of a Late Account of New Smyrna. The Columbia Magazine, December 1788: 685-688.
USDA (United States Department of Agriculture)
 1941 Climate and Man. Washington: Department of Agriculture.
Vignoles, Charles
 1823 Observations Upon the Floridas. New York: E. Bliss and E. White. [Facsimile edition, University Presses of Florida, 1977].
Wallace, David Duncan
 1961 South Carolina: A Short History, 1520-1948. Columbia: University of South Carolina Press.
Whitaker, Arthur Preston
 1931 Documents Relating to the Commercial Policy of Spain in the Floridas: With Incidental Reference to Louisiana. Deland: Florida State Historical Society.
Wickman, Patricia R.
 1974 The Minorcan Phenomenon. Unpublished manuscript.
Williams, John Lee
 1837 The Territory of Florida. New York: A. T. Goodrich [Facsimile edition, Gainesville: University of Florida Press, 1962].
Wolf, Eric
 1959 Sons of the Shaking Earth. Chicago: University of Chicago Press.

Woodland, Naaman J., Jr.
    1989 The Minorcans of Florida: A Neglected Chapter of American
        Frontier History. Beaumont TX: Lamont University-Beaum-
        ont.
Wright, J. Leitch, Jr.
    1975 British St. Augustine. St. Augustine: Historic St. Augustine
        Preservation Board.
Wrigley, E. A.
    1969 Population and History. New York: McGraw Hill.

Index